Coming Clean

Coming Clean

TERRY NEWTON WITH PHIL WILKINSON

VERTICAL EDITIONS

www.verticaleditions.com

First published in the United Kingdom in 2010 by Vertical Editions, Unit 4a, Snaygill Industrial Estate, Skipton, North Yorkshire BD23 2QR

www.verticaleditions.com

ISBN 978-1-904091-41-7

A CIP catalogue record for this book is available from the British Library

With thanks to the *Wigan Observer* for help with a number of photos used in this book

Cover design and typeset by HBA, York

Printed and bound by Cromwell Press Group, Trowbridge

This book is dedicated to my mum and dad who have done so much for me, my wife Stacey for her love and support, and my two adorable girls, Millie and Charley-Mia. And to my sister Leanne who I miss more than I could have imagined.

CONTENTS

Foreword by Brian Carney   11
Prologue   15
1.   The Great Coca-cola Robbery   20
2.   Cheap Cider and Girls   26
3.   Turning Pro: a Tale of Two Teams   37
4.   Me, a Hooker?   46
5.   Fancier than Benidorm   58
    Andy Griffin   66
6.   Grand Ambitions   69
7.   Wonder of Wembley   82
    Adrian Morley   96
8.   Signing for Wigan   99
9.   Lam the Shepherd   107
10.   Our Stacey   118
11.   The Wigan Victory of the Decade   126
12.   Pulling no Punches   136
13.   Greg: 'Rip and Tear'   144
14.   High Tackles and Test Matches   154
15.   Losing Leanne   161
16.   Tackling The Volcano   166
17.   'Bring Back the Biff': Thoughts on the Game   173
18.   Boxing Clever!   179
19.   More High Tackles and a Record Ban   184
    Sean Long   199
20.   Running With the Bulls   202
21.   Dreamteam   213
22.   More Bans and Brushes with the Law   219
    Paul Deacon   231
23.   Going West: M62 Travels   235
24.   Finding Leanne   244
    Stacey Newton   250
25.   An Undetectable Solution?   254
26.   Cock-watchers and Coming Clean   262
Epilogue   282

ACKNOWLEDGMENTS

I want to thank those who have contributed to this book. I asked a person from every major stage of my life to write a piece, which they kindly agreed to do, and I'm grateful to Andy Griffin (childhood friend), Adrian Morley (Leeds), Brian Carney (Wigan), Paul Deacon (Bradford), Sean Long (Great Britain) and my brilliant wife, Stacey, for their words.

Last but not least, special thanks go to Phil Wilkinson for the efforts he made in writing this book.

FOREWORD

HOW DO I best describe Terry Newton?

He's one-third pantomime villain, one-third loving father and friend, one-third cage-fighter, and one-third Del Boy.

And that sums up Terry's mathematical skills for you!

I first came across him when I was starting my rugby league education at Gateshead, and he was playing for a great Leeds team. I used to wonder who the fat lad was who'd bash everyone around before Lee Jackson came on. Two years later, I ended up playing alongside him.

When I signed for Wigan in 2001, I was surrounded by champion players including Brett Dallas, Andy Farrell, Kris Radlinski, Adrian Lam, Matty Johns and Gary Connolly. Terry Newton was another.

Terry was one of those players you wanted on your team— not on the opposition's team. He was professional, meticulous in his preparations, and he took his game seriously. People forget just how good a rugby league player he was. Saying he was just about aggression is like saying Dallas was just about speed, or Faz was just about goal-kicking. He was a smart player and he had that quality that all players crave— consistency.

Terry was rarely *not* on his game. I never turned up for a match thinking, 'I wonder if Terry feels like playing today', because he always felt like playing, and that's inspiring. He'd prowl the dressing room beforehand, and you only had to look into his eyes to know just how desperate he was to win. That's one of the reasons that opponents hated playing against him. Another reason, of course, is that he was a pest. An absolute bloody pest.

Many players have asked me over the years what Tez is like as a person, and they don't believe me when I tell them he's a champion bloke. I have to convince them! Because when he was playing against them, Terry got under their skin. He niggled at them. He was in their ear. Talking, tormenting, terrorising. He didn't make it easy for anyone; from the assistant referee trying to check his studs, to the opposition scrum-half feeding the scrum. He tortured them.

And team-mates and coaches were not immune to his mischievous side! One time, when Andrew Farrar was our assistant coach, he came in early to do some video work and Tez and I were in the gym, doing an extra session before training began. Andrew had a reputation for being an intimidating, no-nonsense player, and he was the same as a coach. No-one dared risk upsetting him. No-one, that is, but Terry.

While we were sweating away, Terry spotted Andrew walking out of his office to go and make himself a brew. Terry said to me, 'Come on,' and sneaked into the office. He paused the video on Andrew's computer, launched the internet explorer and put some porn on his screen (for the life of me, I don't know how he knew there was filth like that on the web!) Then we dashed back into the gym to the weights bench, just before Andrew walked past with his cup of tea. 'Morning lads,' he said, as he ducked into his office. A few seconds later, he erupted. 'What the hell is this?!'

He stormed into the gym. We were the only people there, so he knew who the culprits were, but we just played dumb and managed to contain our laughter, so Andrew let it drop. Terry didn't.

He sloped off to call Mary Sharkey, who works in the Warriors office, to let her know about our practical joke and persuaded her to join in. A few minutes later, she called

Andrew to tell him they'd had a call from the IT department about some obscene material he'd been looking at! Poor Andrew thought he was going to get hauled over the coals, but to his credit, he took it in good spirit when Mary finally admitted she was joking.

Tez is pretty vain, which is surprising given his looks. He spends a lot of time on his appearance. He used to think he looked like Frank Lampard. Then, when he started getting a few grey hairs, he modelled himself on George Clooney. But I think we can all agree he looks like a fatter version of Tyrone from *Coronation Street*! We met the guy who plays Tyrone, once. We were in Blackpool and he came over to us—he's a big rugby league fan—so we took a picture of him with Tez and they looked like twins.

I mentioned a Del Boy part of Terry. Well, if there's a deal to be done, he will be there. He's a wheeler-dealer, Tez, and he will never be scammed. I've never known a more street-smart bloke in my life. And he's certainly got a colourful past—I discovered that for myself when he stole my car.

Our prop, Neil Cowie, had a toy frog, a gift from one of his kids, which he loved; for some strange reason, he took offence when I nicked the fake reptile and strung it up from the chin-up bar! But Neil didn't get mad, he got even—more than even, in fact—by recruiting Terry to steal my car and drive it to his house. There, the pair of them unscrewed my hatchback boot, and then put it back in place before driving my car back to my home. Of course, I was tucked up in bed, oblivious to all of this. I had no idea. Until the following morning when I was driving down the M6 to training, chatting away to Matty Johns alongside me, when—all of a sudden—half my car flew off!

Yeah, Terry sure loves a practical joke.

He's calmed down a lot in his old age but he's still the same fun-loving, trusting, bloke I first met all those years ago. I can't speak highly enough of him; I love him to death.

And yes, that's despite the way his career ended. When he phoned to tell me he had some important news, the first words out of my mouth were, 'Terry you fucking idiot'.

I trained with Terry for years at Wigan. I saw how much sweat he spilled in extra sessions that no-one else saw him do, and no-one had asked him to do. He says he was clean back then, and I'm convinced he's telling the truth. I hope this book explains why, years later, he felt the need to cheat.

That's what he did—cheated. He is a drugs cheat. My great mate, the one who had a career and success that others could only dream of, might only be remembered as a cheat. I find that sad, and a sobering lesson for anyone contemplating such a shortcut in their training. Terry knows my thoughts on what he did; he also knows he will always get my unwavering support. He is, and will remain, first and foremost my friend.

He's a bloke who can't do enough for those he likes. Speak to anyone who knows him well, and they'll tell you the same. He's got a beautiful family; two lovely girls who he dotes on, and 'our Stacey', a great woman he's devoted to.

That's the Terry Newton I know. He's the kind of guy you want alongside you in the trenches. The kind of guy you want alongside you at the bar. The kind of guy I'm lucky enough to call a good mate.

Brian Carney
Former Wigan and Great Britain team-mate

PROLOGUE

'BOLLOCKS, I'm late,' I shouted to Stacey as I rushed through my front door.

I'd been to my doctors, and though I'd had the first appointment of the day it'd still run over. It was half-eight on a wet Wednesday, February morning; I was supposed to have set off 10 minutes ago for training. I've always been one to try to arrive at training early. Not once had I been fined for being late in a decade-and-a-half and while I was only meeting two mates for an extra gym session—it was our day off at Wakefield—I didn't want to break my habit now.

I grabbed my bag from the bottom of my stairs and did the usual two-second bloke check at the door—patting my pockets to check for my phone, keys and wallet.

'I'm off, see you later love,' I said to Stacey.

I kissed her goodbye, and as I turned to head out the door, she said, 'Terry, there's a letter on the side for you'. I was about to ignore what she'd said, until she added, 'I've just had to sign for it'.

That got my attention.

I went into the kitchen and looked on the table and there, sat on top of the usual mess of junk mail, was a big envelope from UK Sport. It was quite a thick folder. I just presumed it was a booklet of new guidelines or something like that. Maybe there was a new cough medicine that players couldn't take. I didn't even think back to the last drugs test I'd taken three months earlier.

I quickly opened the envelope, all the time thinking, 'If I put my foot down, I should still make it in time'. Within reading one sentence of the letter inside the envelope, I'd stopped worrying about tackling the M62 traffic. The letter said I'd tested over the baseline amount for human Growth Hormone, (hGH), a banned substance. I was instantly suspended, and I had to notify my club and the RFL within 48 hours.

I read the letter again. And nearly dropped through the fucking floor.

I was devastated. A hollow, nauseous feeling started in my gut and spread throughout me. 'This can't be happening,' I thought. 'It's hGH, it can't be detected. Someone's fucked up.' I started panicking. It felt like I was drowning. I bent over the kitchen table like I'd been hit in the ribs, trying to take in deep breaths. It's a cliché, but it was as if my whole world was collapsing around me.

Stacey walked past the kitchen. She could see I was upset. 'Terry, what's up love? Are you okay?'

She didn't know that, for the past few months, I'd been taking hGH. I hadn't told her. I hadn't told my mum, or my dad. I couldn't—they were so proud of me. Apart from a small group of players who were also taking hGH, no-one knew.

'Terry?' Stacey said. She was obviously concerned.

'How do I tell her?' I thought. 'How do I tell the woman that I'm providing for that I've just kissed goodbye to six figures over two years? How do I tell her I cheated? How do I tell her that she is going to get stares from people in the street, all thinking, "She's married to Terry Newton, the drugs cheat."'

'Look love, I've got some bad news here,' I said. She started worrying, fearing the worse. But she could have never guessed what was coming. 'I've been done for taking growth hormones. I'll be banned for two years.'

She stood in our kitchen, shaking her head. 'How? It must

be a mistake . . .'

But she could tell from the look on my face it wasn't a mistake. In an instant, she went from shocked to shit-scary— she just flipped her lid. 'How could you? How could you?' She went mental. She was crying. Hysterical. I tried to give her a hug, but she just pushed me away—she was disgusted with me.

I knew the sight of me was making her worse, I started panicking even more, and so I walked out the front door, got into my car and drove to my mum and dad's house.

I've never bullshitted my dad. Never needed to. But in the five minute drive to his house, I kept thinking, 'How do I tell him?' By the time I'd pulled up onto his drive, I still didn't know. I walked in and as soon as I saw him, I knew that if I didn't tell him straight away, I never would.

'Dad, I'm in the shit here,' I said. 'I've been banned for taking growth hormones.' His chin could have hit the floor.

After travelling to Wakefield, and informing all the people I needed to, I went to bed at about 7pm that night. My head was up my arse. I wasn't thinking straight. I switched my phone to silent and left it downstairs—I didn't want to speak to anyone. Didn't want to read any texts. I certainly didn't want to see myself on the news.

Before midnight, I was woken by a knock on the front door. I heard Stacey answer, and the brief murmurs of her talking to someone. Then the door closed and it all went quiet, and I thought, 'Thank God she's got rid of 'em'.

A minute later, my bedroom door opened. It was Brian Carney. He'd just flown up from London, where he'd appeared on *Boots 'n' All*. People who had seen him on the programme later told me that Brian was obviously cut up about what I'd done. Well, if they thought he was upset on the TV show, they should have seen him standing at the bottom of

17

my bed that night. He gave me the mother of all roastings. He absolutely tore me to shreds.

As I tried to get back to sleep that night, I couldn't stop thinking about how upset I'd made him, Stacey and my parents. I wasn't thinking about what I was going through, about not playing again, not earning. What killed me was seeing how upset I'd made the people who care about me.

If I could have pictured their pain, back when I first started taking hGH, I wouldn't have done it. But I hadn't really thought about the consequences. I hadn't been thinking straight. My mum and dad had been anti-drugs for years. They had seen how heroin had taken a grip of my sister Leanne. They'd seen it choke her of a normal life, transform her into a person they didn't recognise until it eventually killed her before she'd reached 30. And they'd also seen how rugby league had got me away from that. The game had set me off down the right path, away from crime and drugs. My sister died; I made a name in—and a good living from—rugby league. It brought a tear to me eye that—having been through so much—I'd pissed it all away.

This book wasn't supposed to start like this. I'd practically finished it when I had to break the news to Phil Wilkinson, my ghost writer, that, 'I think we might have to re-do the ending'. He's another one who was pissed off with me!

I decided I wanted to release my autobiography shortly after Leanne died. I knew I'd been involved in enough pranks, fights and finals to make an interesting read, but I also wanted to open people's eyes about heroin, and the importance of choosing the right paths in life. The fact I became the first person in world sport to ever get caught taking hGH has, of course, changed the focal point of this book. But I hope, ultimately, it still serves the same purpose that it set out to do.

Hopefully I can make sure someone, somewhere, doesn't make the same mistakes I've made. I've not shied away from the reasons why I started cheating, 14 years into a first-team career that had brought me Challenge Cup honours and Great Britain Test caps. I hope, by the end of this book, it will be clear why I threw everything away. That's why I've named the book *Coming Clean*—I've not held back. There's no point bullshitting anyone. I genuinely hope that some good can come from the fuck ups I made.

But this book is not all about hGH. That doesn't define my life.

As well as everything I've gone through in my personal life, I'd like to think I've enjoyed a pretty good career, too. I'd played in every Super League season up until 2010. I played for four clubs (and signed for a fifth). I played and lost in four Grand Finals. I won at Wembley. I played with some of the game's true greats. I've seen Leeds rise, Bradford fall, and Wigan do both. I've pissed off the Aussies, a few at St Helens, and hit one of my own team-mates. I've been stabbed, arrested, threatened, punched, married, suspended, cautioned, fined and nearly imprisoned. And in between all of that, I've had a few laughs along the way.

1

THE GREAT COCA-COLA ROBBERY

WHEN I WAS 11, Ellery Hanley was God.

I worshipped him from the Central Park terraces and tried to emulate him on the pitch, and I used to be glued to the TV screen whenever Wigan were on. After the 1991 Challenge Cup Final, when he helped Wigan to yet another Wembley win, I remember my dad ruffling my hair and saying, 'Don't worry son. One day, you might be on the telly too.'

And he was right, my old man. A week later, I was on TV. Not for my rugby, mind . . . but for nearly killing myself during a foiled break-in.

Bored one Sunday afternoon, a small group of us climbed up on the roof of a distribution centre near to our house in Worsley Mesnes, a couple of miles outside Wigan town centre. One of the lads broke the skylight, and when we peered in we saw all the shelves were loaded with boxes upon boxes of Cokes, Mars bars, crisps . . . you name it! Our eyes lit up. We were only kids, and we felt like we'd stumbled across heaven. We had no idea how we were going to get in, until someone hit on the idea of getting a rope and lowering one of us down. Excited, we legged it round to a mate's house to find some rope, but the best thing we could lay our hands on was a piece of washing line. I was probably the lightest and definitely the daftest, so on the way back to the centre, I was nominated to be the one to go down. We climbed back onto the roof and tied the washing line around my waist. It was a decent sized building, probably two stories high, and I was happy to do it—I wanted to get my hands on all those treats.

I only felt nervous when I looked through the gaping hole where the skylight had been. 'You sure this'll work?' I asked, to reassuring murmurs from the three or four others.

Remember that scene from *Mission Impossible*, when Tom Cruise is lowered into a room on a rope? Well, years before he had done that, there was a chunky, daft 11-year-old lad doing the same thing in Wigan. Only I wasn't lowered. After inching from the ceiling, my mates lost their grip and I crashed to the floor. I was out cold.

My mates told me later that they thought I'd been killed. I'd fallen two stories, and they'd never seen anyone knocked out before. My mates panicked and scattered, but luckily one of them ran home to tell his mum, who called an ambulance. Apparently, the fire brigade had to break the door down to get to me. I didn't know any of this, because I only came to hours later in a hospital bed with a broken nose and a broken collarbone. I was groggy as hell. I saw my mum, dad, a nurse and a policeman waiting at my bed.

It took me a minute to remember what had happened, and why I was in bed with four people, two of them strangers, staring at me. The copper asked me what I was doing on the roof, and instantly it came back to me.

Think, Terry, think. 'I erm, was on the, erm, roof . . .' Work, brain, work! My dad'll bollock me! '. . . coz my ball had gone on it. Yeah, that was it, we were playing football nearby and the ball had gone on the roof, and so I went up to retrieve it when I fell through the skylight.'

I was quite proud of that one. I don't think they believed me—the fact a length of washing line was tied around me probably gave me away—but they saw how much pain I was in and didn't question it. I got away with it. That wasn't the end of it, though. A day later, there was a story on the regional TV news about a poor little primary school pupil who fell through a warehouse roof while getting his ball back!

I was born on 7 November 1978, to parents Val and Tony, and spent my first two years living in Norley Hall, in Wigan. When my sister Leanne was born, we moved to a bigger house in Worsley Mesnes, where I spent the rest of my childhood.

I was a mischievous sod growing up, but I wasn't a bad lad. I got into bother, but nothing too serious. I was never a bully, never a thief. I was always a bit of a free spirit—my mum tells me that, when I was seven, I disappeared out of the garden and caught a bus on my own to Wigan town centre. I caused a bit of mischief as a kid, but apart from trying to steal a few cans of Coke from a distribution centre, the only bad things I did was start fires across the field or 'borrow' motorbikes and take them for spins around the estate. I didn't know that was such a bad thing, because that's what it was like on my estate.

Whenever my mum and dad found about any bother I'd been in, they'd come down on me like a ton of bricks. They're great, my mum and dad. They're as solid as a rock, and while we weren't rich growing up, I never wanted for anything. They taught me right from wrong. But they couldn't keep their eyes on me all the time, and once I was out of their sight and with my mates, I'd be in mischief.

That's probably why my dad always encouraged me to do sport, to give me something to channel my energy into. Growing up in Wigan, rugby was everywhere. It was impossible to ignore. These last few years, Wigan Athletic have been in the Premier

League, but back then no-one knew of Latics, and apart from the odd Man United or Liverpool top, everyone seemed to wear Wigan's cherry and white shirts.

My dad played a bit of rugby when I was a kid, and even had a spell at Chorley Lynx. I used to go along and watch him, and he'd also take me to Central Park to watch Wigan, who had a great side loaded with stars such as Shaun Edwards, Andy Gregory, Joe Lydon and Dean Bell. My favourite was Ellery— he was the man. With my dad's passion for rugby league, and my love for Wigan, it was inevitable that I would start playing the game as well.

When I was eight, Bernard Long, the dad of my future Great Britain team-mate Sean, ran a summer camp at St Jude's amateur club and my dad took me along to have a go. I loved it, and when the summer was over, I carried on training at St Jude's with the 10-year olds, who were coached by Paul Liptrot. I had a short-temper as a kid, so playing rugby was perfect for me. Tackling players and driving the ball in allowed me to release my aggression legally! I couldn't do that in football, running or any other sport.

I was in the perfect environment. I was messing around in the mud, having a laugh with my mates and playing rugby. The only problem was that I used to lose my rag a bit, and that was definitely my downfall—I stormed around like a spoiled little brat some of the time!

I carried that on for a while, but there was no Under-9s side back then—all the lads were one or two years older than me— and after a while I got sick of not playing regularly. I'd been doing well at wrestling, so I jacked in rugby and went wrestling at Billy Chambers' gym in Wigan.

After a few months, Bernard asked me to give rugby another crack. My dad had known Bernard for years, and my mum was friends with Sean's mum. They lived nearby and apparently,

Sean and I used to play together as toddlers. Years later, I knocked about a bit with Longy on the estate, but only occasionally as he's two years older than me. When Bernard told me he was starting an Under-10s team, I decided to give it another go, and I never looked back.

He was great, Bernard. Because I was fearless (some would say daft) and I liked the rough stuff, I always played prop, though I was never as big as the other props. I soon learned I needed to develop my skill if I was to be as good as them. At that age, some lads are massive, and can barge their way through and score a try with every touch of the ball. I was never like that, so I learned to pass, sidestep and support runners. Being shorter than the other props definitely helped my game, and within a year I'd been picked for the Wigan town team, which was coached by Mick Mullaney. I was also playing for my primary school side, St James', coached by Dennis McHugh, and I was doing well. I loved school—which surprises a few people, because, believe it or not, I'm not really an academic—but outside school, I was getting into more and more trouble. I spent my late afternoons and weekends with the same group of lads and as I grew older, I got into more bother. There were flats near where I lived in Worsley Mesnes, and because the residents couldn't take their motorbikes upstairs, we used to break into their sheds and 'borrow' them. A few times the police chased us, but they never caught us as we could go over the footbridges and they couldn't. To this day, I don't know who taught me how to hot-wire them—I wouldn't have a clue how to do it now—and I always took the bikes back when I'd finished. Usually in good condition.

But my mum and dad always seem to find out about what I'd been up to, and after I ended up in hospital—and on the TV news—for my botched great Coca-cola robbery at the distribution centre, they decided to do something about it. Most of the kids from my primary school—including the group of mates I was hanging around with—were going to Cansfield High, in Ashton, a few miles from where I lived. I wanted to go there too, but my mum and dad wanted me to get away from them, and told me I'd be going to a different school, Hawkley Hall High, instead.

I was devastated.

My mum and dad were honest with me. They told me that my mates were leading me astray, and they wanted me to get away from them. I only had one mate who was going to Hawkley, Craig Young, who years later would be my best man at my wedding. I was pleased he was going to Hawkley—I clung to him as we rocked up for our first day, only to find we'd been split into separate forms. I was terrified. Absolutely terrified.

Everyone else in the class seemed to have their own little groups. All except one lad, who—like me—didn't seem to know anyone else. I went over to talk to him. His name was Andy Griffin, and he went on to have a great career in football at Stoke and then Newcastle. We hit it off straight away. Griff lived for football, I lived for rugby, but we had everything else in common. We had the same sense of humour and we both loved PE. He's a tough little bugger and fast, and he'd have made a great rugby player . . . though I'm not sure he'd have made as much money as he did in the Premier League!

Back then, Hawkley Hall High was effectively split into two campuses, so the first and second year pupils—today's Years Sevens and Eights—didn't really see the older kids. Even so, word filtered through to us first years about who the hardest lad of the school was. We never saw him, but we knew him by reputation. He was a fifth year named Andy Farrell, and the word back then was that he was going to be a big star in rugby league.

2

CHEAP CIDER
AND GIRLS

MY DAD taught me to fight. He never showed me how to throw a right hook or land an upper cut, but when I was 11, he taught me that there are times when you need to use your fists. Talking doesn't resolve all problems—not where I grew up, at least. I'd not been at high school long, and a group of us were playing rugby on the school field. A lad who was a lot older than me—I think he was 15 or 16—came down and started picking on a few of us. We were scared stiff, because he was a lot older and bigger than us, and so I ran into my house. I was petrified he was going to beat me up.

My dad could tell I was upset, and asked what was wrong, so I told him, hoping he'd come out with us and sort this bully out.

'What are you doing in the house, then?' my dad asked. 'Go outside and knock his head off.'

I thought he was joking at first. 'Dad, you don't get it,' I told him. 'He's older than me.'

My dad looked at me with a deadly serious look, and said: 'So am I, and if you don't go outside right now and sort him out, I'll knock your head off. Now go and leather him.'

I didn't want to go. All my mates were terrified of this lad, but I sheepishly went back onto the field. At this point, it seemed half the street was out, including my future wife Stacey, who hung around with my sister. The lad started on me again, pushing and calling me names, so I told him to stop. I tried to do it in a deep voice, but I must have sounded like a mouse, because he burst out laughing. 'Make me,' he taunted.

So I did.

I knocked his bloody head off. He went down with my first punch. It was like the scene in *Back To The Future*, when George McFly hits Biff and knocks him spinning. I wasn't proud of what I'd done, at first. I went back into the house in tears. My dad came to see me and said, 'If you back down, you'll be walked over for the rest of your life'. And he was right. I realised that I'd rather take a beating than be branded a coward—and that's how I've been ever since. I know some people will say what I did was wrong, but I bet they've never been in that position. Talking only gets you so far, especially when you're 11-years old and an older kid is bullying you.

Once I settled into my new school, I saw less of my old mates. They were getting into trouble with the law, stealing cars and breaking into people's houses, and I took my dad's advice and stopped seeing them. Of course, that wasn't the end of it. As soon as I distanced myself from them, they started treating me like an enemy. It all came to a head a few days before Christmas. I'd been late night shopping on a Thursday in Wigan, and as I was walking home I saw flashing blue lights outside my house. As I got closer, I noticed a couple of police cars and a fire engine parked outside. But that's not what caught my attention—the arse end of a single-decker bus was sticking out of my house!

It was one of the weirdest sights ever. Luckily, no-one was

in our lounge when it crashed through the wall. It turned out
that the group of lads that I used to mate around with had
nicked the Little Gem bus from Wigan and driven it to
Worsley Mesnes, and then crashed it into our house. My dad
had collared one of them and given him a good hiding. I was
pissed off like you wouldn't believe. A few days later, my dad
was driving me to training, and as we rounded a corner I saw
one of the lads responsible. 'Stop the car,' I told my dad. He
pulled over, I got out and ran at the lad. As soon as he saw
me, he turned and legged it, but I caught him and started
battering him. I threw him to the floor and landed punches
on him. He was thrashing back, but I was so angry, he had no
chance. His mate ran over, but he didn't try to pull me off, he
just stood there—soft git.

I carried on laying punches into the lad's face. There was
blood everywhere. I wanted to get him back for driving a bus
into my house—it was a miracle he hadn't killed one of us.

'That's enough, Terry,' my dad yelled at me. But I was so
angry, I carried on smashing him, until my dad reached
around me and pulled me back. Reluctantly, I gave in and
let him drag me off. As I stood, I thought I saw the lad swing
a punch at my leg, before crawling away and legging it. I
didn't feel anything at first, as I walked back to my dad's car.
Then I felt a wet patch around the top of my leg. I looked
down, and blood was everywhere. Suddenly, I went light-
headed. I didn't know what had gone on, until my dad said,
'I think you've been stabbed.'

It didn't hurt, but I was bleeding badly. My dad helped
me to his car and rushed me to the A&E at Wigan Infirmary.
He'd stabbed me twice—once in my hip, and once across the
thigh. The only saving grace was that he didn't cut my dick
off! The police got involved but I couldn't be doing with
that—I just lied and said I didn't know who had knifed me.

I didn't want to get into bother—after all, I'd been the one who'd given the lad a well-deserved pasting in the first place.

Looking back, I shudder to think what might have happened if I'd carried on hanging around with the same mates. It wasn't long before a couple went to young offenders' prisons. The fact that they'd stolen a bus, crashed it into my house and stabbed me—all within a few months of me not being with them—says a lot. From then on, they got worse, and became involved with social drugs. Pot, pills, stuff like that. I'm not saying I'd have gone around carrying a knife and I'd like to think I wouldn't have become involved in popping pills or smoking spliffs, but who knows? Crime's a slippery slope and fortunately, I got off it at the right time. I was definitely better off at Hawkley Hall High. I enjoyed my first couple of years at school and kept my nose clean. In my third year, my sister Leanne started, and she got me into a few scrapes. We were typical brother and sister—always arguing. She's two years younger than me and she used to wind lads up the wrong way, knowing I'd be there to sort them out if need be. Maybe I should have let her fight her own battles, because she was a cheeky little thing and the more I got her out of bother, the more bother she seemed to cause. I was never any good at school, which is probably why I mucked around in class a bit. Except at PE—I loved PE, and tried really hard at it.

Jeff Clare, who'd played for Wigan a few years earlier, was my PE teacher and he really encouraged me. When I was 13, he entered me into the England Schools Athletics Championships and I finished second in the shot put. Mr Clare had won it himself when he was a pupil—he's a bit of a local legend in Wigan for his athletic records.

I was good at all sports, but rugby remained my main passion, and when I reached Under-13s level, I felt like I needed to get away from Wigan St Jude's to improve. There were two great teams in Wigan at that age group, Hindley and Orrell St James. At first, I tried to go to Hindley but their coach, Cliff Peters, didn't really see me fitting into the set-up then—which tells you how strong they were at the time! In fairness to him, he said it was probably in my best interest to go somewhere else, so I joined Orrell St James. We had a great team, and our games against Hindley were epics. Orrell had an aggressive pack, while Hindley had the gun backline with players like Paul Johnson, Tony Stewart and Paul Deacon, who all turned pro and enjoyed successful careers. Deacs was a master kicker then—any penalty inside your half, and he slotted over the two points, no problem. Jon Clarke, who also turned pro, was with Hindley and we always seemed to end up scrapping. I vividly remember one of our better fights, during a final at Bury football ground. My dad warned me that Hindley could run rings around us, so my plan was to kick-off with Clarkey early on, to rattle their cages. Sure enough, at the first scrum, as soon as I saw the referee looking elsewhere, I threw a punch at Clarkey. I caught him right on the side of his face. But he must have been expecting it, because he lashed straight back at me. Tensions were already high, and the whole scrum erupted. Warren Stevens, who I was next to, and Martin Carney were exchanging blows with Hindley's props David Webb and Andrew 'Moggy' Morris. But the best thing was, when it all settled down, the ref sent two players off and didn't cite me. I ended up scoring two tries and winning the man of the match award!

Those games between Hindley and Orrell were ferocious affairs. The only other games that came close to that intensity were when we played the amateur sides from St Helens, though we usually won comfortably. I remember one game, after we'd given a St Helens team a good pasting on the field—I can't remember if it was Thatto Heath or Blackbrook—a group of their players barged into our dressing room and started kicking off with us as we were getting changed! I waded in and threw a few punches, not realising I was hitting the coach. I later found out he was a policeman, but thankfully nothing came of it.

When I wasn't scrapping, I played well. I kept in the Wigan town team—which was basically a combined Orrell St James-Hindley XIII—and we were unstoppable. At Under-13s level, our record was: played 13, won 13, points for 887, points against 18. We were awesome. My dad has kept the coach's report card from that year and I got As and Bs in most areas. Under the header 'improvement areas' are scribbled two words: 'control aggression'!

A load of the lads had already signed up for professional clubs but no matter how well I played, it seemed no-one was interested in me. My boyhood dream was to sign for Wigan and plenty of my peers were signing for them, including Mike Peters, Paul Johnson and Jon Clarke. I stood out in loads of the games, but no-one ever approached me. Apparently, when a team-mate's parent asked Wigan's scout about me, he said that he didn't think I was big enough to make it in professional rugby. I wonder if that scout realises he cost Wigan £145,000 a few years later!

I kept plugging away and my performances even earned me a place in the England Schoolboys side that played France. I captained the team, which was a huge honour because I wasn't even Orrell's captain—Martin Carney was. We won the game, I scored two tries and was named man of the match. Past winners of that trophy read like a who's who of rugby league, including Andy Platt, Lee Crookes, Shaun Edwards and Andy Farrell—I was made up. Mind you, as confident as I was on the pitch, I was still a bag of nerves off it: when presented with the trophy, I was asked to say a few words, but I couldn't. I shook my head, and got off the stage as quickly as I could!

I've always been painfully shy. I've improved a bit over the years, but I was awful as a kid. When I watched Wigan, I'd hang around Central Park afterwards with my mates. They'd all ask for players' autographs—Frano Botica, Jason Robinson, Gary Connolly—but I never could. I'd just stay at the back and watch them. I desperately wanted their autographs—some of those players were my heroes—but I was too afraid to ask. I was a big lad with a big reputation who was too scared to say, 'Can you sign this please?'

I once went to a Graeme West summer camp, taken by the Kiwi great himself, and at the presentations at the end all the lads asked to have pictures taken with him, or have him sign their shirts. My mum nudged me forward. 'Go and get his autograph Terry.'

'No,' I said.

'Go on, don't be soft.'

She knew I was shy, I knew I was shy, but I didn't want to admit it.

'I'm not soft, I just don't want his autograph,' I said, as cocky as I could. 'Besides, he'll be asking me for my autograph one day.'

I disappeared to the toilet, and when I got back, Graeme West walked up to me with a pen and paper. Now Westy is a mountain of a man and when you're a kid, he looks even taller. He towered over me.

'Oh my God,' I thought. 'My mum's told him I'm too shy to ask him for his autograph.'

But before I could say anything, Westy asked, 'Hi Terry, can I have your autograph please?'

I was stunned. 'You what?'

'I hear you're going to play for Wigan one day,' he said. 'Can I have your autograph?'

I signed some paper. 'Thanks mate,' he said, smiling at my mum and dad. They'd obviously had a word with him while I was in the toilet and he'd played along. I've never asked Westy whether he's still got it—I very much doubt it!

I didn't need my school grades to tell me I was never going to have a high-flying job; I knew rugby league was my best chance of making something out of my life. But when I turned 14, my ambition to turn pro faced its biggest obstacles—cheap cider and girls!

I'd spent the summer labouring for a plasterer, and it was bloody hard work. After the first day I thought, 'They're making it tough for me because I'm the new lad.' But they weren't—it was a regular day! I'd carry the plasterboard, scrape the ceilings, get the toolboxes, fill the buckets with water, brush the floors . . . it was exhausting. The work I did that summer was the toughest I'd ever done, and my respect goes to anyone who regularly works so hard for so long. Never let a rugby player tell you he's got it tough. I don't think some of them realise how good they've got it—getting paid to do something they love. I already had my heart set on making it in rugby, but that summer's labouring made me want it more.

Like many lads at that age, when the weekends rolled around, the in-thing was to meet up and get pissed on Merrydown or Diamond White cider. My dad always used to let me go out with my mates—he wanted me to have a social life away from rugby—but he always told me not to drink before a game if I wanted to do well.

One weekend, it had been lashing down for three days

solid, and Orrell St James were due to play against Wigan St Patrick's, one of our derby rivals, on the Sunday. On the Saturday evening, dressed in my trendiest rags and stinking of Lynx deodorant, I told my dad I was going out. I've always been honest with my old man. I never had to lie to him. 'There's a party at one of my mate's house—his parents are away,' I told him.

As usual, he told me not to drink. But it was peeing down outside and I convinced myself the pitch would be water-logged. I told my dad that the game would probably be called off and he replied: 'If you drink, you're not playing tomorrow.'

I didn't listen to him. I was already in his bad books, because I'd borrowed his brand new, dead expensive trainers that week, even though I'd promised not to. I'd have got away with it, too, had I not crashed my bike and ripped the soles off the bottom!

Anyway, that evening, I went out and got smashed. The following morning, I woke up nursing the mother of all hangovers, with the sun shining through the gap in my curtains. Bloody typical—the monsoon from the day before had dried up. I went downstairs and asked my dad whether he'd heard from the coach if the game was on or not.

'Yep,' he said. 'The game's on.' He knew I'd been drinking—I stunk of ale and my eyes were like piss-holes in the snow—but he didn't say anything. Instead, he let me get dressed as usual and go to the game with him. When we got to the ground, I thought I'd got away with it. But he went up to the coach, told him I'd been out drinking the night before, and said I wouldn't be playing.

I begged him to let me play. 'I promise I won't do it again,' I said, but he wouldn't listen, and so I ended up watching the whole game from the touchline. It was one of the hardest things I'd ever done. It killed me.

Thankfully, we won the game, but I was still gutted, and moped around for ages. My dad didn't say anything to me on the way home, and he didn't need to. He knew I wouldn't make the same mistake again, and I didn't.

I still went out with my mates, but I stayed off the booze. Everyone was drinking and trying to impress the girls, and I was there, armed with a can of Tizer and a ready-made excuse of: 'I can't drink, I've got a big game tomorrow.' Of course, as soon as everyone was pissed, I was the easy target among my mates, and the girls were probably thinking, 'Who's the goody-two-shoes?'

I know this may sound stupid now, but that was one of the hardest times of my life. It was so tempting to say, 'Screw it, give me the cider', but I never did. At least, I never did when I had a game the following day. On the rare occasions I didn't have a match, I'd be smashed after two swigs!

Honestly, when I think about how many lads were as good as me at that time, but didn't make that same choice that I did—and didn't make it in rugby league—it's startling. Sure, some of them might have peaked when they were younger and not progressed, no matter how well they trained. But I'm convinced many of them could have made it as professionals. No question. I truly believe in the saying that you make your own luck, and that's a perfect example. I'm not getting on my high-horse here; there are plenty of drunken stories later in this book, but they never happened the day before a game and they occurred after I'd already made it. When you're at such an important stage of your development, you can't afford to go and get smashed—certainly not the day before a match.

People say you have to make sacrifices to make it in sport, but playing games didn't seem like a sacrifice to me. Training five times a week wasn't a sacrifice. I loved doing those things, more than anything else. The big sacrifice for me was not going down that pathway when my mates started on the booze. If I had, I honestly don't think I'd have been offered a pro' contract. And God knows where I'd have ended up.

3

TURNING PRO: A TALE OF TWO TEAMS

WIGAN MAY have thought I was too small, but I must have been doing something right—I signed for two professional clubs before I left school. And what a real shit-storm it caused!

It's a lesser known fact about me that Warrington, not Leeds, were my first professional club. When I was 14, I was still playing for Orrell St James. A scout named Jim Reider asked if I would be willing to chat to Warrington. Most of the better players my age had already been signed up by local clubs. Even at 14, I was thinking maybe I'd been overlooked, so I was thrilled that Warrington were keen on me. My mum, dad and I went for a meeting with Brian Johnson, their Australian coach, at his house. Brian and the chairman asked me questions but I just shook with nerves—my mum and I didn't say a thing through the whole meeting—we left all the questions to my dad. I was sweating, I was so nervous.

But I liked what they said and when they made me an offer of £12,000 over four years, I signed there and then. I was so proud. It was like all my Christmases rolled into one—I'd have signed for a tracksuit at the time. They gave me a tracksuit anyway, and I wore it every time I left the house . . . I was like a walking, talking Warrington billboard wearing my club emblazoned gear! Warrington were a decent sized club, even then. They had just been to Wembley, they had a heap of big-name players like Kevin Ellis, Jonathan Davies and Paul Cullen, as well as Mike Gregory. Although he played at Warrington, I think every Wiganer liked Greg because he was from the town and he did so much for Great Britain. I didn't meet any of the Warrington players or train with them, I just went back to Orrell St James, and I was to carry on playing for them until I finished school.

Our Orrell team was the best team in Lancashire (former Hindley players may dispute that—but this is my book!) We played a game against Stanley Rangers, who had Chris Chester in their side, and while it was only a friendly, they were the best team in Yorkshire so we knew bragging rights were at stake. To 15-year-old lads, it felt like a State of Origin game! We ended up losing narrowly, but I was having a good game until I had to go off with a cut on my face. Later that afternoon my mum and dad got a call from a scout from Leeds, Dave Robinson. He'd been at the game and said he knew that I'd signed with Warrington. Then he said that I couldn't be tied to the deal because I couldn't agree professional terms while still a schoolboy. We had no idea. Everyone else seemed to be doing the same thing at the time. We panicked at first, because we didn't know if we'd done anything wrong. We even had a meeting with a solicitor, but he assured us we'd done nothing wrong. A guy from Leeds called a few days later and said, 'Look, we'll back you all the way if you want to sign for us instead'. I'd jumped in with two feet—I'd been seduced by the thought of playing professionally, without thinking about other clubs possibly being interested in me. I was happy to stay with Warrington but the more I thought about it, the more Leeds appealed to me. As big as Warrington were, Leeds were bigger.

Leeds also offered me a YTS scheme, and said I could work

in gyms, which I think my mum and dad liked the sound of—I was only young, but they realised playing rugby league wouldn't last forever. Warrington, if I remember rightly, didn't have a YTS scheme. I think my dad also knew some of my mates were still knocking around on the estate where we lived, pretty much doing nothing with their lives, and he probably worried that if I was at Warrington I'd come back from training and fall back into my old ways with them. He didn't want me to go down that path—he realised a fresh start in a new town would be good for me.

My mind was made up. I agreed a deal with Leeds that was to run from my 16th birthday, and with the signing on fee, I did something sensible for once—I bought my mum and dad's house off them, to rent out. They wanted to move off the estate, because my sister was getting into strife as she got older, and my dad made me see the logic of having an investment property. Not many people can say they're on the property ladder when they're 15, can they? See—I'm not *that* daft!

While I made my decision to sign for Leeds pretty easily, it wasn't the end of the matter. Warrington were furious with me, furious with Leeds, and they wouldn't let it drop. In their eyes, they'd spotted me first, and they protested to the RFL to stop Leeds from registering me as their player. The bickering carried on for a while, but it was going nowhere. Eventually, the RFL said a tribunal would need to decide who I would play for.

At first I was flattered—two massive clubs were in a tug of war over me, and it wasn't costing us anything in solicitors' fees. I was one of the last of my peers to sign professionally, and for a spell I thought no-one wanted me. Now I had two big clubs fighting over me! The worst case scenario was I'd join Warrington, which wasn't too bad, but my heart was set on

Leeds and they were confident the case would settle in their favour. As I waited for it to be sorted out, I moved in with Dave Robinson—the scout who'd spotted me—and his family in Wakefield. I'd never lived away from my mum, dad and sister before, and it was terrifying. I can still remember how lonely I felt when they dropped me off for the first time; that first night was like being locked in a police cell. I was 16, living in a strange town with a strange family. Forget being a tough lad—I literally cried myself to sleep that night. After a few days, though, I settled into a routine. I never felt fully comfortable being away from home, but it became bearable.

The Robinsons were great. They washed my training gear and cooked my meals—I can't thank them enough for what they did for me. Their son, Craig, was also on Leeds' books. He was a cracking lad, and each morning we had to get up at about 5.30am—I'm an early-bird, so that was fine by me—to catch a bus to Wakefield centre, then we had a half-hour train ride to Leeds, followed by a bus to Headingley to start training at eight. It was a two-hour trip, door-to-door. A few lads were on the YTS scheme at Leeds, including Nick Fozzard and Marvin Golden, and everyone got on—it was brilliant.

I think the game's gone backwards by scrapping that programme, because as well as training, we all worked, coached, did apprenticeships or went to college: these days, lads don't do anything else, and those who don't make it in rugby league are left to fend for themselves with nothing to fall back on.

Leeds had a great programme. We all did weights in the morning and trained together, and then sometimes we'd go out into the schools in the afternoons to coach the local kids. That was the scariest part—I was terrified of public speaking, and I'm not much better now. Back when I was at school, when a teacher made all the kids stand up and read a little passage out in turn, I used to get the sweats, shake my head and say, 'I'm not doing it'. The teacher could threaten me with detention and I still wouldn't change my mind! As confident as I was at rugby and hanging around with my mates, I just couldn't speak in public. I'm so shy like that, it's untrue.

When it came to coaching the kids while I was at Leeds, I assured myself that I would be speaking about rugby—a subject, unlike the ones at school, that I was good at. But when I got into the schools, it was a completely different story. I was scared to death. Put a few 16 stone men running at me on the rugby pitch and I was fine, but put a few young kids in front of me and my confidence melted. What made it worse was the fact that when we went to the schools, many of the pupils hadn't heard of Leeds rugby league club.

There were so many kids from Pakistan and India, they didn't even know what rugby league was! Some of them could hardly speak English, and when we showed them rugby balls, they laughed and said they were the wrong shape.

Once, I was introduced as a player from Leeds, and I saw one Indian lad's eyes light up. 'Thank God,' I thought. 'At least one of them is showing some enthusiasm.'

This little lad looked at me and said, 'You play with Gary Speed? You play with Rod Wallace?'

'Who the bloody hell is Gary Speed?' I thought. It was only afterwards I found out he played for Leeds United, who were big at the time!

It was totally different to the life I was used to. For a start, there weren't many black or Asian kids in Wigan when I was growing up—it's not much different now. Plus, when I was a kid, *everyone* played or watched rugby. It chooses you, you don't choose it, and I thought everywhere was the same. Yet there I was, an hour down the M62, trying to coach lads who knew little about the game, and cared even less.

After our afternoon jobs—coaching in schools, helping out around the ground—I'd return to the Robinsons' pad at about six, kill time playing computer games and then head to bed at about 8pm. I'm no different now in that respect—it's only with the invention of Sky Plus that I've been able to watch grown-up programmes!

While I liked the family I was staying with, I didn't enjoy being away from home. I was missing my mates and my mum—there was no Facebook or mobile phones back then, so it was harder to keep in touch than it is these days. I was cut off. Because I couldn't play while the legal wrangle was going on, I'd go home as often as I could. Often, I'd leave Leeds on a Friday afternoon and catch a train back to Wigan, and at 5am on Mondays, I'd catch a train back to Leeds.

The RFL tribunal was no closer to resolving my case, meaning I still couldn't play. The year 1995 was a good time to be involved in rugby league. There was Wigan's eighth (and last) Wembley win on the trot, which I'd gone to watch with the Leeds academy lads. Then there was the Centenary World Cup, plus a shortened season in readiness for Super League, which had everyone talking. The whole game was buzzing about the switch to summer rugby and full-time professionalism. But for me, it was a wipe-out. I was frozen out of the game.

The weeks turned into months, and the situation dragged on. When I asked what was going on, I was told it would be sorted out next month, and then another month would go by. Have you ever been delayed for a flight and been told it'll be an hour late? And then the hour passes and they tell you it'll be delayed another hour? Well, it was like that . . . only much worse. I didn't know when it was going to end. And to rub salt in the wounds, back then some academy games were televised on Sky Sports, so when I was at home, I'd see my mates and lads I used to play with, and against, on TV. It was really upsetting. I didn't see an end to it.

Leeds must have thought highly of me, though, because as well as training with the academy lads, I'd do the odd session with the first-team as well.

Doug Laughton was the Leeds coach when I signed, but I didn't actually meet him. The first time I trained with the first-team, Mike Forshaw—another new signing, though he's a few years older than me—and I went to Doug's office and the media guy, Stuart Duffy, came down and said, 'What are you two doing here?'

We told him we were there for Doug and he said, 'You'll not find him here, he's gone'. So with no coach, Mike and I had to walk into the room where all the first-team lads were and introduce ourselves—God it was embarrassing. Mike's a Wiganer too, and before I could drive, he helped me out giving me occasional lifts across the M62. I'd sit in the back and listen to him and Phil Hassan chat, too shit-scared of talking in case I said the wrong thing!

One of my regrets was just missing out on training with my childhood hero, Ellery Hanley. He moved to Australia just before I started training with the first-team lads, but there were still plenty of big-names. Garry Schofield, a former Great Britain captain, was coming to the end of his career but he was still class—he fired passes like bullets, and they always hit the targets. You couldn't coach that talent. I was a bit star-struck at first and although that faded after a while, I never felt fully comfortable around them. Truth was, I was petrified of making a mistake. I took it deadly seriously. I used to think, 'Do they think I'm good enough to be here?'

One of my other duties was cleaning the first-teamers' boots. It was humbling, because I'd train with them, and then just as we'd finish they'd chuck me their boots and say, 'Clean them, lad'.

Did I mind? No. I had respect for them—I looked up to them, and wanted to be where they were. Sadly, respect is another thing that has been lost from rugby league over the years. Some lads don't have that same respect for the older players—and it's probably not their fault, it's the fault of the system they've come into. For example, when I was at Bradford, we were at a training camp and as Mike Worrincy— a senior player—went to sit down, one of the young lads, who must only have been 15, moved his chair out of the way. Mike fell down on his arse in front of everyone. The young lads laughed, and nothing was said. I don't think Mike minded, either—he can take a laugh—but I thought, 'If I'd have done that when I was 16 to George Mann or Garry Schofield or Gary Mercer, my life wouldn't have been worth living'.

I was training hard at Leeds, but I was gradually losing my match fitness. I was also dying to play a game, to vent my frustration at being sidelined. I said to my coaches, 'Look, I need to play a game, this is killing me.' They agreed, but said it would suit everyone if it was a low-profile match. My old amateur coach, Colin Nicholson, was involved at Orrell Rugby Union club, so I mentioned that I was looking for a match and he invited me to have a crack with them, playing for their Colts.

I'd never watched or played rugby union before and Colin put me at inside centre so I wouldn't have to learn the complexities or the rules of rucks, mauls, line-outs and other areas that I didn't (and still don't) understand. Needless to say, I didn't last long in union—I got sent off in my first game! I shoulder-charged a lad in my first tackle, and cleaned him out.

In my defence, it would have been a legal tackle in league, but the ref just looked at me and said, 'You can't do that in this game, son', and sent me off. I couldn't believe it . . . red carded in my only match! Frustrated, I went to Wigan St Judes and had a couple of games for their Under-18s, which was fun, but I was itching to play for Leeds.

Warrington, though, really dug in their heels and prevented Leeds from registering me. I missed the entire Centenary season because of the dispute and it certainly soured relations between the two clubs: I even read that the Leeds board weren't welcomed into the directors' box when they played at Warrington, because of me!

After a frustrating year, the case was finally resolved—in Leeds' favour. I was happy it was all sorted out, because Leeds had been threatening to sue the RFL for not registering the contract, and I didn't want that. I knew more legal action would mean more delays. I was 17-years-old, I'd just spent a year on the sidelines and I was desperate to play.

Warrington had already paid me an instalment of £3,000 for the following year, and Leeds told me I'd have to pay them back. I told my dad about it and he said, 'Tell Leeds you've spent it'. I did, and they ended up paying Wire back instead!

4

ME, A HOOKER?

WHEN THE NEW Super League season began in March 1996, my first game for Leeds academy was against Warrington—the team I'd signed for and walked out on. I knew they were still pissed off that they'd lost out on me. In fairness, I could sympathise—they'd spotted me first, paid £9,000 and failed to get a single training session out of me!

It was a curtain-raiser to the first-team game and Headingley was packed. I was a nervous wreck before the match. I thought, 'I'm going to get my head caved in here'. I was at my usual position of prop, and the only games I'd played in over a year were a couple of games for Wigan St Judes. Plus, of course, the briefest of cameos for Orrell Rugby Union! I was up against Warren Stevens, one of my good mates who is, cruelly, nicknamed 'Brains'. He was a real aggressive player, Brains, but so kind-hearted off the pitch. He later lived with me for a while and, because he spent all of his spare cash on bandit machines, he never had any money to buy food. Once, I came in to find him eating a jacket spud with mushy peas! 'You dirty git', I said, to which he shrugged his shoulders.

He replied, 'What was I suppose to do? We had no beans'. How can you argue with logic like that?

Another time we were in a pub, and he got a call from his brother. I only heard half the conversation, but it went something like this: 'How'm I s'posed to know? Not a clue.

I've not. See ya.'

I asked what was wrong, and he told me his brother couldn't find one of his brown shoes. I looked at him and said, 'Brains, look at your feet you dickhead!' He hadn't realised he had one brown shoe and one black one on!

Brains was tough as hell, and as all rugby players know, it's great to go up against your mates. I knew he'd try and rattle me. He took in the first drive and I tackled him high—I don't know how, because he's massive. Luckily, I stayed on the pitch and went on to play well.

By this point, I'd moved out of the Robinsons' and was commuting between Wigan and Leeds. I'd bought an old Astra with my signing on money from Leeds—I got £25,000 —although after I'd bought my mum and dad's house I only had a few hundred quid left for a motor—and, when I was still 16, my dad took me out on to Southport beach to practise. He'd say, 'You're never going to drive son, you're shocking!' That was another reason I wanted to pass, to prove him wrong.

When I turned 17, my mum and dad booked me into a five-day crash course for my birthday present. The course was in Wigan, so I phoned up Leeds and told them I had 'flu. It was stupid, really, because I started on the Monday and on the Friday I drove to training—I'd passed my test, five days after my birthday, so I think they realised what I'd done!

I loved having my own set of wheels. Having a car also meant I could bring some of my Yorkshire team-mates back to Wigan and show them the sights! One night, after we'd played an academy game in Lancashire, I persuaded Nick Fozzard and Marvin Golden to stay on in Wigan for a few beers. I was a proud Wiganer—I still am—and I was determined to show them a good time. These days, Wigan's King Street is packed with bars and clubs but back then there was only one place that everyone wanted to go, and that was Prince's Nightclub.

We had a few scoops in a pub first, and turned up at Prince's to find a queue snaking down the street. We joined it at the back, and it wasn't long before I noticed the bouncers eye-balling us.

Nick said, 'They're not going to let us in here.'

'Of course they are,' I said. 'They'd tell us to bugger off if they weren't.'

One of the bouncers regularly walked down the queue to check other people's IDs and speak to them, but they didn't say anything to us. I took this as a good sign because, being 17, we'd have been screwed if they asked us to prove our age. It must have taken 45 minutes to get down towards the front of the queue. Nick and Marvin were getting a bit restless, they just wanted a beer. I said, 'Don't worry it'll be good, it's great in here. Everyone goes here.' We got nearer the front—a few people in front of us—and the bouncers kept looking at us.

When we got to the front, to walk in, a bouncer put his arm out and said, 'You're not coming in'.

'What do you mean?' I said.

'You're not coming in.'

'You've seen us in the queue, if you weren't letting us in why didn't you say something?'

'Fuck off pal, you're not coming in.'

I was furious. We'd spent ages queuing up to get to the front. I was a hot-head, back then, and I lost my rag big-time. 'Listen mate, we're coming in,' I said. Why do blokes say 'mate' to people they don't like?

The guy just shook his head and said, 'You're not from round here.'

'I'm from Wigan, these are my mates from Leeds. We're not going to cause any bother.'

But every time I said something, he just kept repeating, 'You're not coming in.'

Me, a Hooker?

The people behind us were getting pissed off by this point, but I wasn't for shifting. Then, the bouncer pushed me down the steps in front of everyone. People behind me started giggling, which brought a smile from the bouncer.

I stepped up to him and said, 'Look, don't push me again, we're coming in.'

He shoved me again, but I was prepared for it. I swatted his arms away, and punched him in the face.

Crack.

He dropped like a ton of bricks, straight on to the floor. His mate next to him rushed over to me, so I put him down too! It all happened in the blink of an eye.

They closed the doors, and before anyone could say anything, I legged it. Nick and Marvin scattered, too.

I got a cab and went straight home. Nick and Marvin were staying at a hotel on the outskirts of town, and when I picked them up the morning after, Nick said, 'You're a mad bastard, Terry. What did you do that for?'

I said, 'If he wasn't going to let us in, why didn't he say earlier? He just did it to try and make himself look good in front of everyone.'

That episode taught me an early lesson about how rugby lads get targeted by pissed up blokes or bouncers. I was a hot-head back then, I admit it. I had a few scrapes.

But rugby lads get their aggression out in training and matches; we don't go out wanting any trouble or looking for fights. I certainly didn't. Unfortunately, too often there are blokes out there who like to have a crack, and embarrass players to try to make themselves look better in front of their mates.

Players are targets. Being so young, I was buzzing after I'd put two bouncers down, but the morning after I was worried in case Leeds found out about it. I was only 17, I'd only just

49

started playing again after a year out of the game, and I didn't want to piss Leeds off.

On the drive back across the M62 I said to Nick, 'Look don't tell anyone, I don't want to get any shit off Leeds'.

'Fair enough,' he said. But one thing I soon learned about Nick was that he couldn't hold his own piss, and within a day I think everyone at the club knew about it! No-one said anything though.

I played well for the academy in my first couple of games. I was still quite compact for a prop, but I was making a name for myself and I wondered how long it would be before I made the step up to the 'A' team, which was the level below the first-team.

Dean Bell had taken over from Doug Laughton as first-team coach, which was great for me because he was one of my boyhood heroes. Dean had captained Wigan when I was a massive fan, and after Ellery, he was probably my favourite player. He came over to me one day after training and asked, 'Have you ever played hooker?'

Before then I'd mainly played prop, with the odd game in the back-row. But I don't think Mick Shaw, the Leeds No. 9, was looking too hot in the first-team, and there weren't really any other hookers at the club. Dean must have seen something in me that convinced him I could do it. I was tempted to lie, but I didn't. I told him I'd never played hooker, and he asked if I fancied playing that position because there might be a chance for me to play in the first-team.

I thought, 'I'll play on the bloody wing if it gets me in the first-team.' We shook on it, and agreed that I'd switch to hooker in training. He also advised me to watch videos of Keiron Cunningham and study him. I think Dean realised that Keiron and I had similar builds. Keiron's more powerful, and I don't think he'll mind me saying that I'm a bit quicker, but we're both stocky and robust. Dean respected Keiron enormously, and told me that I'd learn from watching him play. In an instant, I became an avid fan of St Helens. Or, more precisely, a fan of Keiron Cunningham. I watched every Saints match I could, and I'd not even watch the game—I'd just watch what Keiron was doing. When he passed, when he ran, where he stood in defence . . . it was the best education a young hooker could have had because Keiron was—and has been—the best modern-day hooker by some distance.

Though I was stocky like Keiron, I don't know for the life of me what Dean saw in me to think I could play hooker. It would be the modern day equivalent of picking a compact prop—Wigan's Eamon O'Carroll, perhaps—and suggesting he switch to hooker. No other coach, team-mate or friend had ever suggested switching positions. The only other person who'd ever said I could be a hooker was my mum! I was skilful as a prop, I had good hands and I supported well, but it's a completely different skill to pass a ball from the ground, rather than from standing up.

I began training at hooker with the first-team and I struggled. I really struggled. I was okay passing the ball right to left, but the other way, I was dreadful. The passes were slow and looping; some went to the first-receiver's head, others around his ankles. I began having doubts about playing there, but I practised all the time and I spent hours—literally hours—on my own, in the garden, before training and after, just passing the ball from the floor to imaginary targets. Bend down, pass. Bend down, pass. Bend down, pass. Over and over. It was my job to take our family dog, Ella—a Staffordshire Bull Terrier—for a walk every day, so I'd take her to a nearby school field, with four balls. I placed the balls in line with the posts, a few metres apart, and practised hitting the post with the ball. When I got all four on target, I'd turn

51

around and repeat it from the other side, passing left to right. It was my ritual, and I wouldn't leave until I'd nailed all four from both sides. Once, it was absolutely pissing down, and I couldn't hit the post for shit. Ella was staring at me with her puppy dog eyes as if to say, 'Hurry up and hit the bleedin' post, Tez!' Sometimes I would be at the field for two hours. Then, one day, it just clicked. I did it the first time. I lined the balls up . . . ping, ping, ping, ping. Both sides, all the passes were right on the money.

I started putting the balls further away, and improvising—adding a spin, or a press-up, before passing. The other people walking their dogs must have thought I was mad! Passing from the floor is a fundamental skill for a hooker, because you're the first person to touch the ball from the play-the-ball and if that first pass to the first receiver—often the scrum-half or stand-off—isn't crisp, then every other pass is off.

Once I'd mastered that skill, Mick Shaw and I took turns running at hooker in training and I started enjoying it. But just as I thought I'd overcome my biggest obstacle, I had to learn different game plans too. I kept messing them up, I felt so stupid, but the lads were understanding, especially guys like Adrian 'Moz' Morley and Barrie McDermott, and after a few sessions I managed to get my head around the different calls.

I played an academy game at hooker against Leigh, which we won 34–8, and I eased into my new role. It felt natural; like I was meant to be a hooker. I could still get stuck in and hit lads, but it also allowed me to talk and to direct play and pass the ball. I even scored a 65-metre try in that game, which turned a few heads, and I kept my place at hooker in the academy side for the next couple of weeks. I continued to train at hooker with the first-team, too.

Then, one day, Dean gathered the lads together after training as usual to name his team for their next game. When he got to hooker, he said, 'Terry Newton'. I was stunned. Mick Shaw was out with a head injury, but I didn't expect a call-up so soon. I'd not even played in the 'A' team—I was going straight from the academy side to the first-team, just a few weeks after changing positions. All the lads began clapping, Dean shook my hand and then the players started chanting, 'Speech, speech, speech'.

I didn't give the greatest speech ever heard—I believe the words I uttered were, 'No fucking way!'

We were playing Sheffield Eagles at Headingley, which today sounds like an easy two-pointer, but at the time it was a tough match. Sheffield had been in some good form while we'd been playing crap. We'd lost our last five matches, including a 25–16 humbling at Oldham which really had the fans worried. It was only April, but there was already talk about Leeds being in relegation trouble because we were rooted to the bottom of the table, on zero points: our only wins, at the start of the year, had been in the Challenge Cup.

I started the game at hooker, and I didn't exactly make a dream start. My first touch of the ball was when we got a penalty inside our own half. I just picked up the ball and tapped it against my foot, as I'd always done, but I think there'd been a recent rule change and I should have tapped the ball while it was on the ground. The ref blew his whistle for a penalty, and I handed Sheffield an easy two points on a platter.

After that, I was petrified of doing something wrong, and I don't think I ran the ball in once. The speed of the game was the big difference. It was so fast, I was blowing out of my arse and thinking, 'I'm not fit enough for this'. Sheffield had some decent players in lads like Keith Senior and Paul Broadbent. Paul was one of the biggest props around at the time, and I tackled him early on to try to put him off his game. I probably didn't, but it gave me confidence.

We won the game 36–22, much to the relief of the 9,000 fans at Headingley, because it gave us our first competition points of the historic summer campaign.

I went off at the end of the first-half, with the fabulously-named Marcus Vassilakopolous replacing me. I dropped back to the 'A' team after that (I must be one of only a few players to make their 'A' team debut after their first-team debut) but after Leeds lost their next game—at home to London—Dean called me back up for the first-team to play Paris St Germain. The game was on Sky, which was great, because all my mates and relatives could watch it. I was buzzing—the fact we murdered them 40–14 made it even sweeter.

I kept my place in the side for the next two matches, and though we lost both—against Halifax and Bradford—I was determined to keep my place in the team because our first match in June was a home match against Wigan. Every player will tell you that there's nothing like playing against your hometown club to get you fired up. I knew that all the people I grew up and went to school with would be watching.

And when your hometown club are the biggest side in the game—and also the reigning champions—that feeling is doubled. If there was one game that I wanted to make a big impression in, this was the game. I was happy at Leeds, but I'd not forgotten that Wigan had overlooked me as a kid. I was too small, apparently.

Well, we lost 40–20, but I had a good game. I'm not being big-headed—honestly, I'm normally a fierce critic of my own performances. But I ran my blood to water in that game, and won my first man of the match prize. Wigan had a great team, with players like Kris Radlinski, Henry Paul, Martin Offiah, Gary Connolly and Andy Farrell. They were awesome.

The rugby league paper, *League Express*, gives two man of

the match awards—one for each side. I can't tell you how made up I was when I opened it up on the Monday morning to find I was Leeds' star-man, and the other one, for Wigan, was Jason Robinson! There I was, a 17-year-old lad playing his fifth first-team game, and I was mentioned in the same sentence as Jason—probably the world's greatest winger.

Players may tell you that they're not bothered what the press say about them, but that's crap, especially when they're first starting out. My mum and dad got all the papers, and they've kept the reports in a scrapbook.

'Newton, a Wigan lad, came of age, topping the tackle count and running the ball bravely at the champions,' read one. Another was: 'Terry Newton's all round contribution in exalted company was nothing short of heroic.'

My favourite one said: 'Newton's virtuosity allowed an immediate riposte.' I wasn't sure what 'riposte' meant, but it sounded good!

I hate to admit it, but those headlines went to my head a bit. I was dropped by Dean—at first to the bench, and then altogether from the first-team. Dean probably realised I needed to keep my feet on the ground. At the time, I didn't feel like I was getting above myself; what happened next suggests maybe I was.

I dropped down to the reserves for a home game against Saints, who were one of the better sides at that level, but because I'd been in the first-team I thought, 'I'm too good for this'. I didn't train properly all week, and I binned the extra sessions that I usually did religiously before, and after, training. That weekend, I probably had the worst game I'd ever had. I missed tackles, dropped balls, gave away penalties—I had an absolute nightmare. If it could go wrong, it did.

I was devastated, and after the game, I was the last one left in the dressing room. I didn't speak to anyone. It was only a reserve game, but I couldn't look my team-mates in the eye.

When everyone else had gone, Dean came to me and said, 'What's going on?'

I was in tears. I said, 'I don't ever want to play hooker again.' It wasn't true, but I blamed my bad game on playing hooker when, of course, it was really because I hadn't trained and prepared as I should have done. It was a heat of the moment remark—and I regret saying it to Dean, because he'd been nothing but supportive, and I didn't want him feeling bad for switching me to hooker.

The day after, I had another meeting with him and he asked me whether I'd prepared correctly for the match. I was honest, and I told him I hadn't. I told him I didn't think I needed to, because it was a reserve match. Dean didn't even say anything—it just clicked in my mind that I was to blame for my shocker, not the position I was playing. That's when I realised the importance of preparing for a game—I was looking to blame other things for my poor game, but it was all my fault. From that day, I always prepared well for a game— whether playing against Australia or an amateur side in the Challenge Cup. I always kept my same routines and discipline. It's not easy to treat every game as your last, but that's what I tried to do.

Leeds were really struggling, and the crowds just fizzled away—one of our home Super League matches pulled in less than 5,000, which is shocking. We had a decent squad, with blokes like Adrian Morley, Barrie McDermott, Tony Kemp and Graham Holroyd, but we just couldn't string two wins together and kept losing games we never should have lost. Everyone else was stressing about it, but not me; I just focused on my own game and, after busting my nuts in training, I managed to force my way back into the first-team's starting line-up for a home game against Paris.

Any player will tell you, no matter how young he is, that once they've tasted the first-team, anything else just doesn't compare.

I was made up. And just when I thought things couldn't get any better for me, they did. I walked into the dressing room, and glanced at the shirts that were hung up on the pegs in order as usual: St Hilaire, Golden, Iro . . . and then I saw it: Bell. Our coach, my boyhood hero, had picked himself! He hadn't told any of the lads, and hadn't named himself in the squad when we'd met the day before.

'Fucking hell, how mad is this?' I thought. It was surreal. Because I always played in the pack as a kid, when I watched Wigan I tended to look out for and admire the forwards, rather than the backs. Yet while Dean played at centre, he was as tough as any player—he had such an aggressive, unforgiving style, it was impossible not to admire him. I'd only just got my head around the fact that he was my coach; suddenly, he was my team-mate! It was incredible. His mere presence lifted the whole side, and we won 34–12, which practically secured our Super League survival. We finished 10th; I played in 13 games in total, which was roughly about 13 games more than I could have ever hoped for as a 17-year old.

The rugby Gods scripted that game against Paris perfectly. Not only did we win, in front of the Sky cameras, but I put Dean over for his final ever try of his brilliant playing career. Whoever said you shouldn't meet your heroes is talking shit— I sent mine in for his last ever try! And whenever I've bumped into him over the years, he's always thanked me for it—which I still get a buzz from, even now.

5

FANCIER THAN BENIDORM

MY YEAR wasn't finished. I was picked for the Great Britain academy tour of New Zealand at the end of 1996. There were a few Leeds lads on the tour and we were all thinking how good it was going to be—a six week-long lads' holiday!

I'd never been on a long-haul flight before. I hated it. I can't sit still for two minutes, and it felt like we were on the plane for three weeks before we touched down. 'Thank God we're here', I thought. Then the announcement came over the loud speaker that we'd landed in Hong Kong, and I remembered we had a bloody connection.

We had a few hours to kill in Hong Kong, so the coaches decided to organise a training session in a park in the middle of the city. They probably didn't realise how bad the weather was going to be, though. It was so hot and humid, I could hardly breathe, so they cut it short and let us have the day exploring Hong Kong.

It was a real eye-opener—talk about a culture shock. The most exotic place I'd been before then was Benidorm. People were cooking food we didn't recognise out on the streets— God knows what it was. Deep fried dog, probably. Of course, rugby lads being rugby lads, we headed straight to the nearest KFC!

A few hours later we hopped on another plane and 12 hours later landed in New Zealand. It took us nearly two days to get there with the stop-over, and when I got off the plane I thought, 'We've come all this way and it's just like the bloody Lake District. Only colder'. The New Zealand people were all friendly, welcoming and polite, but the weather was awful—it seemed to be pissing down all the time.

We played seven games on that tour—four club matches and three Tests against the Junior Kiwis—and I'm pretty sure I was the only one to figure in every match. I was one of the smallest forwards in our side, and I played everywhere from hooker to loose forward to prop. I'll never forget when the Kiwis walked out for the first match—they all had beards! If they were under 18, they didn't look it. The games were brutal—their players were far more physically mature than us, and it proved to be the difference. We lost the three Tests against the Junior Kiwis, but gave a decent account of ourselves and ran them close.

I found it hard on that tour. I was still only 17 and I'd done a decent job in my first Super League season, especially against Wigan, so I probably went over there thinking I'd made it. But the Kiwis were a lot quicker and more physical than me. It made me realise just how much progress I still had to make when I saw how far some of the Kiwi lads—like David Kidwell and Lesley Vainikolo—were ahead of me. It wasn't quite men against boys, but it was a good yardstick for me to judge myself by. It came at a good time for me because it ensured I didn't become complacent like some 17-year olds can get after a good debut season. Ever heard of second season syndrome? Believe me, it's got nothing to do with teams wising up to young players and everything to do with the players getting ahead of themselves. Luckily, being humbled by the Kiwis made sure I stayed hungry to get better.

The full Great Britain team were touring at the same time as us, and one of the perks of our tour was being able watch their Tests against New Zealand. I'll never forget Terry O'Connor running out in white boots in one of those matches. Back in 1996, everyone wore black boots—I think Henry Paul was the first to start with the white boots in Super League. But Henry had all the silky skills to pull it off. Terry was a prop, not a stand-off, and when I saw him facing the Kiwis in those boots I thought, 'He's going to get bloody murdered'. And he did! The Kiwi front-rowers battered him, and I'm convinced to this day it's because he was wearing white boots.

We didn't really mix with the GB lads. We had different schedules and we were in different hotels across town. I often saw Andy Farrell and Denis Betts out jogging on their own. Just those two. They'd done all their training with the team and there they were, probably our country's two best forwards, doing extra training on their own. None of the academy lads went for runs off their own backs; I realised then that the reason they'd got to where they had was because they went the extra yard. When I was looking to improve to get up to speed with the Kiwi boys, just seeing Faz and Denis out jogging like that was one of the defining things that shaped my early career. From then on, I started to do more of my own extras.

John Kear was our coach on that tour and he was brilliant at keeping the lads together. For all the confidence and cockiness that 17 and 18-year-old rugby lads like to portray on the surface, there were plenty who were soon missing their mums and dads—me included. John realised that, and he knew when to have a laugh and when to put an arm around a player's shoulder. His man-management was brilliant. He balanced and split rugby with social time, which is crucial on a long tour like that. If it's all about rugby, you get suffocated by it.

At the end of the tour, we all went out with the Great Britain boys for a few beers and I got chatting to James Lowes. A few New Zealanders in the bar took offence to us and started having a go at a few of our players, taunting them about their 3–0 series defeat. Before I knew it, it had all kicked off. In a blink of an eye, Lowesy jumped in and started scrapping with the Kiwi lads. Everyone jumped in until it became a full-on brawl. I was only a young lad and thought, 'I'll have some of this', so I got a few punches in before the bouncers cleaved between us, and kicked us out.

I was back down under the following year. In 1997, the powers-that-be expanded the World Club Challenge so that it included all the 12 Super League teams from England, plus the 10 teams down under that had broken away from the ARL to form their own competition. It was widely panned by the media, and with good reason; the British teams performed shockingly. The fact that Penrith Panthers won all their six matches and didn't make the quarter-finals says a lot about how one-sided it proved to be. It was great to play in, though. I loved it.

At the time, rugby union had just turned professional and there was a lot of talk about all our best players switching codes because they'd have more travel opportunities and so on. Balls to that—I'd been to Hong Kong, New Zealand and Australia in six months. That was good enough for me.

I was excited to be playing against the Aussie teams, because as a kid, all I'd heard was how much better they were than us. But I'd watched Wigan beat Brisbane Broncos three years earlier in a one-off World Club Challenge match, and I genuinely fancied our chances. I was also excited about going down under again; I'd been to New Zealand just a few months earlier, and loved it. Although it took a lifetime to get to and the weather was crap, New Zealand was beautiful and the people—aside from the knob-heads in the bar on our final night—were really friendly and welcoming. I thought Australia would be the same.

How wrong I was.

Australia is a nice place. The beaches are great, the weather's warm and the beer is freezing cold. But sadly—and this won't shock you—the country is full of Aussies. I don't know what's wrong with the Aussies, but they hate us Brits. This doesn't apply to all Aussies—just the majority.

Everywhere the Leeds lads went, we met hostility; the Aussies looked at us as if to say, 'What are you doing over here?' I've nothing against the Aussie lads who've come over to Super League and played here—some of them are good mates of mine. But I've got a theory that the Aussies who come to Super League are open-minded, want to see some of the world and meet new people.

Yet many Australians haven't left their own state, never mind their own country, and I found them arrogant and ignorant. Many of the Aussies I came across—young lads, old ladies, it didn't matter—didn't like the English, and they weren't afraid of saying so. And I soon discovered that there is one thing worse than an Aussie, and that's a pissed Aussie. If you go into a bar over there, all you hear is, 'Pommie this, Pommie that'. They're horrible.

When I hear about Brits wanting to emigrate to Australia for the sun, I feel like telling them, 'Go to Spain instead'. The nice weather doesn't make up for having to put up with Australians every day.

We arrived in Townsville first to play the North Queensland Cowboys. I wasn't selected for the first game but I was glad to be left out because it was red hot. It was a physical game and the Aussies were giving it to the Leeds lads.

We lost narrowly; the game was played at night and I had so much admiration for the lads playing in that heat. I sat on the bench wearing just a vest and shorts, and I was still too hot—it was horrible. I don't know how the lads played in those conditions.

After that, we flew down to Adelaide for our second match, against the Adelaide Rams. I was named as one of the substitutes, and came off the bench with half an hour to go. I was desperate to make a big impact. Whoever I tackled first was going to get hurt. One of their forwards drove the ball in, I whacked him—job done—but in trying to get him to the ground, I ended up spear tackling him.

I knew what was coming—a red card. It must have been one of the quickest sending offs in history! We lost the game and I was thoroughly pissed off. I'm a home bird anyway, and I was dying to get back to Wigan. The two losses and my sending off made me crave home even more.

Dean approached me after the game. I apologised for being sent off, and he said, 'Don't worry about that, these things happen. But you're going to have to stay here on your own for a week for the disciplinary'.

A week? On my own, in a country I couldn't stand?

I was bricking myself, thinking I'd go mad. I know it sounds like paradise for some people, but not for me. What would I do for a week in Oz? I'd go mental on my own, and if I didn't want to be alone I'd have to talk to Aussies!

'Bloody hell,' I thought. 'I'll end up in jail for punching someone!' Luckily, before I broke down into a fully blown panic attack, the sniggers from Barrie Mac a few yards away told me that Dean was winding me up! They'd got me good style.

Leeds, like most British teams, were exposed in the World Club Challenge. As well as losing down under, the Cowboys and Rams beat us at Headingley, too. Everyone wrote the competition off as a huge flop but in hindsight, it had its benefits, because it opened our eyes to how good the Aussies were. As much as I don't like most Australians, I have to admire how good they are at sport.

They had two rugby league competitions, the ARL and the Super League, running parallel at the same time—we effectively only played half their pool of first-team players—and so, in some respects, it was the best thing that could have happened to Super League because it showed us how far behind them we were. I'd love to see the competition repeated. Having seen how much our game has improved over the last few years, I'm convinced it would be a different story now.

Bradford beat us in the Challenge Cup semi-final, and practically walked away with the title in 1997, but we had a much better season at Leeds. We finished fifth in the end, which was a massive improvement considering we'd scrapped against relegation the year before.

I was still only 18 but I began to feel like a key member of the first-team. I was earning a bit of extra cash, so I decided to move in with Phil Cantillon and Phil Hassan, two other Wigan lads who were travelling over to Leeds with me.

We rented a flat in Headingley which was owned by the Kiwi great Richie Blackmore. Though Moz was actually living with Neil Harmon, he effectively moved into our pad. He came around every day, slept there as often as any of us and ate all our food! We used to go out drinking on Mondays, Tuesdays and Wednesdays—nothing daft, only a few pints—but I don't know how we did it. We couldn't do it now.

When people find out I used to effectively live with Moz, they usually raise their eyebrows as if to say, 'Oh yeah, you must have some stories to tell!' They must form their opinions of us as people based on how we play. Because we're both hot-heads on the pitch, they expect us to act like that off it—like home life would be fighting and smashing up furniture. Well, I can assure you that's not the case. Moz is a terrific fella, and a Christian, who went to church on Sundays when he could. We were pretty sensible.

The most decadent thing we did was break Phil Cantillon's bed when we were wrestling! The thing just snapped in half, which we felt bad about. I suppose, in that sense, we did smash up a piece of furniture while we were fighting! We apologised to Phil and offered to get him a new bed, but Phil told us not to worry. Six months later, he was still sleeping on it and when he left Leeds, he took the bloody thing with him!

Andy Griffin
Ex-classmate, ex-Newcastle United

ON MY FIRST day at my new school, Hawkley Hall High in Wigan, one boy stood out a mile. Terry Newton. He was big, he looked tough, and his head was the same size it is now. I'd recently moved across Wigan, from Winstanley to Worsley Mesnes, and I didn't really know anyone in my new class. Terry didn't know anyone either, so we hit it off straight away. It was September, 1990, and it's incredible to think that, before the end of the decade, we had both played at Wembley Stadium—Terry at rugby league with Leeds, in a Challenge Cup Final, and me at football for Newcastle United, in an FA Cup Final.

The more I got to know Terry, the more I realised he's a person of great contrast. At times he was bubbly, mischievous and a bit of a prankster in class, yet at other times he was shy, guarded and secluded. The biggest contrast about Terry, of course, is the fact everyone thinks he's a rough, tough hard-man. Well, he is on the rugby field, but behind that facade is a real gentle giant. He's a big softy who is very generous, and would do anything for anyone. At school, he got into the odd bit of trouble but I felt sorry for him a lot of the time, because he never caused the bother. He had a (well-earned) reputation for being as hard as a tank, and often older lads would pick a fight with him. Needless to say, on those occasions, he knew how to handle himself.

Terry was a very good rugby player back then. I went along to play rugby with him a few times and I enjoyed it; I was nippy, so I usually played at full-back or centre. Unlike me, Terry loved the rough stuff, so he would be in the middle of the field, doing the bulk of the tackling and driving the ball in, and then I would be there to run down the wing . . . a bit like now! I dragged Terry along to play football. He will tell you he's awful but he's modest, because he's not got a bad left peg, and he was never afraid to tackle. But rugby league was always his calling, and I wasn't surprised that he carved out a professional career.

In the years that followed, as my career took off—first at Stoke City, and later at Newcastle—I always looked out for Terry. If I'm honest—and this may surprise a few people—I prefer to watch rugby league rather than football. It's a real man's game, and you get a lot more entertainment throughout the match.

On many occasions, I've talked team-mates of mine into watching the Friday night Super League games on Sky Sports—it was either that or Casualty—and whenever Terry was on, I'd proudly tell whoever was watching with me: 'That's my mate, Terry.' Terry probably doesn't realise this, but there are loads of Premier League footballers out there who all looked out for him when he was on TV!

I can't count the number of times a team-mate said something to me along the lines of, 'Your mate Terry had a good game last night'. And every time I heard this, I smiled, because he fully deserved the success he had.

I know how much he sacrificed to get to where he did. He always had great enthusiasm and a driving will to win, but any sportsman will tell you it's not just about talent, training and desire—it's also about the sacrifices you make. And Terry—and his mum and dad—made plenty of those along the way. Terry's a nice, decent lad, and it's good to see someone so young fulfil his ambitions and potential. We're both from rough backgrounds, and we both had dreams to make it professionally in our sports, and we both did. I'm proud of what he achieved in his career. Even in his final years at Bradford, I always looked out for him on TV. 'You see him, with the ball,' I used to tell whoever was with me. 'That's my mate Terry . . . and his head was that big when he was 11.'

6

GRAND AMBITIONS

I BROKE my leg twice, was loaned out to Bramley, feared my career was over, played in the first Grand Final and made my Great Britain Test debut. Oh, plus I battered one of my own team-mates. To say 1998 was an eventful year for me would be an understatement!

Dean wanted to step down and take a role developing young lads—I think he realised the coaching move had come too soon for him—so Australian Graham Murray was brought in at the start of the year. When a new coach joins a club, it gets everyone buzzing. Everyone trains hard, because everyone wants to make a good impression. Yet typical of my bad timing, I broke my leg in training just before we flew out to Lanzarote for a warm-weather camp. It was the last thing I needed, because Muzz didn't know me, he didn't know whether I could play or not—and I didn't have the chance to show him. I had a plate inserted into my ankle and went along to Lanzarote anyway; I could still do weights, even if I couldn't do my usual early-morning routines with the rest of the F Club—that's Fat Club: Barrie Mac, Dean Lawford, me and any other lads who struggled with their body weight.

I hated being on crutches. On one occasion, all the boys were by the pool, and as I hobbled past my crutches slipped on the wet tiles. My crutches split either side of me and I fell flat on my face—cue the sight of 20 unsympathetic blokes pissing themselves with laughter!

Over the years I've been on countless overseas training camps, and every time I went I'd tell journalists and fans and friends and even family members how tough they were. Most people didn't believe me. They just rolled their eyes as if to say, 'Yeah, yeah, whatever . . . enjoy your holiday'. Well, honestly, they really are hard, and usually consist of two or three tough sessions a day.

Muzz must have been pleased with the amount of work the lads had got through because when we got back, he took us to Blackpool for a team-building session.

God knows why he chose Blackpool, because usually bonding sessions are at quiet places! We stopped in the chalets at the Pontin's holiday camp, and hit the town for a few beers. It wasn't long before we were all pretty tuned in, and in one bar, Barrie McDermott had a bit of a scuffle with Jamie Mathiou. Jamie had a way of rubbing people up the wrong way. I never really liked him too much, but I could tolerate him. Barrie couldn't. Those two never got on. Someone started a silly pub game of putting a condom on a team-mate's shoulder. They'd see how long it'd take before they noticed it, and then he would have to put the condom on someone else's shoulder, without them noticing, and so on.

Baz took offence when Jamie got him with it, and they ended up scuffling. It was nothing major, but Leroy Rivett, Moz and I took Baz out of there and decided to go to a different pub. We figured it wouldn't do Baz any favours with our new coach if he ended up fighting with one of his own team-mates in a bar.

'Hold up lads, I'm just going for a piss,' I shouted, and headed down an alley between two pubs. Barrie came too, and pissed on the wall next to me. He was still in a bad mood because he'd had that scuffle.

I said, 'Come on Baz, cheer up. It's not the end of the world.'

Still he wouldn't smile. So for a laugh—and looking back now, I still can't believe I did it—I pissed on Baz's hands.

'What you doing, you dickhead?' Baz asked and, outraged, turned and pushed my shoulder.

We both still had our todgers hanging out at this point.

'I'm only having a laugh with you,' I said. 'Calm down will you, I'm not starting with you.'

He shoved me again and I let it go—I'd just pissed on his hands, after all—but he was getting worked up and I said, 'Baz don't shove me again, I'm not going to back down to you'.

He was in a foul mood already and being pissed on hadn't calmed him down. Funny that.

He said, 'Come on then', and I knew he was going to come for me. As I've explained earlier, I'd rather lose a fight than be a coward and run away—even if it's against someone as big as Baz.

He was absolutely raging. I thought, 'I better hit him before he hits me', so I whacked him.

Barrie's head is as thick as a wall, but my punch connected sweet, I hit his chin and he went straight down on the floor, right next to the puddle of piss.

I sobered up in an instant. 'What have I just done?' I thought. Moz and Leroy saw what was going on. They jogged down the alley and, as Baz was getting to his feet, rubbing his chin, they took me back to the chalet where we were staying before Baz came round and had a chance to get me.

I wasn't proud of putting Baz down, I was ashamed. Baz had been Dean Bell's first signing at Leeds, and I'd looked up to him long before he had become a team-mate. He used to knock the living daylights out of the Aussies—he even cleaned out one of my favourite Kangaroos players, the Balmain forward Paul Sironen, while playing for Wigan in '94—and I thought, 'I'm going to love playing alongside him'. And I did love it—we'd become good mates. I was devastated that I'd hit him.

On top of that, we had a new coach and, as I lay in my bed in the chalet, I started worrying about what he'd think of me if he found out. Players have been fired from clubs for much less. Bust-ups among players in training are not unusual, because rugby lads are aggressive and competitive by nature, but usually it's a shove here or there and that's it. Pissing on— and punching—a team-mate outside a pub is, I'm happy to say, not common in our game.

Barrie, in his autobiography, said I ran off after I'd whacked him but that's not true. I'm not saying he's lying, but his recollection must have been a bit dazed after I'd hit him!

I was lying on my back, Leroy in the next bed, replaying what I'd done in my head. I was ashamed of myself. A few minutes later, I was just nodding off when I heard a loud 'boom'. I looked up and the door shot open, crashing against the wall.

Baz stood in the doorway. Our room was dark, and all I could see was his silhouette against the doorway. He looked massive! Before I could say anything, Baz jumped on top of me and hit me, but somehow I managed to turn him on his back and I started hitting him again. The lads broke it up, Barrie left, and that was it.

I avoided him the day after, and that's how it carried on. We didn't speak to each other for about three months after that. We couldn't even look each other in the eye, because we were both so ashamed of what had happened. The other lads noticed it in training. There was a frosty atmosphere whenever we were together in the same room.

If it happened now, at my age, I'd like to think I'd go over and apologise to him. But I was still a young man then, and I think the fact I didn't swallow my pride was one of the worst mistakes of my career.

Eventually, after weeks of ignoring each other, it all came to a head. I went for a sandwich after training and as I pulled up outside in the car, I saw Barrie inside the shop. I decided to wait until he'd gone—the whole thing had escalated to the point where I couldn't be in the same room as him. Barrie came out of the shop and saw me. He came over to the passenger's side window, put his big head through and said, 'Look Terry, whatever happened, let's forget about it. We can't go on like this. Let's shake on it'.

So we did.

And since then, we've been good mates. We've never spoken about that fight to this day—and I've never told him how much I respect him for being the first to break the ice afterwards. It took the bigger man to do that.

Muzza made an instant impression at Leeds. Iestyn Harris, who had come in from Warrington midway through the past season, was playing at full-back and he was on fire—he was the best player in Super League by a mile. When our games were on Sky, the man of the match was given a PlayStation and Iestyn must have won seven or eight of them over the course of the season! We also had a monster pack, with Anthony Farrell, Darren Fleary, Barrie Mac and Mark Glanville, an Australian back-rower who could hardly train during the week because of all the niggling injuries he was carrying, but was awesome on the field. He never gained recognition from the fans but the players loved him. I remember thinking, 'I'm a lucky sod playing with all these meat heads'.

After one awful season followed by an average one, we really started to believe we could actually challenge for silverware, especially after hammering Bradford 26–6 on Easter Sunday at their Odsal ground. A Leeds win over Bradford is nothing unusual now, but at the time, Bradford were awesome. They'd gone 21 games without defeat the year before to win the Super League title, and added the great Shaun Edwards to their side since. I remember bumping into some Leeds fans the day before the match and they said things like, 'Make it a good score', and 'Try your best'. They never expected us to win, but I did. Our forwards ripped into Bradford and on the back of that, Iestyn was superb, and finished the game with a hat-trick.

I was lucky to play in a few Bradford-Leeds derbies, for both sides, over the years and they're always great occasions. I also played for Wigan against Saints, and I've been asked a few times which is the biggest and best. I think it's Wigan-Saints—but I'm biased, because I'm a Wiganer. Yorkshire players who've experienced both, such as Leon Pryce and Stuart Fielden, will probably tell you the opposite.

In mid-season I suffered another injury setback, breaking my leg in training. It healed quickly, but Leeds had formed a link with Bramley and so anyone who had a lay-off got shipped off to Bramley on loan to recover. Bramley basically became a rehab centre for injured Leeds players.

I had to go for four weeks, along with Leroy Rivett and Barrie Mac. I wasn't happy about it. When I got there, I thought, 'This is where my career ends', because I was always hearing about lads who'd get injured, drop down a division or two and never returned.

It was horrible playing in that division—no disrespect to those lads, they were a good bunch who loved the game. But they were part-timers and I knew I was better than them.

I played two games, against York and Doncaster. We were beating York by four points and we were attacking their line, then one of my passes got intercepted and York snatched the win. Bramley didn't get promoted that season and their chairman still jokes with me that I cost him £200,000 because of that intercepted pass! At least, I think he's joking.

I was only 19 and, in hindsight, I can see the logic of Leeds loaning me out like that to get my match fitness. But at the time, I couldn't see the bigger picture. I felt unwanted. I was low, and it got to the point where I considered packing it all in. I nearly walked away from it all. Barrie knew what I was going through, and he helped me sort my head out. He told me to be patient and to keep plugging away, and within a few weeks I was back in the Leeds side.

Muzz had really transformed the side. We went from losing games we should have won to winning games we could have lost. The fans were pleased with the turnaround, but Muzz wasn't satisfied. Our form dipped mid-season—we were winning games without playing particularly well—and Muzz decided we needed another team-bonding session to bring us together. It showed what a great man-manager he was. He hired a canal barge, filled it with ale and put the team in it. No-one else was allowed in—no mates, no staff, no girlfriends.

We were just in one long, open room, getting drunk, going down the Leeds-Liverpool canal, taking part in one of the best team-bonding sessions I've known. No-one could get off and go to the next pub, or talk to other people or chat up girls; we were all together, and if you had a problem you aired it. It was a brilliant idea.

We all clicked, and really kicked on in the league. My form was beginning to turn a few heads, and with a few weeks to go until the end of the season, I was named in the provisional Great Britain squad for the end-of-season series against the touring New Zealand side.

Wigan, who had been revived by John Monie, and Leeds were pretty much neck-and-neck all year, though it didn't really matter who finished top—that was the first year of the play-offs, with the Grand Final deciding the champions. It was strange getting my head around the Grand Final concept. For as long as I'd known, the team who finished top of the league were the champions. The RFL decided to copy the Aussies and bring in a Grand Final instead, which I was excited about.

They scrapped the end-of-season Premiership, which was dying a slow death, and I could see that the play-off system was going to keep the interest and excitement there all year. Since then it's taken off, and every player I speak to loves it. Occasionally, I'll read remarks from a player saying they don't like it, but I reckon they do that just to get their name in the paper. If you took a poll of players, I bet every one of them would keep it, because I've never once heard a player say, 'How shit are these play-offs?'

We lost four games all year. Wigan lost two. We finished second behind them on the ladder, earning us a trip to Central Park in our opening game of the play-offs. Though I was playing for Leeds, part of me was still a Wigan fan. I looked at what they were doing. Don't get me wrong, I always wanted to beat them, but I still checked out their results. Old habits die hard. It was a massive occasion for me to play at Central Park; I'd played there at schoolboy level but it was unbelievable to play in front of the Wigan fans, because I knew there were people I went to school with still standing in the same places I used to stand with them, cheering Wigan on.

We'd already beaten Wigan 15–8 back in August at Central Park, in a game best remembered for Mick Cassidy trying to remove Adrian Morley's head with his forearm! I don't know what Cass was thinking, normally he had such a good, copybook tackling style—maybe he got scared of Moz running at him. A lot of the Wigan fans thought, 'Good on Mick' because Moz had cleaned out Robbie McCormack in a previous game.

We lost our play-off match to Wigan, but then we eased past Halifax and St Helens to get to the final to set up another date with my hometown club at Old Trafford.

It seems ludicrous thinking about this now, but before the first Grand Final, plenty of people were edgy and wondering if it was going to take off or not. The rugby league officials tried to convince everyone it was going to be a big event like an American Football Superbowl—but plenty of fans thought it was going to be, well, crap.

As a player, I was unsure which way it would go, until I walked out of the tunnel at Old Trafford and was hit by a wall of noise. 'How good is this?' I thought.

I was so hyped up. I was 19-years-old, playing at a packed Old Trafford, alongside some great players and against some of my boyhood heroes. It was definitely the biggest moment of my career. As soon as it kicked off, the game was fast and ferocious. We scored first when Richie Blackmore went over for a try. We were leading 6–4. That was only a slender lead, but I honestly felt like we were on top: I remember at one stage, we kicked a ball down field and we had Wigan on their line. We were bashing the hell out of them, and there didn't seem to be one player who wanted to take the ball in. We beat their pack, no question: they had some decent players and a superb leader in Andy Farrell, but in general, our forwards were better than Wigan's. They had a gun backline, with players like Henry Paul, Gary Connolly, Kris Radlinski and Jason Robinson, but luckily the wet conditions did their three-quarters no favours.

They looked down on their feet when—and I can still

vividly picture it—I looked up and there, at dummy-half, was Jason Robinson. I looked at our defensive line and it was ragged in front of the play-the-ball, with Jamie Mathiou still getting back in position. Bollocks.

Jason was lightning from a standing start. An absolute freak. He ran at our line, sidestepped past Jamie and I thought, 'Bloody hell, that's the game'. In fairness to Jamie, no-one else could have scored that try. We'd put so much into that game and one lapse of concentration—and one freakish act by Jason—cost us dear. We were gutted. It was like someone had ripped our insides out. Everyone said afterwards that the Grand Final concept was going to be a hit, but we weren't thinking of that. I'm not even sure we bothered having an end-of-season drink, we were just so down.

Within a week, Jason Robinson went from chief tormentor to team-mate. A phone call from someone at Leeds informed me I'd kept my place in the Great Britain squad to play against the touring Kiwis. No fanfare, no fuss—I'm still surprised at the informal way such call-ups are announced to players. They're never built up, but they should be—especially for lads getting their first call-up, because it's a huge honour. I was only 19, and I'd already resigned myself to not playing. There were plenty of quality players in the squad, including Keiron Cunningham, but I was excited to have the chance to learn from them, even if I wasn't picked.

When we met up at the team hotel, and I was with guys like Andy Farrell, Jason, Gary Connolly and Kris Radlinski, I knew I must have been doing something right. I loved being in that environment. I was still shy, so I stuck with mates such as Darren Fleary and Francis Cummins. I wish I'd had the confidence to ask Keiron if he could do some one-on-one training with me, but I was too scared to say anything to him other than the occasional, 'Alright'.

It's normal for lads from different clubs to stick together during international camps. They made a bit of a fuss about it after the 2008 World Cup, with plenty of people saying the reason they did so poorly was because the Leeds and St Helens lads didn't mix. It got blown well out of proportion—things like that were happening when I first got into the GB squad in '98, and it's no big deal. It's natural to stick with your mates, but that doesn't mean there's a problem—everyone still gets on. It's certainly not an excuse for being caned by the Aussies.

Although I stuck with my Leeds mates, I kept a close eye on what the Wigan lads were up to, just because I was in the squad with players who were heroes of mine. Faz, just like on tour in New Zealand two years earlier, always seemed to be doing extra training.

Sean Long was also in the squad, which was great for me because I'd known Longy since we'd been kids growing up on the same estate. As expected, we didn't get picked for the first two Tests. The games were on Saturday nights, and obviously everyone had a lie in. Even so, the management told the players who weren't in the team that they weren't allowed to go out on the Friday night. For some reason, they were worried the noise of a few pissed up fellas coming in at 3am may disturb the lads who were playing!

Still, not the type to pass up a chance to have a few drinks, Longy recruited Harvey Howard and between us we hit on the idea of going out via the service lift—which the cleaners and maids use—so no-one would see us. I wanted to go, but I was a bit nervous.

'What if someone sees us?' I asked.

'Don't worry, I'll get disguises,' said Harvey.

So the three of us sneaked off through a hotel fire exit and headed for Love Train—the seventies night at Leeds' Town and Country Club—wearing ridiculously over-sized shades and afro wigs! We felt like mischievous little school kids, knowing we weren't supposed to be out, but when we got back to the hotel we were careful not to wake the lads up, so no harm was done.

GB lost the first two Tests, which I didn't figure in; the senior lads were pissed off about the results but to be honest, I was just made up to be in the squad. I knew my only chance of playing was if Keiron got injured. No player wishes injury on someone else—no matter how much they stand to gain—but at the same time we know we're playing rugby league, not tiddlywinks, and injuries are part and parcel of it.

Sure enough, before the third Test, Keiron got injured, so I got my chance in the game, which was played in Watford of all places. Andy Goodway presented me with my shirt and cap in front of all the lads—I didn't let on how proud I was, but afterwards I went straight to the phone to tell my mum and dad!

The Kiwis were coached by big Frank Endacott—my future Wigan coach—and they had an awesome side with players like Ruben Wiki, Richie Blackmore, Henry Paul, Craig Smith and Quentin Pongia. I had an immense amount of respect for Quentin. He was an animal. I remember Darren Fleary cleaning him out with one of the hardest tackles I've ever seen in one of the other Tests. I thought, 'There's no way he's getting up from that', but sure enough, Q got up, dusted himself down and played the ball . . . and I'm sure he had a smile on his face as he did!

Half my family came down to Watford for the game. We'd lost the series, so there was no pressure on us and that helped me, on my debut for Great Britain. Goodway was brilliant—I really rated him as a coach—and he told me to relax and just to play my normal game.

As we walked out, all sorts of emotions passed through my mind. It was an awesome feeling. Adrenaline was running through me. I'm definitely no karaoke king, but as we lined up for the national anthem I thought, 'I best pretend to sing this, in case my mum's watching me', so I mimed along with it! Before the game kicked-off, the Kiwis did their traditional Haka. I can see why the Haka unsettles some players. Even Robbie Paul looks like a scary sod when he's doing it! But for me, it had the opposite effect. It fired me up.

I did alright in the match, but I had to leave the pitch just after half-time because, as Goodway said in the press conference afterwards, 'He was knackered, but we got him back on and it started to go well again.' Bloody right I was knackered—have you seen the size of those Kiwi boys? It was a great experience and I was pleased with how I played. Tony Smith kicked a late drop-goal to earn us a draw, which made it even sweeter.

It was a great way to end my year. I'd come back from two broken legs and a loan spell at Bramley and finished as Great Britain's starting hooker. For a time, everything felt good. Until I heard who Leeds were signing for the following season—another bloody hooker.

7

WONDER OF WEMBLEY

I WENT INTO my fourth season as a first-team player and as a Great Britain international. So you can imagine how pissed off I was when Graham Murray signed Lee Jackson at the start of 1999. I thought Muzza mustn't rate me as a hooker—why else would he sign a hooker?

This was at the time when teams only used one hooker, not two. It's common-place now to carry a hooker on the bench, but Muzza was the first one in Super League to employ that tactic. Before then, coaches rarely put another hooker as a substitute, so when Jackson was signed I thought I was destined for a year in the 'A' team. If ever anyone asked me about it—and there were a few—I was diplomatic: 'Everyone wants competition for places, I'm happy about the signing.' But I didn't mean it. I was proper pissed off.

Lee won a Grand Final with Newcastle in Australia in '97, and was a good player. He had many good qualities, but he wasn't renowned for his defence. By contrast, I could hit blokes and hurt them, no problem, but I was still learning the craft of a hooker—when to pass, when to run from dummy-half, when to work the blind-side. Muzza must have realised that, and decided to use us both in a game, which usually meant I'd play the first 30 minutes and then Lee would come off the bench. Looking back now, it worked brilliantly, and it highlighted what a great tactical coach Muzza was.

But was I happy about it? No. Even though I was playing regularly, it did my head in that I started games and did all the donkey work, made 20 tackles and bust a nut trying to hurt players, and then Lee came off the bench to carve open the same defences that I'd helped wear down. Lee was taking all the limelight. I didn't blame him—it wasn't his fault—but it annoyed me that no-one noticed I was the one softening teams up before he came on and did all his fancy work.

The Leeds squad headed off for a pre-season training camp in Tunisia at the start of the year. While there, Barrie McDermott hit on the idea of shaving everyone's hair off. The Olympic great Daley Thompson was on that camp; he must have thought we were nutters.

Phil Cantillon, as the new bloke, was a prime target for a prank, and when Barrie started shaving Phil's head he deliberately left tufts of long bits everywhere. He said, 'Don't worry Phil, I'll get them in a minute', but then Baz turned the clippers off and told Phil they'd broken! I'm not sure if Phil believed him, or was too scared of him, so he didn't say anything, but at the time Phil fancied himself as a bit of a ladies' man so he wasn't thrilled with his new look.

To make matters worse for Phil, later that evening we had a game of spoons which did nothing to improve his looks. Spoons is a silly game, where you put a spoon in your mouth by the handle-end, leaving the head prodding out. Then players take turns to hit each other on the head with them: one player would dip their head and the other would 'nod' their head as hard as they could to see who could do it harder. I hid a spoon behind my back, and when Phil dipped his head, I put my arm behind my back, grabbed my spare spoon out of my pockets and whacked him on the head!

'Bloody hell Tez, how can you do that so hard?' Phil said.

I just shrugged. 'Strong neck, mate.'

By the end of the game, he had as many bumps and bruises on his head as he did tufts of long hair!

Mind you, with Phil having such a unique look, at least Muzza could recognise one player in the side. After our first pre-season game, he did the video review and he couldn't tell who was who because all the white lads in the team looked the same with their heads shaved! Every time there was a forward pass or someone did something wrong, the player just denied it. It was one of the funniest video sessions I've ever seen.

Muzza was a great man-manager and coach, and another string to his bow was that he was a brilliant motivator. This was back when the Cup Final took place in April or May, so the early rounds were at the start of the season. He got all the lads together before the Cup draw, and talked about Wembley. It was to shut down that year to make way for a new stadium, meaning that year's Challenge Cup Final would be the last at the famous old ground.

'You've got a chance to go down in history,' Muzza told us. 'Imagine being the last team to win the trophy at Wembley. Imagine what it would mean to your families.' He got us all pumped up.

We all bunched around a small TV to find out who we would play first up. At various stages during my career, I was asked by reporters for my reaction to a draw, and usually I came out with the same diplomatic response that most players recycle—'You've got to beat the best at some point' and 'We'll respect lower division sides, it'll be like a Cup Final for them'.

It's not true.

Everyone wants to get one of the remaining amateur sides or lower league teams rather than one of the bigger Super League sides, of course they do. And with the Leeds squad dying to get to Wembley, we hoped Lady Luck was wearing blue and amber.

We got Wigan, at home.

Muzza wasn't deflated, though. 'You're going to do it,' he said. 'And you're going to do it the hard way.' We knew we were capable of beating Wigan.

They'd lost two of their pivotal players, Henry Paul and Robbie McCormack, in the off-season and not really replaced them, and we were still stewing over our Grand Final loss to them just a few months earlier. We had a score to settle.

On the day of the game, we were fired up like you wouldn't believe. Within the first few minutes, Barrie Mac was sent off for a high tackle on Simon Haughton, reducing our side to 12 men. Losing a player is always tough; losing a big player like Baz, and so early in the game, even more so. But we were so angry about the circumstances that it actually worked in our favour.

Barrie will be the first to admit he caught Simon high, but I wasn't happy with the way he went down and started rolling around on the floor like a footballer. The ref saw it was a high tackle, so for Si to make it look even worse by staying down . . . well, to say we were furious is an understatement. It sparked us up, we gave it to them physically, and we went on to win 28–18. After the heartache of Old Trafford a few months earlier, it was a sweet victory.

Barrie, though, was still furious and after the game, while we were all having dinner, he clocked Simon across the room. He went straight up to him to confront him about his Oscar-winning dramatics—Baz was a raging bull, and lost his head a bit. Whatever happens on the field should stay there, and usually does; you should always be able to shake an opponent's hand afterwards. Baz eventually calmed down, but God knows what he would have been like had we lost the game!

That win, in the first game of the season, really gave us the confidence to think we could go on and do something special. Muzza introduced a call—'78'—that we'd shout out any time we felt under pressure. For someone who doesn't know the game, that may sound stupid, but you can't play a full match at 100mph. Inevitably there are lulls, and times when blokes tire, so when the '78' call went out, we stepped up. The name of it referred back to the last time Leeds had won the Challenge Cup—the year I was born.

I'd never heard a call like that, but it worked a treat. We beat Saints and Widnes in the Cup, and then played Bradford in the semis at the McAlpine Stadium, in Huddersfield. Bradford had gathered some momentum that year, and so it was an epic derby. During the match I tackled Brian McDermott under the sticks, and accidentally caught him with my knees in the ribs. He stood up, and I could tell from the pissed off look on his face he was going to have a go at me. I thought, 'It's on'. I totally go along with the theory that the best form of self-defence is to get the first shot in—that way you can take your opponent by surprise and, hopefully, stop them in their tracks before they've had a chance to hit you. That day, I didn't get the chance. Brian hit me with a swift punch that sent me spinning like a bloody ballet dancer. A couple of my team-mates rushed in to back me up and Brian got them with the fiercest, fastest four punch combination I've ever seen. Respect to him. It was only later that I found out he used to be a boxer in the Royal Marines—he's one I never went for again!

We won the game, 23–20, and everyone at Leeds went Wembley crazy. Everyone, that is, but me. The RFL reviewed the incident, and even though I knew I'd caught Brian with my knees by accident—and had been on the receiving end of his own form of retribution—I worried it would cost me my place in the Cup Final. Even if I only got a two-week ban, someone else would get my place before Wembley and I may not have got back into the team. Luckily, the disciplinary panel saw sense and let me off, and I was cleared to play in the Challenge Cup Final.

Leeds had been to Wembley as recently as 1995—when Wigan had beaten them 30–10 in the last of their eight final wins on the trot—but hadn't lifted the trophy in 21 years. For such a massive club as Leeds, that was a hell of a long time between drinks.

Muzza had completely transformed us. He took us to a Grand Final in his first season and then to Wembley—it spoke volumes of the impact he made at the club, especially when you consider that we'd battled relegation in my first season.

We went into the '99 Cup Final with the previous season's Grand Final loss on our minds. That defeat hurt us like you wouldn't believe, and none of the lads wanted to go through that suffering again. We had plenty of confidence, and luckily our opponents were the London Broncos. London were a decent side back then and had some great players like Martin Offiah and Shaun Edwards, but we expected to win.

Muzza probably realised that our greatest obstacle was complacency, and so the night before the game, he came up with a great idea. He gathered all the lads together, handed out slips of paper and pens, and asked us all to write down what we thought of each of our team-mates. He asked us not to sign them, to keep them anonymous.

There's no-one worse than me for taking the piss at arty-farty ideas like that, but I went along with it and wrote down what I thought of each player. I thought it was a bit daft. Like something primary school kids would do. When we went for dinner, the coaches copied out what had been said about each player onto a single sheet of paper, underneath a picture of the player, and then later that evening they slipped them under each player's door. Mine had comments like, 'a great player', 'a future Great Britain captain', 'good skills', 'always gives his all'—I didn't know who the comments had come from, but they inspired me. They made me feel about seven feet tall. I was still relatively young—21—and I thought I might have been nervous the night before the final, but after reading those comments, I went to bed completely calm. I slept with that comments sheet under my pillow and read them again the next morning. We went for breakfast and the mood was incredible. We were all best mates and a tight unit. Muzza's ploy had worked a treat.

We talked about London's key players, and the big threat was undoubtedly Edwards—everything went through him. I couldn't believe I was playing against him, because he'd been in the Wigan team when I'd gone to Wembley a decade earlier to watch Wigan beat St Helens 27–0, and he's practically a God in Wigan. And rightly so.

Our game plan was to take as much energy out of him as we could by channelling the forwards' drives at him. Muzza told us that the secret to winning a Cup Final is to carry on doing what you usually do, and not to look for the Superman plays—that's when you come unstuck. Apart from wearing the nice Hugo Boss suits that Leeds had bought for us, we kept our usual pre-game routines; some lads listened to their Walkmans—these days they use iPods—and some lads played cards on the way to the ground. I never played cards—I'm too tight to risk losing money! I like my music, though. Moz is a massive Bob Dylan fan; he got me liking him, and The Jam as well. But before a match, I listened to hardcore dance music. I've never really liked it, but it got me pumped up before a match. The lads took the piss out of me for it and said things like, 'Get your glow-sticks out, Terry'. They wouldn't let me play it in the changing rooms, so I put it on at home instead.

Barrie Mac was always nervous before a game and often vomited, in between pacing around the dressing room. I had to tell him to calm down and not to burn up energy playing the game in his head, well before kick-off. I'd played at Old Trafford a few months earlier but I'll never forget how I felt when I walked out at Wembley. It seemed massive! All the dimensions seemed bigger—even the pitch, though it was only a full-size one.

It felt like it took half an hour to walk from the tunnel to the middle of the pitch, in front of the Royal Box, to meet the special guests. It was surreal—it hit me like a sledge hammer. I remembered all those times on the school field when my mates and I would re-enact Wembley moments—we did what all lads that age did, complete with our own running commentary. And now it was happening. I was actually at Wembley. Muzza told us before we went out to concentrate on playing the game rather than on the occasion. He also told us not to look for our families. I still had a glance, but I couldn't see them.

Leeds' fans were unreal that day. They'd not won a trophy in two decades, and the fans could sense something special, just like we could. Challenge Cup Finals always attract fans from various clubs—not just the two teams involved—and that day, I think there were more 'neutrals' than usual: they wanted to pay their farewell to the famous Wembley stadium.

The match nearly got off to a great start for me. I'd never scored for Leeds before, and from acting half-back, I saw a small gap open up and I darted through. I was in the clear. In my mind, I'd scored, but out of nowhere their full-back Tulsen Tollett came across and stopped me about an inch or two short—if I'd gone for it and pinned my ears back, I reckon I could have scored. I was furious with myself, though not as mad as my dad. He later told me he had £20 on me at 40/1 to score the first try, and I think half his local pub had the same bet on! Tulsen's a good bloke, but I don't think my dad ever forgave him. London shocked us a bit by scoring a couple of tries, including a great Offiah effort, and actually led 16–12 early in the second-half. But our pack was awesome and we blitzed them in the second-half. Leroy Rivett became the first to score four tries at Wembley and he got a £10,000 bonus, plus the Lance Todd Trophy as man of the match, so he was over the moon.

The game went by so quickly; it was a case of blink and you'd miss it. With a few minutes left I knew we had it in the bag, which gave us a chance to relax a bit and soak up the atmosphere, and the magnitude of what we'd done. When the final whistle went, the feeling was sensational. I didn't want it to end. It's hard to describe just how good it was. It was one of those brilliant, amazing feelings you wish all your close mates and family could experience just once in their lifetime. We did a lap of honour and collected the scarves, hats and flags that had been thrown onto the pitch—the fans were going mental. I scanned the crowd for my mum and dad, and just before I went to the tunnel, I caught sight of them. They were happier than I was, and I went over and gave them a kiss.

I'd been to Wembley not long ago as a fan; I'd watched all Wigan's Cup Finals, some live, and some on the TV. In my eyes—just like in many fans' eyes—Wembley was a special place.

Inside the dressing room, the press came in—they're usually allowed in to interview the winning team after big games—and before the interviews were completed, we cracked open the Champagne, which I poured down my neck. I can't stand the stuff, but it was free; I've never been one to turn down a free drink!

That evening, we had a formal meal and function in our hotel. Most of the lads had their wives or girlfriends with them, and were on best behaviour. I was single at the time—Moz, Andy Hay and Leroy were also unattached—and so we headed to the bar early and began necking stupid amounts of shots. Leroy must have been especially drunk, because before heading to bed at about 5am, he suggested we go for a swim. I must have been fairly drunk, too, because I remember thinking what a great idea that was. So the pair of us walked down to the pool and dived in—still dressed in our Hugo Boss suits. Needless to say, the suits were ruined, and I was devastated when I sobered up. It was the nicest suit I'd ever had!

The homecoming, the day after a Challenge Cup Final, is as much a part of the occasion as Wembley. We got up early on the Sunday, all nursing monster hangovers, and loaded up our coach with booze for the journey back north. Everyone was still in a great mood, despite the lack of sleep and pounding heads. What made our achievement even more special was the fact it was nearly an all-British line-up. We only had three overseas players—Kiwi Richie Blackmore and Aussie pair Brad Godden and Marc Glanville. As we approached Leeds, we calmed down the drinking a bit—we didn't want to appear slaughtered in front of our own fans. We switched coaches to an open-top bus for the parade through Headingley. Our stadium was packed with fans. I remember holding the trophy up and Iestyn Harris gave a great speech to thank the fans for their support—they were ecstatic. That's when my joy gave way to panic: when I'd been to Wigan homecomings at Central Park as a fan, players used to get up and sing a song each. For a brief moment I thought, 'Please God, tell me I don't have to sing on stage'. Thankfully I didn't!

A few weeks later, perhaps realising we needed freshening up before our play-offs charge, Muzza gave all the lads a few days off to recharge their batteries. Most of the lads did the sensible thing and went away with their families. But 'sensible' and me don't always go hand-in-hand, and I talked Moz, Iestyn and Leroy into going to Ibiza for a lads' holiday.

One night, when we were all tanked up, we decided to go diving in the harbour. It was a silly thing to do, but in our drunken state we thought it was funny, and we must have spent about an hour jumping into the sea from the harbour wall. Suddenly, Iestyn and I clocked a couple of policemen heading our way. We wanted to warn the other two, but they were in the water and we didn't have time. So, without making a fuss, Iestyn and I calmly walked away, leaving the other two to deal with the local police. I expected them to get a rollicking in Spanish—I couldn't believe it when they were taken away to spend the night in the police cells. I felt bad for them. The following day, they were released, and Moz told us that when they were taken back to the station the policemen battered them with truncheons. Moz is a big fella and everyone knows he can look after himself, but against the Spanish law, he realised the best thing to do was act like a coward—so he did, and they went easy on him. Leroy, though, stood up to them and every time they hit him, he gave them more stick—and so they carried on beating him! He showed me the bruises the next day and he was black and blue all over!

My form for Leeds remained good. I was learning the finer points of a hooker's craft and—in the process—attracting a bit of praise, too. Everything was going great. I'd played for my country, in a Grand Final and won the Challenge Cup at Wembley—and all before my 21st birthday. I thought my life couldn't get much better, but it did . . .

I'll never forget the day when Wigan first approached me—I told them to 'piss off'.

It was a Sunday, and I was around at my mum and dad's house having tea when the phone rang.

'Get that, Terry', said my dad.

I answered it, and a fella asked, 'Is it possible to speak to Terry Newton?'

'Speaking.'

'Hi Terry, I'm David McKnight. I'm calling on behalf of

Wigan.'

I listened while he went on to ask whether I'd be interested in signing for Wigan. I was convinced it was one of my mates mucking around. 'Piss off, you dickhead,' I said, and hung up.

I sat back down and my dad asked who it was. I had just explained that someone was playing a prank when the phone rang again.

I picked the phone up, and it was the same fella. He assured me he really was serious, and asked if I'd have a chat with them about joining Wigan.

It was completely out the blue, and at first it felt too good to be true. It was surreal. There had been a newspaper story the year before, when Lee Jackson had signed, saying Wigan were keen on me, but I heard nothing at the time and I'd seen nothing in the papers since.

Funnily enough, the only person who'd even mentioned the possibility of me joining Wigan was Gary Connolly a few weeks earlier. I was in a club called Embargo, in Wigan, and he was in there with a few of his mates. I'd met him in the GB camp, though I'd never really had a conversation with Lager (that's his nickname, and for good reason).

He came over, asked how I was doing and said that Wigan were going to come in for me. I thought nothing of what he'd said until that phone call from David McKnight. A few days later, my dad and I arranged to meet him—David, not Lager—in the Middleton Hotel in Manchester. He laid it on the table and told me that Andy Goodway, the Wigan coach who'd given me my Test debut, really rated me and that they wanted to sign me. He told me that it was an exciting time because they were moving to a new, 25,000-capacity stadium, currently being built on the outskirts of Wigan town centre. He did a great job of selling the club, but to be honest he didn't need to. My mind was made up before I'd walked into the meeting—all I'd wanted to do since I was seven was play for Wigan.

It didn't take long for Leeds to become aware of Wigan's interest; they were keen to keep me, and offered me a new three-year contract. It caused a shit-storm in the papers. Gary Hetherington, the Leeds chief executive, told the press: 'He won't be going to Wigan or anywhere else for that matter.' He accused Wigan of using the media to unsettle me and called them the 'league leaders when it comes to arrogance'.

I don't know if Gary was trying to scare Wigan off, but if he was, it didn't work. David put a deal on the table from Wigan, and it wasn't great. It wasn't even as much as Leeds had offered me to stay. I told them that, and they upped it by a couple of grand. My heart was set on moving to Wigan, but the experience of jumping into bed with Warrington too quickly a few years earlier had taught me to make sure I didn't rush into anything. I spoke to my dad and weighed up the pros and cons. He pointed out that it made sense to play at Wigan—I was spending a small fortune on petrol driving between Leeds and Wigan every day. I'd loved my four years at Leeds but it was getting a bit stale and, to be honest, ever since the first call, I couldn't get the thought of playing for Wigan out of my head. In the end, it was the easiest decision I'd ever made.

I was out of contract at Leeds but under the Bosman ruling, clubs could request fees for off-contract players under 24. Leeds put a six-figure sum on my head. I was flattered at first, then that feeling turned to worry because Wigan only offered £40,000, and I thought the move might fall through. Peter Norbury, the Wigan chairman at the time, and Hetherington continued their slanging match in the papers, until eventually it went to a tribunal. In the end, the tribunal settled on £145,000! Wigan didn't moan about it, and forked up the cash. But I remember thinking, 'They could have had me for free, four or five years ago.'

I was excited about working with Andy Goodway. He'd given

me my Test debut a year earlier and I thought he was a good coach. So it's typical of my bad timing that, no sooner had I signed a three-year contract with Wigan, they showed Andy the door. I thought, 'Bloody hell, what if the new coach doesn't want me?'

Wigan hadn't won a trophy that season, which was the first time in 19 years they hadn't landed a piece of silverware. For Wigan's fans, that was a crisis—how times change!

When Wigan started back for pre-season late in '99, half the team was away—the overseas players and the Great Britain lot— but I was still a nervous wreck at my first training session. I knew a couple of the lads but I kept to myself because I was after respect, not popularity. Marty Hulme was the conditioner and his fitness sessions were great. I knuckled down and got as fit as I could, because we still didn't know who the new coach was going to be.

Maurice Lindsay had taken over as chairman, and he arranged a friendly against Saints on Boxing Day. My first game for Wigan was a derby at the new stadium. I couldn't believe it. As if it couldn't get better, a few minutes before kick-off, Maurice came into the dressing room and said, 'I'm going to give you £750 each if you win'.

We won our money and I had a decent game. It was only a friendly, but the new season was just around the corner. The country was going mental about going into the new Millennium, and I was going mental too. I was about to start playing for my hometown club.

Adrian Morley

I KNEW Terry Newton had guts before I'd even met him.

I'm a couple of years older than Terry, and I was already on Leeds' books when we heard that he was signing for the club. Trouble was, he'd already signed a contract with Warrington, but he wanted to come to Leeds and he wasn't afraid to fight for it. I remember thinking, 'For a lad of 15 to take on a big club like Warrington, he not only knows what he wants—he's got the balls to do something about it.'

It took ages to sort his wrangle out, meaning he could train but not play with us for months. He was an absolute caged animal, just desperate to play—and he took that anger out by training like a maniac.

In one session, doing 400m runs, the players were split into a few groups, depending on how fast they were. The quick outside backs were in the top group, and then all the way down to the forwards in the last group. Terry started off in the last group and worked his way up four or five groups within the one session—it was amazing to see how much determination he had, just in 400m runs. He had a tremendous work ethic and he loved doing all the hard stuff. I knew from the start I was going to love playing alongside him. Tez signed as a prop and then played a bit of back-row and loose forward, but his body type probably wasn't best suited to those positions, and when Dean Bell moved him to hooker, he took to it like a duck to water. That wasn't just because he had a good engine and good handling skills, but because of the hard graft he put into training in his new position. He didn't want to look like a back-rower playing hooker, he didn't just want to 'do a job' at hooker—he wanted to be the best. It wasn't long before he was representing his country with distinction.

Tez is the first to admit that, especially when he was younger, he was 'all guns blazing, ask questions later'. He never went looking for trouble but he was often in it—and when he was, he'd usually be the one finishing it!

When he was 17, he came drinking with me in my hometown of Salford. We were in a pub with one of my best mates, Carlo, when a few bouncers came down looking for Carlo's brother. I don't know why they were after him, but they were all big lads and they were looking for trouble, and it wasn't long before it all kicked off.

It was like a scene from a Western, with fists and bodies flying everywhere. Tez was only a young kid and I was the one who'd invited him out, so I felt like I had to watch his back.

I looked for him to check he was alright—and found him taking on two massive bouncers! He put them both down. I thought, 'This lad has dynamite in his hands'. I knew he was a tough lad anyway, but that day I realised just how tough. Since then, I've always felt like Terry has had my back.

On the field he was one of those players you wanted on your side. He loved irritating other players and putting them off their games. Rugby league's brutal, and you have to have a streak of nastiness in you to play it. In the heat of the moment it's very easy to cross the line, especially if you're an aggressive player like I am, and Terry was. There's a line, and he occasionally went beyond it because he's so competitive, he just wanted to win, and people could see that every time he took to the pitch.

What fans didn't see was what Tez was like off the pitch— an absolute legend.

He's matured over the years. I know some people probably

think of him as a bit of a wild lad—truth is, he spends his spare time playing with his kids and is usually in bed before the watershed!

He still likes a drink like we all do, but the sessions aren't as often these days. When we toured with Great Britain in 2006 he missed his family so much—he'd be on the phone all the time. He's big on family, but he'll never forget his mates. If Terry's your friend he'll do anything for you. When I was 20, I got banned from driving, which made getting from Salford to Leeds for training tricky! But Tez picked me up for training every day. He went out of his way, driving from his house in Wigan to Salford, then on to Leeds, even though it put many miles and many minutes on his journey. That's the kind of bloke he is—he can't do enough for you. Nothing's too much for him.

8

SIGNING
FOR WIGAN

AT THE START of 2000, Wigan staged a press conference to officially unveil their new signings. I stood on the pitch with three Australians—Brett Dallas, Steve Renouf and Willie Peters. Willie was a cracking lad and an efficient half-back. He was about my age and just at the start of his career.

The other two, though, were dead-set legends. They were already huge stars of the game and had both played for Queensland in the State of Origin series and for Australia. Steve, especially, was a superstar. He brought the nickname 'Pearl' with him from down under, and he lived up to it. I'd seen Brett play on TV, he was one of the quickest wingers around. I soon discovered he was also one of the toughest; I used to call him Robocop because he was an absolute machine.

Stood on the JJB Stadium pitch, freezing my balls off while photographers took our pictures, I looked across at my new team-mates and thought, 'I'm going to enjoy playing here'. Wigan had a new coach that year. I knew of Frank Endacott by his reputation, the Kiwis had been doing well under his control—they'd beaten GB in a series, when I made my Test debut in '98—and we were all excited about playing for him. From his first day, he made an instant impression. He walked in and he was so nice to everyone, he made every player feel good about themselves. Frank always went out of his way to say hello to the players, and also to the players' families and friends. He has a great ability to remember everyone's name. If I bump into him now—he's an agent, who spends a bit of time each year in England—he'll always ask, 'How's your dad, Tony? And what about Stacey?' And on and on. I still don't know how he does it!

Usually, early in the New Year, teams will go away for pre-season training camps. But Frank thought that, with a new coach, two new Australian three-quarters plus a new half-back and hooker, we needed to get to know each other off the field, so he organised a trip to Dublin. When he ordered us to leave our boots at home . . . it was obvious we were there for the beers, not the bleep tests.

I roomed with Tez O'Connor. On our first night, I got up to go for a slash, careful not to wake Tez up. I went to the end of the bed, opened the door for the bathroom, felt around for the edge of the toilet bowl and emptied eight pints down it. But I must have been drunk because the following day, I was woken up by a mental Terry O'Connor moaning that I'd peed all over his shoes! I'd pissed in the wardrobe by mistake.

Mind you, that was nothing compared with what happened to Steve Renouf.

Pearl and Gary Connolly had probably been the best two centres in the world over the past few years. I'm sure Lager won't mind me saying that Pearl probably edged their duels, but there was one area where Gaz was far better than Pearl— drinking!

The pair of them went pint-for-pint all day, and Steve got absolutely smashed. He was completely off his face. Neil Cowie volunteered to put him to bed, so he picked up Pearl and walked off towards his hotel room with his new team-mate over his shoulder.

'I'm going to be sick,' Pearl uttered. As soon as he said that, Neil dropped him. Pearl crashed to the floor. I expected him to scream in agony. He didn't—he didn't make a sound. He didn't move, either.

We all began to panic.

'Oh my God, Neil,' yelled Marty Hulme, our conditioner. 'You've killed the Pearl!'

Neil looked worried. 'But he was going to be sick on me,' he wailed.

Lager and Rob Ball picked Pearl up, and he made a sound that no-one could understand. At least it convinced us that he wasn't, thankfully, dead. They helped him to his room, and no sooner had they got in there than Pearl threw up. Everywhere. It was like someone had blown up a family sized tin of Heinz vegetable soup.

Rob was one of the young lads in the side—a real nice fella who never really got his chance at Wigan—and was rooming with Pearl. The vomit went all over Rob's towel. Gaz did the right thing and helped Pearl clean up in the bathroom. As he came out, Steve was so apologetic. As a diabetic, he obviously wasn't a big drinker and he was embarrassed that he'd got into such a state in front of his new team-mates.

'Sorry Rob, sorry Rob . . . I've been sick on your towel. I'll get you a new one,' he said.

But Rob was having none of it. 'Are you kidding?' he said. 'This is Steve Renouf's sick on my towel. I'm going to treasure this forever.' Rob's probably still got that towel to this day. He certainly still gets reminded of it, whenever he bumps into any of his old Wigan team-mates!

Pearl must have been ill. The morning after, Gary went to wake him up to tell him we were back on the drink. He was having none of it and stayed in bed!

As well as joining a team containing some of my heroes, Wigan also had a player who I didn't like—Neil Cowie. I'd always admired him as a player but I'd never liked him.

I must stress, though, that I formed that opinion of him without ever having spoken to him. One of my biggest flaws—and I try and stop myself from doing it now—is judging people before I've met them, which is ironic, given how much it annoys me when people do the same about me. When I was at Leeds, all I'd hear from Barrie McDermott in the build-up to games against Wigan was how he wanted to smash Cowie. Those two had a fierce rivalry and I—wrongly—judged Neil as a person on the back of that. I thought it might be awkward playing beside a bloke I didn't like, but I soon discovered he's a top bloke. Honestly, he's one of the nicest fellas I've ever met, and he really helped me out.

I'd enjoyed my time at Leeds, but playing for the club I'd supported all my life was a different, better, feeling altogether. Every game at the JJB felt like a final to me. We made a dream start to the season, hammering Whitehaven at home 98–4 in the Cup (I was gutted we didn't post 100 points).

I'd scored six tries in four years at Leeds; at Wigan, I scored 14 in my first season including a hat-trick at Warrington, my first since my amateur days. I also earned plenty of praise. Yet though my first season with my hometown club was a success on the field, I didn't feel completely comfortable in my new surroundings until my second year.

Signing for Wigan was a funny situation because I looked up to the likes of Faz, Denis Betts and Gary Connolly, and I was so nervous being in their company that I didn't really socialise with them for the first 12 months. I fitted in well as far as the team's performances went, but I was still in awe of many of my new team-mates, and I avoided situations where I'd be in conversations with them. I kept my head down. I didn't feel like one of them, not straight away: I felt like I had to earn their respect.

There were players in that team who didn't need coaching. Frank realised that all they needed was a bit of guidance, so he concentrated on turning us into a close-knit group, and that's what we became. He didn't give us many ideas on how to beat teams but he made us want to play for him, and for ourselves. Frank didn't really coach us, in the true sense—and that's not an insult, it's a compliment. Many coaches, in that position, would have allowed their egos to interfere and start telling the players what to do. Well, if you look at our backline at the time—Jason Robinson and Brett Dallas on the wings, Steve Renouf and Gary Connolly in the centres, plus Kris Radlinski at full-back—Frank knew he didn't have to tell those guys what to do, and he didn't. He left them to it. Wigan's players were as immense off the field as they were on it, and just by rubbing shoulders with them every day, my habits improved and I became a better player. Faz was the ultimate professional. He was as talented as any forward I've ever met and of all the players, he could have afforded to turn up sometimes and think, 'I can't be bothered today'.

But he never did. Not once.

Just like when I'd seen him out doing extra fitness sessions when I'd toured with the GB academy side in '96, he was always one to put in the extra yards.

Terry O'Connor was another. He wasn't the most skilful player in the game but he was one of the fittest props I came across, he worked on his fitness every day—people talk about the professionalism of blokes like Faz and Rads, and Terry was the same.

We'd resigned ourselves to losing one of our best players

at the end of the year. Everyone knew Jason Robinson would be leaving to switch codes, but nobody talked about it. Some fans presume that, as players, we know everything that is going on at a club. Not true. Players tend to keep to themselves when it comes to contracts and so on—they may tell a close mate or two, but not the whole squad.

I liked Jason a lot. He never did a great deal of weights but he had the physique of a Greek God, and he was unbelievably fast. I was one of the many team-mates he left for dead in training matches. Everyone knew he was a Born Again Christian, but it's not as if he preached to us or anything like that. He had a wicked sense of humour and was just like one of the lads. He didn't drink, but he'd still come out with us when we went on the lash. He used to help our partially sighted masseur, Andrew Pinkey around. That's the kind of bloke he is. He was also, of course, an awesome winger. He loved nipping into dummy-half and taking runs in—who was I to stop him? I just tried to keep up with him in support!

We only lost three matches out of 28 all season. Some weeks we'd rack up 50 and 60 point wins; other times we'd scrape victories. Our best win was definitely against Bradford at the JJB. We were trailing 19–14 with seconds to go, and were pinned on our own line.

The ball started on our right, we swung it across the line and Pearl made a trademark break from deep inside our own half. He had scorching pace, and the presence of mind to find Rads in support with an inch-perfect pass, to put him over under the sticks. Faz's conversion made it 20–19, and it was probably the best try I've ever seen. Certainly better than that St Helens 'Wide to West' one that Saints fans prattle on about!

Saints were having a decent season, and had beaten us twice already during the year. We blitzed them 42–4 at their place to finish top of the ladder, but bizarrely, they reversed it and won 54–16 at the JJB in the opening game of the play-offs the following week.

We regained our confidence and composure by battering Bradford 40–12, to set up a Grand Final date against Saints. After our past two results between us, no-one could call it.

We'd been awesome that year but they'd been a thorn in our side throughout, and in the Grand Final, Saints out-played us. I'm not making excuses, but I think Frank made a big mistake in that match. Lager was injured, and rather than put David Hodgson at centre against Sean Hoppe or Paul Newlove, he put Hodgy on the wing and switched Jason to full-back, so that Rads—our regular full-back—could line-up in the centres.

Jason's strength was in playing 100mph for short stints, which made him a deadly winger; but he wasn't a rugby league full-back. It disrupted our attacks and we weren't the same side. Frank shouldn't have changed things. We had the better players—we shouldn't have been worried about St Helens.

It was my second Grand Final, and my second defeat. But unlike my loss for Leeds two years earlier, we'd finished top of the table and not won the trophy. Some fans couldn't get their heads around that. They were still used to the old, 'first-past-the-post' way of deciding the champion, and felt that we were the true champions. I didn't. The players accepted it—there was no bitterness from us whatsoever. Saints beat us on the day, fair credit to them. The Grand Final winners are the Super League champions. End of.

These days they present the team that finishes the season top with a league leaders' shield, but I'm not really a fan of that. It takes something away from the Grand Final. If anything, maybe the club that finishes top should be given a financial bonus, maybe to invest in their youth policy, so there's an incentive to finishing top without taking anything away from the play-offs and Old Trafford.

There was a World Cup at the end of the season, but I had to withdraw because of trouble with my left knee. Rob Harris, Wigan's physio, took me down to see a specialist in Wales. One thing about Wigan is they never cut corners on the medical side, they always took players to see the best surgeons and specialists. My left knee was scanned and it was revealed I had an inch-long piece of cartilage missing. On the specialist's advice, I underwent a micro-fracture, in which they drill the bone next to where the cartilage is missing. The bone bleeds and forms a scab—so the scab, in effect, carries out the function of the cartilage (rugby league players become medical encyclopedias by the end of their careers!)

I had to stay off the leg for six weeks, and so I missed the World Cup. I was gutted because I'd been playing well and I wanted to play for England in the tournament. On the plus-side, it meant I was fully fit for 2001. And with the signings Wigan had made I couldn't wait to play again.

9

LAM THE SHEPHERD

FRANK'S REWARD for taking us to the Grand Final was a new, two-year contract, which all the players were made up about. We'd gone alright the previous season, but Maurice was desperate to deliver success to the fans—he had promised them a return to the good days when he returned to the club. He made some brilliant signings that year in Adrian Lam, Matty Johns, Dave Furner and Brian Carney—we were more than capable of winning something.

Once again, Frank opted against the pre-season training camp and for another bonding session, this time in Edinburgh. It wasn't a training camp, it was a training piss-up!

The team had some new faces and the best way of getting to know each other was after a few beers. It sounds like an excuse, but some rugby league players are quite shy, and when other lads are already in established, close-knit groups, it's hard to get to know them. Give them a few beers and everyone soon talks. They don't always make much sense after a few pints and Sambuca shots, but at least they're talking!

No sooner had we arrived in Scotland than Frank told us to disappear into Edinburgh to raid the charity shops for fancy dress clothing. I stuck to the safe 70s option. Carney managed to find a wrestler outfit from somewhere—in another life, he must have been a wrestler. He loves all that, Brian.

The best (or worst, depending how you look at it) outfit

belonged to Simon Haughton. He turned up in a tight, Lycra black catsuit—the scary thing was, he actually managed to pull it off! Si's built like a brick-shithouse, and dressed in his catsuit he looked like Batman with blonde hair.

Everyone knows there are some Australian players who come over to Super League for a big pay-day before they retire. And frankly, I don't blame them—I blame the clubs for signing them without doing their homework. Well back in 2001, no-one could say we had a load of journeymen chasing the coin. Wigan had five Aussies—Steve Renouf, Brett Dallas, Furner, Johns and Lammy. They were all at Wigan to win trophies, and none more so than Lammy.

He had a real passion for the game and on top of that, he was so knowledgeable. I probably played the best rugby of my career that year, and a large part of that was down to Lammy's influence. He was like an extra coach, and a bloody good one too. Until then there was no real logic to whether I ran or passed the ball from dummy-half—but Lammy changed that.

He said to me, 'When I want the ball, give it to me'. It made sense. As a hooker, I was always at dummy-half, bent over, waiting for the ball to be played. At best, I could afford a quick look up at the opposition defence and maybe a glance left and right. Lammy said, 'Terry, you're a hooker. No disrespect, but your head's up someone's arse. How are you going to spot any gaps? When I call for the ball, I want it.'

And he was right. Lammy, as first receiver, had time to look at the other side before the play-the-ball and no-one read a game as well as him. Lammy also taught me that when our forwards were on the front foot—that is, we had momentum and quick play-the-balls—not to pass the ball from the ground, but to pick it up and run a few steps over the advantage line and then pass it. That way, everyone else would be on a roll and—on occasion—it also allowed me to earn my side penalties by deliberately running at offside defenders and making it look like I was being blocked.

His game-sense was faultless, impeccable, and he taught me so much. One of Lammy's many other talents was that he was a champion break-dancer! We only discovered that when the TV pop group, Hear'Say, came to visit for a promotion. We showed them a couple of drills while the cameras filmed them going through the motions, passing a ball, and then they volunteered to show us how to dance.

We all backed off. There was no chance I was going to dance, especially when it was going out on TV—that *Popstars* rubbish was massive at the time! Lammy stepped up to the plate and began break-dancing and he could move, too. Before I knew it, he was spinning around on the floor. It was one of the funniest things I've ever seen.

For such a glamorous squad, we had a very unglamorous opening, with a pre-season friendly against Chorley Lynx. It was one of the coldest games I've ever played in. It must have been –10°C, and at half-time, Pearl sat next to me shivering away, trying to warm his hands on the radiator. He didn't want to go back out for the second-half.

We battered them, as we expected, but our season got off to a nightmare start. Our first competitive game was a Challenge Cup match at St Helens, and we lost 22–8. We were crushed. We'd set our hearts on winning a trophy that year, and one of our two chances had been blown in our first real game.

We put it behind us with some good wins in Super League, and we'd only lost one of seven games—to Bradford, who were killing it that year—when we were beaten at London Broncos. Their Kiwi full-back, Richie Barnett, absolutely ripped us apart in that game.

Still, we'd made it to May with only two defeats in the league and we were all feeling good, especially after running half-a-century past Wakefield in our next match. I still don't know how, but we lost the following game at Salford, 31–30. We just didn't turn up. Credit to the Salford lads that day, they really put on a display, but with the star players we had we should have murdered them. It highlighted the fact that if you don't turn up in rugby league, you can be beaten.

Right at the death, Matty Johns had a chance to scrape us a draw but he pushed a drop-goal attempt wide. We were angry with ourselves, but we didn't panic. We were still third in the league, and only four points off Bradford, who were top. It was hardly a crisis, unless you were Maurice. He was livid. It seemed every time we were beaten—and we'd only had two losses in the league before then—Maurice would call a crisis meeting and tell us it wasn't good enough.

'We're Wigan, we shouldn't be losing to these teams . . .'

What Maurice didn't realise, or chose to not mention, was that all the other teams were catching us up. Gone were the days when Wigan could run away with everything; there were now a handful of clubs spending the same amount on players' salaries, and those players were training the same programmes, in the same type of facilities—it was inevitable that a few teams would become more evenly matched.

I know Maurice wanted success but I think he struggled to grasp how hard it was to get, with the improvements other teams were making. The day after the loss at Salford, we were in training and due to have a first-team meeting at 10am. It got to quarter-past, then half-past, and there was still no Frank. He'd never been late for a meeting before. Finally, he turned up, and walked down the middle of us all, a tear in his eye. He had the look of a man trying to remain strong. We all knew what was coming—you could have heard a pin drop. He didn't beat around the bush. He stood in front of us all, and told us that he'd been fired. And then he did something that absolutely tore me up.

He began to cry.

I'll never forget how upsetting it was seeing such a proud, big man, stand up in front of us and break down in tears.

It wasn't Frank's fault, it was our fault. Maurice had assembled a great bunch of players and expected results, but I think he should have looked at punishing some of the players rather than just the coach. It seems the easy option out is to blame the coach—that year, Dean Lance at Leeds and my old team-mate Gary Mercer, who was coaching Halifax, had both been given the bullet. Then it was Frank's turn. And this was still May.

Frank's man-management was excellent but if he had one flaw, he didn't have that side that would bollock players if they messed up. I never once turned up for a video review session afraid of what he would say—even after I'd had a shocker—because he never highlighted those errors. That aside, he was a top bloke and I thought the world of him. I was gutted he got the sack. We were the ones who deserved punishing, not him.

Australian Stu Raper was swiftly appointed. He'd done a good job at Castleford and he came in and got us back on track. Stu was the opposite of Frank in his coaching style and approach, he was abrupt, but he got us doing the business on the field.

The more we played together, the better my combinations got with Lammy, Kris Rads and Matty Johns. We were all playing really well, and all earning plenty of praise from the fans and the press. All, that is, except Matty.

When he'd signed, Wigan hadn't really had a good stand-off since Henry Paul left and the fans had high hopes for him. Matty wasn't the dashing stand-off who cut through defences. He wasn't Brett Kenny, but that doesn't mean he was a bad stand-off. Far from it.

People didn't realise how good he really was, and a lot of

the criticism he attracted was bang out of line. It usually came from people who didn't know what they were talking about.

Faz scored 17 tries that year—from loose forward—that alone should underline how Matty took the burden of organising the side off Faz's shoulders. How on earth could Faz score all those tries, and how could the backs score tries for fun, if our stand-off wasn't doing the business? It wouldn't be possible.

During the season, Matty Elliot, the former Bradford coach, emailed me and asked if I would be interested in playing in Australia. He had recently taken over at Canberra Raiders, one of the big-names in rugby league, and I must admit I was tempted. I'm no lover of Australia or Australians, but their competition is the best, and the chance to test myself against the best players really appealed to me. But when I spoke to a couple of the Aussie boys at Wigan about it, they warned me off it.

They said that if I wanted to go to Australia, I shouldn't go to Canberra. There was little to do there, the climate is like England, it's inland and not by the beach. Had it been one of the Sydney clubs I may have been tempted. There were plenty of rumours the Sydney Roosters were keen on me, too, and it would have been nice to play alongside my old mate Adrian Morley, but they never approached me. I was flattered that Canberra wanted me, but I loved it at Wigan. I thanked Matty for the interest, and said, 'No thanks'.

Saints had won the last two Grand Finals and it was eating up our fans. They hated it. Saints talked like they were taking over from Wigan as the dominant team in rugby league, so it was great to smash them 44–10 in the play-offs to deny them a place at Old Trafford to face Bradford.

We finished level on points with the Bulls that season—they were top on points difference—but I always felt we'd have the upper on them in the Grand Final. A big strength of Bradford's was their home form. They'd moved from Odsal to Valley Parade, home of football side Bradford City, and it had a small pitch. With their pack, it only took two drives from their big props like Paul Anderson and Stuart Fielden to march halfway down the pitch! On top of that, because the pitch was so short, Paul Deacon—a great kicker at the best of times—could literally slot goals over from inside Bradford's own half.

When we'd played them on our turf that season, they were no match for us—even if their giant pack was enough to give Kris Radlinski the shits!

I sent Radders over for a try in a televised match at the JJB, and as soon as he scored he shot up off the ground. We rushed to congratulate him but he just fended us off, and ran towards the bench. At first, I thought he'd hurt himself grounding the ball. But as he legged it past me I caught a whiff of him and I realised it was something altogether different! It turned out he'd accidentally shit himself a few tackles earlier, while he was driving the ball in. He claims he had a dodgy stomach; personally, I think he was scared of big Joe Vagana and Paul Anderson running at him!

Over the course of the season, we beat Bradford twice and they beat us twice. But I thought because it was at Old Trafford, on a wide open pitch, we were going to run them ragged. How wrong I was. Bradford battered us 37–6. They were 26–0 up inside half an hour; we just couldn't handle them. To this day, I have no idea how we lost by that scoreline. Our team read like a who's who of Wigan legends—Radlinski, Dallas, Connolly, Renouf, Carney and Lam in the backs. O'Connor, Faz, Betts, Furner and me among the forwards. It was an awesome side. But like in the Salford game earlier in the season that cost Frank his job, we just didn't turn up. We had ourselves to blame.

That defeat didn't cost Stuey Raper his job, but it cost us—the players—a small fortune. Maurice came into the dressing rooms after the match, and he was livid. He didn't hold back—he said we were an embarrassment to Wigan, and to ourselves. After being embarrassed on the field, it was the last thing we needed. We didn't need the club chairman telling us we'd let ourselves down, but he had our attention when he finished his rant by saying we weren't going to be paid our bonus. We were stunned.

The end-of-season bonus was calculated on where you finished the season. For finishing as runners-up, we should have got anything up to about £8,000 each, depending on how many games the lads had played in. It was divided fairly—a bloke who'd played 30 games would get twice as much as a bloke who'd played 15.

I quickly forgot about it. I was just pissed off with myself for not playing well. I kept asking myself, 'Could I have done more? Did our forwards get dominated because I didn't give them good balls?'

After a day or two, though, I calmed down, and realised Maurice had ripped us off. We finished second and got to the Grand Final, and though we lost heavily at Old Trafford, we deserved the money. We'd messed up because we didn't sign a contract with Maurice—we didn't think we'd need to. We trusted him. Faz—being the true captain—went to see him to fight our corner, but Maurice was having none of it. He stuck to his guns and refused to give us our money.

We were all furious; we were embarrassed by our performance at Old Trafford, sure, but not all the players were on huge salaries. I certainly wasn't a big earner, and there were plenty of lads on less than me. Many had already earmarked their bonus pay for something—maybe for a holiday with the missus, or a new car, or a deposit on a house. I'd always admired Maurice, but I couldn't understand how he could do that to us.

I lost a bit of trust in him, and to this day I don't know why he did it because Wigan still got the money from Super League for finishing second, and there were 10 teams who finished below us whose players, I presume, all got their money.

Steve Renouf's contract ran out after the Grand Final. The players loved him and the fans loved him, and it was a shock to everyone that Maurice didn't offer him a new deal. I loved playing in the same team as Pearl. We made sure we gave him a good send-off, though Pearl—still mentally scarred from Dublin—went easy on the ale. I drank his share for him to try to numb the pain of an arm injury I'd suffered tackling Daniel Gartner in the Grand Final.

It was killing me. I had a feeling it was broken. I knew I should have gone to get it scanned, but I didn't want to miss Mad Monday because I was sitting in a bloody X-ray room. I made the mistake of telling Rads that my arm was killing me and he kept banging it with a bottle and telling me to stop being so soft. I don't think he realised I was in real agony! Credit to him, though. Rads had been given £1,000 by the sponsors for topping the Super League try-scoring chart with 30, and being the champion team-mate he was, he put it behind the bar for all the boys to share on Mad Monday. We had our annual piss-up at my local, The Crooked Wheel, a pub in Worsley Mesnes that was run by my future father-in-law, Keith Holden. I'd suggested his boozer because it was one of those places where anything went. And it did.

We'd not been drinking long when I looked through the window and saw Brian Carney stripping off to just his boxers. 'What's that mad Irishman doing?' I thought. By the time I'd finished my pint and gone outside, he was riding a little kid's bike around outside, wearing just his duds!

His clothes were in a pile by the side of the road. Being the good mate I am, I gathered them up and threw them onto the pub's roof before he had time to stop me! I waited for him to ask me to go and get them, but he never did. He spent the rest of the day in just his underwear.

Looking back now, those were some of the best memories of my life. Not seeing Brian nearly naked, you understand, but the laughs we used to have on those Mad Mondays. We let our hair down, joked, reminisced, drank until we fell over . . . they really were magical times. In the evening, we went outside to flag down a few cabs to take us into Wigan, but couldn't find any. 'Quick, there's a bus!' someone yelled, and as it pulled up we all ran onto it. The poor driver didn't know what was going on; his bus was invaded by the Wigan team, and I don't think one of us paid! We carried the party on in town and then moved onto Gary Connolly's pad; my last memory was dancing on his over-sized fireplace, accidentally knocking people off with my clumsy arms!

A couple of days later, finally sober, I went into the GB camp for the Ashes series against the Aussies. My arm was still hurting, so I went to see the team doctor, Chris Brookes, and he sent me for a scan. My worst fears were confirmed; I had a complete break in my arm. Brooksey told me I might not play in the Ashes, which I was gutted about because I'd been happy with my form. Terry O'Connor told one of the papers, 'For me, Tez Newton has been the Man of Steel this year'. That was nice to hear, especially considering the nicest thing I'd said about him was that he had a bit of a belly on him!

David Waite, the GB coach, must have been pleased with how I'd been playing. He named me in his 24-man squad even though there was no way I could play in the first Test, and I was only scheduled to have the plaster removed three days before the second Test. My chances of taking part were slim at best, but I thought, 'If David Waite's shown enough faith in me to put me in the squad, I owe it to him to be in great shape.'

I worked overtime to get myself really fit. I was desperate to play against the Aussies. I'd not played for GB since my debut three years earlier and I'd improved out of sight as a hooker. I watched as the lads beat the Aussies in the first Test, at Huddersfield, and that was it. I couldn't stand any more. I thought we were going to make history and beat them in a series—no way was I going to miss out because of a broken arm. I was buzzing around, desperate to play. I phoned Dr Brookes and said, 'I'm taking this plaster off, I can play'.

I believe his exact words were, 'Terry. Don't. Be. Stupid.'

'You're the doc,' I replied. I hung up. And then I took a hacksaw out of my toolbox, and sawed the cast right off. My arm felt fine, so I drove to the Worsley Marriott hotel, outside Manchester, where the GB boys were staying.

Brooksey saw me in reception. 'Nice to see you took my advice,' he said, looking at my arm. He told me I needed another X-ray to prove I was okay. Reluctantly, I went for one and—lo and behold—the bone hadn't healed. I couldn't play. GB lost the next two Tests, which made me feel worse. Yet another year went by with no Test rugby league.

10

OUR STACEY

I FIRST asked Stacey to marry me when I was 13.

Believe me, there were no feelings there. She's four years younger than me and, back then, I just saw her as one of my sister's little mates—they knocked about quite a bit on our estate. One day, she was sitting with my sister on one of those green BT function boxes, at the side of the street, just dossing around. I walked past her with a group of mates. I smiled at her and said, 'I'm going to marry you one day'. My mates burst out laughing—that's the only reason I did it. To show off. I laughed and she forced a smile. It was the weirdest thing to say. Weirder still to think that within the next 10 years, I'd asked her to marry me for real.

When I moved from Leeds to Wigan, I started going with my dad to his local, The Crooked Wheel. I didn't always booze—often I'd go along and drink pop, just for the laugh. Stacey's step-dad, Keith Holden, ran the pub, and Stacey started doing occasional glass collecting shifts behind the bar. She was only 16, I was 20, and I fancied her straight away. I couldn't believe she was the same girl who used to mate around with my kid sister.

I only ever used to see her in the pub, so I started going in more. She must have known I liked her. I was dead shy—still am—so instead of chatting her up, I used to pass little notes over on beer mats. It sounds romantic, but it was stupid really; Keith's hard as nails, and if he'd found out I might not be here now!

It wasn't long before we started going out and we hit it off straight away. She was in her final year at school, and I was in my first year at Wigan. She used to watch me play our home games, and then come up to the players' bar afterwards. She met a lot of the players, and their girlfriends and wives, and everything was going well. She'd actually finished school—she wasn't going to classes or anything, but still had a couple of exams left that summer. I said to Stacey, 'If anyone asks, tell them you're a hairdresser'. That was only a small lie, because she started training as a hairdresser as soon as she'd finished her last exams. Besides, she looked—and acted—much older.

As I was in my first year at Wigan, it was hard enough trying to fit in without the lads knowing I was seeing someone who'd just left school. We kept it a secret, and then she left in the summer. She started training as a hairdresser and I didn't have to lie to anyone. She only had to go back to school once more, to collect her Record of Achievement at a presentation.

Later that night, she phoned me up. 'Oh my God,' she said. 'You'll not believe who presented our Record of Achievements.'

My heart sank. 'Who?'

'Kris Radlinski.'

I could have bloody died. I'd kept it secret for all those months, and now she'd actually left school, my secret would be out. One of my team-mates had presented her with her Record of Achievement.

Rads had met her at a few of the games, but I went to bed hoping that maybe he hadn't recognised her. There must have been loads of people at the school, I thought.

Rads, like me, was always an early bird at training. I got in the next day, saw him, and waited for him to start laughing. But he didn't say a word, other than his usual, chirpy, 'Mornin'!'

'Brilliant,' I thought. 'I've got away with it.'

Soon after, we were taking a break from training and having a laugh in the gym. Someone asked, 'What did you get up to last night Rads?'

'Well, funnily enough . . .' I knew what was coming next. 'I had a school presentation and you'll not believe who I saw.'

My face must have been as red as a monkey's arse. All the lads started pissing their sides—Rads had already told them. Everyone thinks Rads is an altar boy but he's got a wicked side and loves a laugh. Of course, as soon as Tez O'Connor and Andy Farrell found out about it, I never lived it down!

By complete chance, a couple of policemen came to the gym that day—I think it was for an anti-bullying scheme we were running in the schools. As the coppers walked in, Faz shouted out, 'Tez, they've come to arrest you,' and everyone cracked up laughing.

Luckily, it worked out between Stacey and me so the stick didn't last long.

My parents were very close to Sandra and Keith, Stacey's mum and step-dad, and it's been great. Keith's like a mate, not just a father-in-law. I hear some blokes who make their mother-in-laws out to be scarier than Willie Mason. Luckily, I've never had that. We're like one big family.

I don't think Keith always thought that way about me. He wasn't too happy about the age gap when we first started going out. Keith's not stupid—he knows some rugby players have reputations. He probably thought, 'I'm not having a rugby player going out with my little girl.' But when he realised I was fully committed to her, he warmed to me.

Stacey moved in with me when we were both young. I

know some people were thinking we'd not make it, but it never bothered us. We just got on so well. We were both as daft as each other, especially after a drink. After a couple of years, we were still going strong, and I knew I'd found the girl I wanted to spend the rest of my life with. I just knew.

We got a six-day break during Wigan's season and I made up my mind that I was going to ask her to marry me. I wanted to do the right thing, so I saw Keith and Sandra on my own and asked for their blessing. I was bricking it. Although I knew Keith had started to like me, Stacey was still only 18 and he could easily have told me to get lost. He didn't, thank God, so I bought the nicest engagement ring I could afford and booked five days in Palma Nova.

It was a great place. On the first night, I took Stacey to a dead posh restaurant—I'm romantic, me—and decided to ask her as soon as we'd had our meal. I was so nervous that I was sweating and shaking. I began sinking back the ale.

'What's wrong with you?' Stacey asked.

'Nothin',' I said. And then I carried on necking the drink.

Stacey must have thought I'd gone mad, I was drinking so quickly. By the time we'd finished the meal, I was really tuned in. I think she was beginning to get annoyed because she knew I wasn't being myself.

'Don't bottle it now, Tez,' I thought, as the waiter cleared our plates. I took a deep breath.

After the amount of beer I'd had, I decided against going down on one knee.

I took the engagement ring out of my pocket and said, 'The reason I brought you here was to give you this.' Then I opened the box, showed her the ring, and she started to cry. Happy tears, mind.

I didn't have a stag do, but I made up for it by having two

weddings. That wasn't my idea. I wanted to get married abroad. I'm shy and didn't want to do a speech, and Stacey agreed it would be a nice way of tying the knot. We booked a wedding in Jamaica, just us, and 20 or 30 of our close friends and family.

But her dad, Harry, has a massive family and they couldn't all come, so Stacey asked if we could have a bit of a night party when we got back. I liked the idea of that, because then I could invite my rugby mates.

It was 2006, and I was away in Australia with Great Britain while she was sorting it all out. I was glad to be picked for that tour, because it meant I had to do bugger all of the wedding planning. The suits, the cake, the pictures, the guest list . . . you name it, I didn't do it! Stacey's always been supportive of my career—it can't be easy for players' wives when the team disappear to Australia for a few weeks at a time. I know some people must think it's a breeze, but it can be tough on players' wives. Every time they want to do or go to something, such as a Christening or a wedding, they have to check their husband's fixtures and training schedules.

That year, with the Tri-Nations abroad, I had my doubts about leaving Stacey at home with our little girl and a wedding to plan. But she told me I should go. The Tri-Nations meant I had no time for a stag do, which was fine with me; even sensible fellas usually end up tying the groom-to-be naked to a lamp post—God knows what my lunatic mates would have done!

We flew out to Jamaica and it all went perfectly. When we returned to England, though, I discovered we had a full wedding again. I think Stacey got carried away and instead of just organising an evening party, she'd gone the whole hog. We renewed our vows—a week after tying the knot—and then we had a sit-down meal for 100 and a couple of hundred at night. I had two weddings to the same girl! But it was a great night out at the Manor Lodge hotel, in Lancashire, and it was brilliant for Stacey, too, because she got to walk down the aisle with Keith, her step-dad, in Jamaica, and then down the aisle with her real dad, Harry, as well. They're both top fellas and she's close to them both, so that meant a lot to her, and to me.

The only down side to having the second wedding was that we had to re-do our speeches in front of a heap more guests, which I wasn't looking forward to.

My best man, Craig Young, was as nervous as I was. He'd been great in Jamaica, but that was only in front of a couple of dozen guests. At my second wedding, it must have been a bit intimidating. It's a pressure at the best of times, but to look out and see people like Barrie Mac, Terry O'Connor and Brian Carney, he was probably a bit star-struck. I could tell he was a bag of nerves, he just wanted to get it over with. So while people were still eating their meals, he got up and started murmuring his way through the speech! It was over before everyone had finished eating. People were looking at each other, not knowing what to say.

Luckily, Tez O'Connor must have sensed the awkwardness—and to be honest, you'd have had to have been deaf and blind to miss it—and stood up and rescued the situation. 'I'd just like to add a few words about Terry,' he started. I thought he was going to rip me to shreds, good-style. God knows he used to in training. But he was brilliant. He said how lucky I was to have Stacey and how much I loved my family. That got a round of applause.

Then Adrian Morley got up and said a few words, and then different players around the table stood up and said a few words. It was so touching. I did my speech then. And I thought I was doing alright. People were laughing and smiling, I was on a roll. Until my mum shouted out, 'Terry, stop swearing!' and

I realised I must have been a bit pissed.

As great as Stacey is as a wife, she's even better as a mum. I've two girls. Charley-Mia was born on 23 October 2003, just after our Grand Final loss to Bradford and three years before our wedding. People told me being a dad would change my life, and it did. It certainly made me grow up and calm down. It's amazing how a little person can take up so much time and so much space in the house! But I loved her from the minute she came into the world. When we had Charley, people said, 'I bet you want a lad next'. Well, if I have a lad in the future, I'll love him to bits, but for some reason I always wanted two girls.

On 21 August 2008, Stacey gave Charley a little sister, Millie Grace.

They're my little princesses. I love having my own family, being a dad and just spending time with them. I know all about Peppa Pig and don't get me started on High School bloody Musical. It wasn't like that at Hawkley Hall High.

I'm lucky—Stacey's great at sorting out all their clothes and meals and school things. I don't know how she does it. I know I've been lucky to have a job that usually lets me get home by mid-afternoon, so I've always spent plenty of time with my girls. They know I played rugby but they're too young to understand, I suppose. When we go out, often people say, 'Hi Tez', but it's normal to them—they just think their dad has a lot of mates!

I tried not to bring rugby home with me. Of course I'd be in a bad mood after I'd lost a match, but I kept my family life separate because it can suffocate you if all you know is rugby. It's important to have a family life away from that.

It's weird to think back to when Stacey and I first started going out. To when Kris Rads went into a school to present my future wife with her Record of Achievement. So much has happened since. We've got married and had two beautiful girls. We've got a great house in Orrell and our parents are nearby. Just like all couples, Stacey and I have our silly little fall-outs, of course we do. But we're great together and everything feels comfortable. It feels right. And before anyone asks, 'Who wears the trousers?' the answer is me.

I do.

Stacey just tells me which ones to wear.

11

THE WIGAN VICTORY
OF THE DECADE

SOME KIDS dream of singing in a band, being famous, or scoring a winning goal for Man United or Liverpool. For me, it was always lifting the Challenge Cup for Wigan, and in 2002 I got that chance. Walking out for your boyhood team in a final and beating the enemy—I'm not sure if it ever gets better than that. It turned out to be Wigan's only trophy win in the entire decade of the Noughties, but what a win it was . . .

We'd come up empty handed in two Grand Finals in two years, but all the lads knew we had the makings of a good side. Jamie Ainscough came over from Australia to replace Steve Renouf, and someone told me he was laid-back. Laid-back? Bloody hell, he was practically horizontal! He wasn't Pearl, but he did the business on the pitch even if, at times, the fans didn't notice it. Craig Smith also joined from St George-Illawarra, and there was a lot of talk among the players before the season about how much money he was being paid. Players are like fans; they hear all the same rumours

The word was that Craig's wife was reluctant to leave their dog, and so Maurice Lindsay paid to have his dog flown over! I don't know if that was true, but the dog arrived, and stayed with them in a nice house on the outskirts of Wigan.

Terry O'Connor wasn't happy about it. He'd given his heart and soul for Wigan for years, and he'd never been a top earner. To bring over a Kiwi at the back end of his career on mega-money, put him in a nice house and pay for his dog to come as well . . . I think it was a bit of a kick in the balls for Tez. But it wasn't Craig's fault, and Tez realised that. The only problem Tez had with Craig was that he was jealous he didn't have his torso! Craig was a man-mountain, who would take his top off at any chance to show off his rig. Did he show off? Absolutely . . . and if I had a six-pack like that, I'd have done exactly the same thing!

We won six of our first seven matches that year but two defeats, to St Helens and Hull FC, were enough to start everyone panicking before our Cup semi-final game against Castleford. We were hardly on fire in that match—we needed two Gary Connolly tries to see them off, 20–10. The following week, Stu Raper fielded practically a reserve side against Warrington to make sure none of his big-name players were injured for the final. Credit to the lads, they murdered the Wire 58–4, but we were huge underdogs for the final against Saints.

They were the Cup holders, and they'd been playing well. They'd already nilled us in Super League that year. To make matters worse, a few days before the final, Kris Radlinski got a nasty foot infection.

When people discuss tough rugby league players, they usually talk about the aggressive forwards. Well Kris Rads may not have been a scrapper or a bruiser—I don't think he's ever had a fight in his life—but he was a tough player. He had no right to play in our Challenge Cup Final. Brian Carney and I went to visit him in Euxton Hall Hospital in the week leading up to the final. He was in bed, on an IV drip, and he was proper fed up. We tried to cheer him up, but it was hard to raise his spirits. So as we left, Brian went up to one of the nurses and said—in a perfect, I'm-embarrassed-to-say-this kind of way—'I'm sorry to bother you but my friend has done a . . . you-know . . . poo . . . in his pants, and he doesn't know what to do.'

I was dying to laugh, but I bit my tongue. The nurse walked into Rads' room, and we tiptoed to the side of his door so we could hear what she said.

'Don't worry, it's nothing to be embarrassed about.'

'A foot infection?' Rads replied, confused. 'I know.'

'No silly, I don't mean your foot infection. Your friends told me you'd had an accident. Don't worry, we get that all the time in here.'

That's when me and Brian pissed our sides and legged it!

When a team leaves for a final, there's usually a bit of a dinner first, and then the fans cheer the players as they board the coach at their home stadium. We had our function at the JJB, with a few club legends there, and it really hit home that we had a chance to make history, like them. We went out to board the coach and I couldn't believe it when Rads turned up to travel with us. He'd been on a drip in hospital all week, his skin was white (even whiter than usual) and his foot was absolutely massive. Don't think he just had a sore foot; he looked drained and knackered, and he could hardly walk. Fair credit to club owner Dave Whelan, he offered to fly him up in his helicopter but Rads wanted to be with the team—he always put the team first. I think that's why he was struggling with it, too, because like me he'd always dreamed of winning the Challenge Cup with Wigan but he wouldn't have been selfish; he wouldn't have played if he thought he was going to be a liability to the team. Missing a final would be gutting, for sure. But nowhere near as bad as playing when you shouldn't

As a toddler, helping my old man out in the garden

Leanne and me at the airport, going on our family holiday to Benidorm

I've made it! Signing my first autograph . . . for Kiwi legend Graeme West

Collecting silverware from one of my heroes, Andy Platt

I've never forgiven Tulsen Tollett for denying me a try at Wembley!

Lining up, between Moz and Barrie McDermott, for the '99 Challenge Cup Final—the last ever played at the old Wembley

The bruise brothers, me and Adrian Morley, celebrating after the 1999 Challenge Cup semi-final win over Bradford

©RLphotos.com

Playing for GB academy with Kris Smith, who is now going out with Danni Minogue. Stacey doesn't realise how lucky she is—I could have had Kylie!

Making my debut in 1996 for Leeds, against Sheffield, shortly after switching to hooker

©RLphotos.com

Making the Great Britain full team. Harvey Howard, Sean Long and me formed the bomb squad!

The Wigan Under-13s town team. We destroyed everyone that year. I'm sat on the front row, third from the left, with Paul Johnson next to me. Paul Deacon is in front on the floor . . . he's hardly changed

Me in a Warrington shirt after signing for them—though I never played for the Wire

I was in my element in my first year at Wigan, playing alongside Jason Robinson, Kris Radlinski and Steve Renouf

Packing down with Adrian Lam, and Suzanne Shaw and Kym Marsh, from the Popstars' band Hear'Say

The Sinner and The Saint, me and Longy in a derby match—a few years before I nearly removed his head!

My dad Tony with my sister, Leanne

and costing your team-mates a win.

We all knew Rads was capable of doing the unexpected, but the night before the game—having seen him in the hotel—I never gave him a chance of playing. I don't think anyone did. The only one who had any optimism was Gaz Connolly, who'd trained at full-back all week. Though he was used to that role, Lager hated playing at full-back, so he was as keen for Rads to play as Rads was himself!

The morning of the Final, our team doctor—Dr Zaman—worked his magic in a makeshift operating theatre. Some of the lads didn't know he was a top surgeon. When they found out, there were more than a few requests as to whether they could sit in the next time he performed a boob job!

Our physio, Alan Tomlinson, squeezed Rads' toes and massaged his foot. Then Doc got a scalpel, and cut the foot. It was disgusting. Tons of green gunk started spraying out of his foot. Andy Farrell filmed it on his camcorder and he bounced around, excited. Doc loved it. 'Nice infection Radlinski. Nice infection Radlinski,' he kept repeating. It was horrible. But it worked. Rads' foot went down, he went to the treadmill to check it was okay and declared himself fit, and it gave us a massive lift.

It sounds silly, but I really felt like the rugby Gods were smiling on us; that it was going to be our day. With Wembley still being rebuilt, the game moved to Murrayfield in Edinburgh. The experience wasn't the same as at Wembley and it took the edge off it.

But at the same time, it was a great atmosphere, and the fact I was playing for Wigan, against Saints, more than compensated for the venue change. I was dead confident ahead of the game, but in the first set we had a scrum off our line, and Lammy passed the ball to Julian O'Neill.

He spilled it. I thought, 'We're in for a long day here'. But things like that only become turning points if you allow them to and we played well that day. My form was good at the time, and I knew there were the usual discussions about who was the best hooker, Keiron Cunningham or me. It always brings the best out of me and if you out-play your opposite number then great, but that's not what drives me.

If you're a prop, or a winger, then it's easier to gauge how well you've played against your opponent. At hooker, it's different; it's one of those positions that, if your forwards aren't playing well, it's difficult to impress, and likewise if they're on top of their game then it makes a hooker's job easier. It's always hard at hooker to play well behind a beaten pack; if you can't get players over the advantage line, you can't make any metres and so you end up having the ball inside your own half, with little chance or position to threaten the opponents' line. It's also a chicken and egg situation. If I had a bad game I always asked myself, 'Have I not played well because the forwards were beaten, or were they not playing well because I gave them poor service?'

That day, we were all on our game, especially Adrian Lam. He was impeccable, and commanded the team with real class. Rads pulled off some great, try-saving tackles in that match and—after what he'd gone through during the week with his foot—it was fitting that he won the Lance Todd Trophy as man of the match. But over the 80 minutes, Lammy was the best player on the pitch; even Rads will admit he would have given the award to Lammy that day. Lammy and BD scored tries to make it 12–8 at half-time, and as soon as Lager went over we all felt confident of winning. Saints wouldn't lie down but Rads pulled off a couple of great try-savers, we all dug in, and we won 21–12. When the final whistle went, I can't tell you what it felt like. It was surreal, dream-like. I zoned out. Beating Saints is always special—for me, anyway. Fans always love seeing their opposite fans upset when they win.

Well, as a player, I like seeing the Saints players upset. I respect them enormously as players, I like some of them as mates, but I've been brought up to treat Saints as the enemy and beating them is the ultimate feeling. Saints feel exactly the same about Wigan. It's been like that since I was a kid—when I was playing for the Wigan Town Team, the one team I wanted to beat was Saints.

The atmosphere at Murrayfield was incredible. Wigan's fans were going mental. They'd been brought up on success, winning the Challenge Cup felt like a birth-right to them, but it had been seven years since they'd last won it. Throw in their shock defeat to Sheffield in '98 and it was easy to see why they were as happy as we were.

I didn't want to leave the pitch. I stayed on for ages, soaking up the atmosphere and the applause, before going into the dressing room.

Many probably expect the dressing room to be a wild place after a big win. Sometimes it is, but that day it was calm. It was a feeling of relief, as much as joy. I guess the players were just enjoying the feeling of beating Saints in a final, and doing it as the underdogs. Later, we dressed in our suits and had a great dinner which Dave Whelan, the club's owner, splashed out for. He gave a speech, and said we were on a bonus of £25,000. I'd spent the money in my head before I was told it wasn't each, it was between the team! Still, it was a nice gesture from him. After the meal, the beers flowed freely—and they tasted so good after the win we'd had! Everyone was happy. No one acted like an idiot. No-one did anything stupid. Then Mick Cassidy told us he'd brought his hair clippers with him and we all went to have our heads shaved!

Mick is renowned for being tight, and rightly so—rumour was he once asked to borrow 99p so he didn't have to break into a £1 coin. I don't know why he'd brought some clippers with him. I guess he must have been doing his own hair cuts at the time to save some cash. Lads started drifting out of the bar, and then returning minutes later with their heads shaved. Mick had opened a makeshift barbershop in his room, and once three or four players returned with their heads shaved, including me, it soon turned into a team-bonding exercise and all the players went up for a buzz cut. Gary Connolly, who is surprisingly proud of his hair despite his big cow-lick, went up to get shaved and when he came down no-one recognised him. He looked so different. His wife, Kath, was practically in tears—she said he looked like a thug. And she was spot on!

The following day, Rads and Brian Carney woke us all up and collected some money from us to buy beer for the coach journey to Wigan. They must have cleaned the hotel's cellar out, because our coach was packed. The soundtrack for the trip home was the God-awful Starship song, 'We Built this City': I don't know who chose it, but it was played on loop constantly for the entire ride home! Ricky Bibey, our young prop, walked around the coach ripping players' underpants off, and then tying them around his head. Why, I don't know, but it was hilarious.

The coach arrived at Abraham Guest High School in Orrell, and we switched to an open top bus for the ride into Wigan. It was great for me, because the route practically went through the area I grew up in. We passed fields I used to play on, the school I went to and people I'd known for years waved from the pavements—I can't tell you how proud it made me feel. It was a great experience. We headed to the town hall for an official council function, and the street outside—Library Street—was literally a sea of faces and Wigan shirts. It was packed.

Jules O'Neill, our Australian stand-off who'd joined that

year, climbed onto a pillar and waved at the crowd. Brian Carney nudged me and pointed at him, so I walked over behind him and pulled Julian's pants down for a laugh—little did I know he wasn't wearing underpants! Ricky must have ripped them off on the coach. His bits were displayed to half of Wigan and, of course, the officials and dignitaries we were with. I don't think Maurice was too happy about it, but he realised it was all good banter.

We had a mid-week game at Wakefield after that, but credit to Stu Raper, he let us enjoy ourselves and we did. I'd grown up dreaming of winning the Challenge Cup with Wigan. I'd grown up seeing Ellery Hanley, Dean Bell, Shaun Edwards and Andy Gregory lifting the trophy. I'd already won it once, for Leeds. To do it for Wigan . . . it was incredible.

Saints will tell you they got revenge later in the year when they knocked us out of the play-offs, and let them believe that. But I know it's not true. Nothing could ever ruin the memories of that magical day in Murrayfield.

After making my debut in '98 for Great Britain, I had to wait nearly four years for my next chance to pull on a Test shirt. My form during that time had been good, and I know I would have been in the frame had various injuries not kept me out of the equation.

It was annoying, but when you've been through a tough season and you need operations, what option is there?

Two months after the Cup Final, Great Britain had a one-off Test against the Aussies in Sydney and I was selected. I'd never played the Aussies before; I'd broken my arm the year before when they'd lost 2–1 in an Ashes series, and I genuinely thought that—with Keiron Cunningham, Kris Rads and myself added to that team—we'd have a chance. I thought we would kick-on from the previous year's narrow series defeat.

We flew over in business class, with on-call food and our own DVDs, and Dr Brookes gave us sleeping tablets on the plane to make us adjust to the Australian sleeping patterns which definitely helped. But after a couple of days there, in a different climate, I was still drained from the flight and I realised it was going to be a tough ask to beat the Aussies on their turf. I'd not been back to Oz since the World Club five years earlier, and that was one reason I was so fired up to win: I knew how arrogant their fans were.

David Waite was the GB coach and his appointment caused a bit of a storm because he wasn't British. Frankly, I wasn't bothered as long as he did a good job. I hadn't come across him until the build-up to that game, and he was one of the most intelligent coaches I've ever met. I would have loved to have had him coach me at club level; he'd have been great over a full season. But maybe, at GB level, he gave us too much information. He overloaded us.

The scrutiny and attention to detail he did on opponents was out of this world—far more advanced than what anyone else was doing at the time. Over a full season, that would have been great, but when you've only got a few days to prepare for a match it was mind-boggling. He was too thorough, and we couldn't take all the information in.

On top of that, we were exhausted from the trip. We only had a few days in Oz before the Test, and our routine was all screwed up. We were having dinner functions when we wanted breakfast; training sessions when we wanted to sleep. We only had about four or five training sessions together. Still, no-one expected us to be battered 64–10 but I'm not laying all the blame for that defeat on our travel.

I came on for Keiron in the first-half when the Aussies were already in control, and they were red hot. Their moves were straight from the training ground. We couldn't have stopped the onslaught that day, no matter how well prepared we were. We just couldn't get into gear. That match was the first time I played against Andrew Johns. I knew he was a genius from watching him for Australia and New South Wales, but I often thought, 'He's only a small bloke, how can he break so many tackles?'

When I tried to tackle him in that game I discovered how— it was like hitting a brick wall! He was putting shots on our big guys and bending them in half, and then on top of that his passing game and kicking game was so precise. Everything clicked for them. In my first match against the Aussies, it was a record defeat. It's something I'm not proud of.

Later that year, GB went some way to repairing their reputation when they drew a three-match series against the Kiwis. Once again, injuries weren't kind to me, and I missed out.

12

PULLING NO PUNCHES

THEY SAY it takes a bigger man to walk away from a fight. I say that's bullshit.

Ever since I learned to use my fists to sort out trouble as a kid, I've carried with me a reputation for being a bit of a hard-case. When I was younger, I needed to be like that to get by.

Where I was brought up, it was either learn to handle yourself or be walked all over. Back then, I had fights everywhere. In streets, at school, on the pitch, off the pitch; trouble's followed me everywhere. I'm not a violent person, but if a situation crops up I'll not walk away. And if I need to hit someone to sort out a problem, I will. I know that's not the cleverest thing in the world but that's me. That's my makeup. I soon learned, though, that as a professional sportsman, acting like that can catch up with you—and can also cost you an absolute packet.

I can still remember the phone call from Mary Sharkey, who worked in Wigan's office. I was coaching in a primary school on a Monday afternoon when she called, and asked me to return to the club immediately. When I got back, two police officers were waiting for me.

The previous Saturday, I'd been out in Wigan and ended up with Wes Davies, my former team-mate, in a bar called the Springbok. Things got messy, and I ended up punching a lad and putting him down. I'd like to tell you what it was about, but I'd be making it up—I was young and I was drunk. I'm not using that as an excuse, but I never expected it to be a big thing. It's something that happens all the time in town centre pubs on a Saturday night.

I certainly didn't expect the police to rock up at Wigan three days later. The coppers told me they were arresting me for assault, and suggested I go to the police station to answer a few questions. I went straight there. I didn't call a solicitor, didn't call my dad. I was naive—I thought that once I'd explained and held my hand up, they'd give me a slap on the wrist and send me on my way. I'd given this lad a couple of black eyes, apparently, but I'd not really injured him. No bones broken. I admitted assault, but I was more worried about what Wigan would do to me than what the courts would do. Luckily, Maurice Lindsay, the Wigan chairman, was brilliant. He sorted out a solicitor and fully supported me, which was a big relief, because I was playing well at the time. I'd been named in the Great Britain squad the previous week.

I went to Wigan magistrates' court on my own. I didn't want my parents or Stacey there—I was dead embarrassed about it all. The court fined me £500 and ordered me to carry out 240 hours worth of community service, which I thought was harsh. I'm convinced they hammered me because I was a rugby league player, and I was in the spotlight. If the average person in the street had hit someone in a bar and given him a black eye, I don't think they would have got such a punishment. In all honesty, if I'd not been well-known I'd probably have got away with it because nobody in the pub would have known who I was. I'd been in far worse fights and never really been in bother with the police before!

But I'm not excusing what I did, and I'm not blaming anyone but myself. It's the law, I broke it, I copped it on the chin. If they want to make examples of people in the spotlight, power to 'em—that's their job.

The community service dragged on but I actually enjoyed part of it. It opened my eyes to how different people lived. I met some colourful characters, and we had a laugh.

My favourite job was taking dinners to the old folk. One lady lived on the top floor in a block of flats, and she was a big Wigan rugby fan. The poor dear nearly swallowed her false teeth when I turned up with her meal on the first day! She'd always ask me what was going on at the club and talk about matches—she was a nice lady, and I enjoyed that.

By the time my community service had finished, I thought, 'Lesson learned. I'm never going through this again'. But within a few weeks, I was back in bother . . .

It was a Bank Holiday, and I'd gone for a drink with Stacey, her step-dad Keith and her mum Sandra to the Fishergate pub in Pemberton, near to where I lived. I clocked a group of lads by the pool table, staring my way. 'Come on, let's go somewhere else,' I said. So we drank up quickly and walked down to the nearby White Swan, where my dad was.

A few minutes later, some of the same lads came into that pub.

If there are two people you'd want with you in a fight, they'd be my dad and Keith. But when Stacey and her mum were there, I didn't want trouble and neither did they. I asked my dad, 'Can you call me a cab?'

'No problem,' he said, and walked out.

My dad had been gone a while, so I went outside to check on him. I opened the door and it was mayhem. He was wrestling on the floor with a bloke. Another guy was on his back, and others were rushing in.

I grabbed the lad who was on my dad's back, and threw him off. One of the other lads shouted, 'You're going down this time, Newton', and ran at me. As he did, my dad just dropped him. The lad went down. He was on the floor, out cold.

Suddenly, a car pulled up, a complete stranger, and he said, 'Jump in here, before the police come'. That sounded good to me. I knew I wasn't at fault but the last thing I needed was the police to find out about this incident, just weeks after I'd finished my community service.

Well, they did find out about it.

My dad owned up to it, and admitted he'd punched one of them. But some of the others claimed it was me so the coppers couldn't let it drop. I pleaded my innocence but they wouldn't listen. They said it would be for the court to decide. The police charged me with 'malicious wounding with intent to cause grievous bodily harm', as well as a lesser offence of affray. In short, I was up shit-creek.

If I was found guilty, I wasn't going delivering meals to the elderly. I was going to prison.

I walked out of the police station and I was nearly in tears. I told my mum, dad and Stacey what I'd been charged with and they were heart-broken.

My dad had put his hand up and admitted clocking the lad and breaking his jaw—with good reason, in my opinion. But some of the lads told the police it was me. Why? I don't know. Maybe they hated Wigan.

Maybe they thought that because I was a Wigan rugby player, and one of the big-names at the time, they could sue me after the courts had dealt with me and get some of my money. Not that I had a load of money. My first contract with Wigan was quite modest, considering what I'd gone on to achieve, and I was coming out of contract that year.

I kept assuring myself I'd be fine, because I knew I wasn't guilty, but it was impossible not to fear the worst. What if I went down? What about Stacey? She was working as a hairdresser but she wasn't earning enough to pay the mortgage and the bills. We'd lose our house. I went to see Maurice, and again he was brilliant. He said that if I went to prison, the club would stick with me. He offered me a new contract and said they'd look after my mortgage and bills if I went down. He had me over a barrel, really, because although I was playing well I couldn't negotiate with other clubs. Let's face it, who'd offer me a contract when I faced a jail sentence?

It wasn't a great deal, but I couldn't argue. Having the security that he'd look after me if I went down was one less thing to worry about. Before my case went to trial, I signed a new four-year contract.

My performances on the field were good and so people thought I was coping well, but inside, I was a nervous wreck.

And the Saints fans didn't exactly make things easier for me—when we played them, the buggers started chanting, 'He's going down, he's going down, New-ton's going down'!

I was a bag of nerves in the weeks and days leading up to the trial. I didn't sleep, I hardly ate. I kept playing different scenarios in my mind. Walking into a crown court is a horrible experience—I wouldn't recommend it. Especially not when you're charged with something that could land you in prison! Needless to say, there were a load of photographers, reporters and news crews there as well.

My barrister, Donal McGuire, was brilliant. He's the brother of Sean McGuire, who was the St Helens chief executive. I don't think the Saints fans who'd been jeering me were aware that their chief exec's brother was defending me!

I've gone over the newspaper clipping of my case and it says:

'Witnesses were criticised by the court because they had been drinking all day before the fight and gave "conflicting versions of events".'

Donal told the court that 'there will always be a small number who are jealous and will pick some type of argument or dispute' with me. He told the judge that I'd grabbed the bloke who was wrestling with my dad and that I regretted it. 'But he didn't deliver any blow,' he said.

Thankfully, the court saw that I was telling the truth.

The charge of affray against me was dropped. I pleaded guilty to a charge of public disorder—a nothing offence, really—and I walked free from court with a conditional discharge. No prison, no community service.

I can't describe how relieved I was. All I'd done was pull a lad off my dad's back, and I'd spent the next few months worrying that I might go to prison and lose my home. It was absolutely terrifying.

It only cost me a few hundred quid in court costs at the time, but in the long run it cost me a lot more.

About £200,000, I reckon.

I'd been named Super League's best hooker and I was the Great Britain hooker, so I probably should have been one of the top earners at Wigan. But because of all of the court bother, I'd signed a pretty modest four-year deal with Wigan. I'm not blaming Maurice, because he'd been good enough to support me and offer me a new contract when I risked going to prison. But had I not had the whole court thing hanging over me, I reckon I could have got an extra £50,000 a year, either with Wigan or with someone else.

I know I've got a reputation, and I know mud sticks. But my problems with the courts took place a decade ago; I've not been in bother with the law since and, touch wood, I won't be again. Having a family has definitely mellowed me. But I'm not going to bullshit anyone and start preaching about 'violence solves nothing' because if someone ever threatened my wife or kids, I wouldn't think twice about hitting them.

I read a case last year about a guy who was jailed for beating up someone who broke into his house with a knife. Trust me, if I found someone in my house, I'd kill them. No question. In fact, I know one guy who'd vouch for that!

A few years ago we lived in Winstanley. It was a nice but secluded house down a country path. It was fine during the day but at night time the area was pitch-black, and one of the reasons we moved was because Stacey was scared of being in on her own.

One night, I was fast asleep in bed with Stacey next to me and Charley-Mia tucked up in the next room.

'BOOM, BOOM, BOOM.'

I leapt out of bed. Someone was trying to break in. The bastards were trying to kick the door down!

Stacey was petrified. It was totally dark—as black as a crow's arsehole—the only light coming from the alarm clock on our side. It was 4.30am.

'Don't worry,' I said. 'If I'm not back in a minute call the police.'

I legged it down the stairs. I deliberately made as much noise as I could, thinking I'll rumble them and get them as they're legging it—rather than on my own doorstep in front of Stacey.

I un-latched the lock, swung the door open and jumped out, ready to leg it outside after the bastard who was trying to break in.

'ArrggghhhhhHHHHH!'

I looked at the fella in front of me, cowering behind his out-stretched hands. He looked familiar. He didn't look like a wannabe-burglar. He was absolutely bricking it, and with good reason—I was raging mad.

'Sorry to bother you Terry,' he said, his voice quaking.

'What the hell you doin'?' I asked.

'I need you,' he said. 'Drugs test.'

My anger instantly turned to embarrassment—I was stood in my doorway with just my Y-fronts on, in front of one of the rugby league's drugs testers! I was full of apologies.

That was my fault, though. When I was in the Great Britain camp, they went through a spell of telling the top players they had to be available for testing during the off-season.

Which sounds fine, but I had to tell them where I was going to be for one hour, every day, for the following month. And they put the shits into the players, stressing that if the drugs testers turned up and you weren't there, it could be taken as a failed test resulting in a two-year ban. The first year I did one of those forms, I had to list the hotel I was stopping at in Mexico. Every day for two weeks, my family went off for lunches, walks or excursions and I had to make sure I was at the hotel from 12pm until 1pm, like I said I would be.

I understood why they did it, but it pissed me off that it ruined my holiday. So the next year, when I was handed the sheet of A4 with all the days for the following month on, I thought I'd be a smart bastard. Every day, 4.30am, bed, bed, bed, bed, bed, bed . . .

Well, at least I knew they took it seriously! I told this story to Stanley Gene when I returned to pre-season training a few weeks later. 'Cuz,' he said, 'next time, tell them you're at my place back home. It's a tree-house in the middle of Papua New Guinea—they'll never find it.'

13

GREG: 'RIP AND TEAR'

WE MADE a decent start to 2003, but it was a tough time for all the Wigan lads. Billy Joe Edwards and Craig Johnson, two of the club's reserve players, died in a car crash at the start of the year. They were two young lads with their lives ahead of them. I didn't really know them well, but rugby league is such a close-knit family, a tragedy like that affects everyone. I'd played with and against Paul Johnson, Craig's brother, for years and the way he dealt with that tragedy was a tribute to what a bloke he is. He wanted to play in our first game of the season, a walk-over against amateurs Halton Simms in the Challenge Cup, but common-sense took over and he didn't play. Still, the fact that he was soon back in the side spoke volumes about the kind of person he is; I was disgusted that, at the end of the season, Wigan nudged him out the door. Johnno was a real player's player. Fans sometimes didn't notice what he did but any player will tell you, Johnno hits as hard as anyone.

Early in the season, Julian O'Neill was shipped out to Widnes. Jules had a reputation for being a bit of a wild-man ever since his early days at the Brisbane Broncos. Trouble seemed to follow him wherever he went; he'd been sacked by a few clubs before he arrived at Wigan. When someone told me he got binned from Souths for shitting in a team-mate's shoe, I thought, 'Who are we signing?'

Maurice probably thought he could tame him. Jules was so funny, it was hard not to like him. When we played games on Fridays, he would come to The Wheel—my father-in-law's pub—on Saturdays, sit with the old men, place bets on the horse races and drink pints of mild!

He didn't really do it on the pitch, and fans questioned why Wigan signed him. But I still say he could have been one of the best signings the club ever made. Seriously. If Jules had the same dedication as someone like Faz, or Kris Rads, he could have been an absolute phenomenon. He had so much talent, he could have been anything. But beer seemed to be his first choice in life, not rugby league, and the lads always knew when he'd been drinking the night before, because the following day he'd be the first one at training to sweat it out—and he'd stink of Jean Paul Gaultier aftershave! I think he had baths in the stuff, to try and mask the smell of booze.

One thing I could never understand about Jules, and Jamie Ainscough, was that after games, they would be in the showers in the dressing rooms smoking. It pissed me off, because they were two senior Australian players and there were young lads like Martin Aspinwall, Shaun Briscoe and Danny Tickle in the squad who needed senior players to look up to. Jamie was a bit out there. Weird doesn't cover it. I liked them both, especially Jules, but the Wigan team wanted to go forward and Jules didn't have the right attitude. He wasn't right for Wigan. Sean O'Loughlin was coming through at the time and it made more sense to give him a run in the team. His attitude and the way he conducted himself, every day, was exemplary, and on top of that he could really play. It didn't shock me that he later became captain of Wigan.

I know coaches like using injuries as an excuse for losing games but early in the season, we were losing players all over the place. I think at one point, we had 10 senior players out.

And they were all match-winners, too, like Faz, Kris Rads, and Brett Dallas.

The doctor told me I needed a knee operation but I kept postponing it to help the lads out. I was glad I did—I won a couple of man of the match awards, on one good knee! Mind you, I ran myself into the ground, and even needed oxygen during games a couple of times.

After scraping a win against Wakefield, we lost three matches on the bounce against London, Hull and then Bradford in the Challenge Cup semi-finals. It seemed it wasn't a Wigan season without one crisis or another, and this was it. The Cup defeat was a sickener—we were the reigning Challenge Cup holders and we'd made it our goal to defend it.

Our next fixture was a derby against Saints on Good Friday. We'd been battered into submission by Bradford the week before, and we'd literally run out of players. Stu Raper was forced to give debuts to four teenagers, including Kev Brown and Dave Allen. He even borrowed Jon Whittle from Orrell Rugby Union club! It was a case of finding 17 fit players and giving them shirts. And it meant Mark Smith—a cracking lad and a good hooker—had to move to loose forward, and Ricky Bibey had to move from prop to the second-row. Every fan thought we were going to get slaughtered, and I could see why. Saints were crash hot at the time, while we'd lost three games on the bounce and we struggled to put a side together. When you lose one or two regular first-team players, it's always tough. Take 10 out of the side and it becomes a worry, and I was wondering whether the young lads who were drafted in were good enough.

I didn't know anything about them and they knew little about us; but what stood out for me was that apart from Lammy and Craig Smith, pretty much the rest of the side was made up of Wigan lads. If they had been from anywhere else, we wouldn't have turned Saints over. But they all knew what it meant to beat Saints.

We were down 22–12 at half-time but pulled it back in the second-half and won 24–22. Beating them that day, with the team we had, was incredible. It was definitely the most unexpected win I've ever had in my life. I won the man of the match and scored two tries, and apart from the trophies I won, that was the best game of my career. If you ask any Wigan fan about which win over Saints was the best, I reckon many will tell you, 'The one on Good Friday with all the kids'.

It was a massive achievement. But it masked the problems we were having with our coach, Stuart Raper.

Different players react differently to different coaches and their styles. I thought Stu had good tactical awareness, but his man-management let him down. One day he would walk straight past you and not even say, 'Good morning'. He would literally just blank you! He was abrupt and rude, and he rubbed players up the wrong way. He could literally not talk to you all day, but then at other times he would act like he was your best mate.

If we played on a Friday, the following night we'd sometimes go to Walkabout, an Australian-themed bar in Wigan. Several times, Stu turned up. It was like he wanted to be one of the lads. It's one thing to have a few beers with your coach, like we used to do with Frank, but you'd never see Frank out on the town with us! I think a coach should keep some distance.

As a coach, Stu had some good ideas. The best thing he did was before one big game—I can't remember which—he wheeled a TV and video into the dressing room and put on a clip from the American Football film, *Any Given Sunday*, when Al Pacino's character gives a speech about 'playing for inches'. If you've not seen it, you should, because it's great. And that speech got me so fired up. It was a great ploy by Stu.

His big problem wasn't how he coached, but the way he carried himself, and some of the players didn't really respect him. On one occasion, we had a golf day but as I'm not a big golfer, Gary Connolly and I went along for a few drinks. Craig Smith's wife was expecting their first child at the time and he wasn't drinking, which was perfect for me and Gaz because he volunteered to pick up our beer in the golf cart! Afterwards, a few of the players decided to go to the Cherry Gardens, a pub on the outskirts of Wigan. We sat outside having a few beers, and who did we see walking down Wigan Lane but Stuey Raper. He was dressed in a white linen shirt and white pants—like all Aussies, his dress-sense was awful.

One of the lads said to Ricky Bibey, 'If we all put £20 in a jar, will you tackle him?'

I didn't think he'd agree to it, but Ricky said, 'Of course I will'. So everyone quickly delved into their wallets and put our cash into an empty pint glass. Ricky ran over and grabbed Stu around his waist in a bear hug. Poor Stu didn't know what was going on. Ricky told him that there was £500 on the table if he'd tackle him, and said how about he allowed him to put him down and they could split the pot, 50–50. Stu told him where to go, but Ricky was undeterred, and so he picked him up and back-slammed him onto the grass like a wrestler. In an instant, Stu's sparkling white clothes were covered in grass stains and dirt!

To make matters worse—I don't know why I did it—I ran over with two pints of Guinness and threw them over Stu. I don't think Ricky played for Wigan again, and he didn't even get his unofficial severance pay-out: we all delved into the pot to get our money back before he could get it!

Luckily, Stu either didn't know it was me who threw the

Guinness on him, or he forgave me.

It was only a silly prank, and I actually felt a bit sorry for him after we'd done it, but the fact we did that to the coach showed that the players didn't respect him. There was no way anyone would have done that to someone like Frank or Mike Gregory.

Quentin Pongia joined the club mid-season and he was great for us. He trained like he played, full-on and aggressive, and he really strengthened our pack. With lads returning from injury, our form was solid and we had some good victories, including a 38–34 win at St Helens' ground. After a win down in London, Stuey told us on the coach home that he was going to be leaving at the end of the year.

He didn't get that chance.

After a loss at Widnes the following week, he was sacked, and I wasn't shocked about it. Players such as Craig Smith and Quentin didn't like him, and I think they had a big say in it. I often heard at Wigan about 'player power' but the sacking of Stu was the only time I noticed it. I wasn't asked what I thought of him, but others were, and they'd lost respect for him. We weren't playing for him, we were playing for ourselves, and Maurice made the right call in sacking him.

Mike Gregory was promoted from assistant coach and he made our game plan simple. He stripped it down to a basic battle between us and them; us and our opponents. Greg was the first Wiganer to coach Wigan in nearly two decades and he had so much passion for the club. He would give a team talk before a game and he'd break down in tears, he was so emotional. He treated us like men, not children. Greg could have a laugh, but he was there to win, and we all responded to that. Lads wanted to play for him.

We never lost a game in our remaining eight fixtures, and we played some tough teams, too, like Warrington, Leeds,

Bradford and Saints. Greg put a lot of emphasis on being physical—he was my sort of coach. His favourite saying was 'rip and tear'. Every training session, every team talk he would say, 'Rip and tear, rip and tear', and it rubbed off on the players. Our defence was ferocious and it gave us so much confidence as we went into the play-offs. Greg was all about aggression and giving your all; I can't remember any stand-out team talks because it wasn't what he said, but the way he put his words across.

He introduced wrestling practice. It's common-place now, but it wasn't back then. One of Greg's old mates, Royce Banks, owns a gym in Ince—named, appropriately, Royce's Gym. Royce is no spring-chicken and he's not exactly ripped with muscles, but he's as fit as anyone, and he's got a reputation around Wigan for being a handy wrestler.

I'll never forget our first session. We all turned up in our normal training gear, except for Brian Carney, who walked in dressed in a leotard and wrestling boots, and wearing a wig with a head-guard on! He couldn't help but take the piss. He looked like one of those old-style American wrestlers, and I think Royce took offence to it, because when Brian was on the mat he threw him around like a rag-doll. After that, I think Brian always respected wrestling—though I'm not sure if he did it again!

I was in good form and loved playing for Greg. After we beat Saints 40–24 in the play-offs, Greg was quoted in the press as saying, 'Without question, Terry is the number one hooker at the moment'. That meant a lot to me, because I knew how highly Greg rated Keiron Cunningham. We had to win one more game, against Leeds at Headingley, to reach the Grand Final.

Our confidence was sky-high but a couple of days before the match, Adrian Lam went down in training with a bad knee injury. We were doing an unopposed session—which is when the team runs through the moves without any defenders against us. Suddenly, Lammy went down in a heap on the floor. I thought, 'What's going on?' He clutched his knee in absolute agony. All the lads were concerned. Lammy was in tears. Not just because of the pain but because he was desperate to win a Grand Final for Wigan. It showed how much Wigan meant to him. Lammy had as much passion for the Wigan shirt as any Wigan-born lad, without question. He'd been on fire that year and he was named in the Super League Dream Team with me, Craig Smith, Carney and Faz.

The game against Leeds was an epic. Brian Carney scored an absolute screamer—not only was it a great score—but the stage was great as well. Danny Tickle kicked a drop-goal with a couple of minutes to go to give us a 23–22 win, and book us a date against Bradford the following week.

In the week before a Grand Final, it's normal for a club to arrange a trip to have a look around Old Trafford, so the players can get used to the changing rooms, the corridors and the pitch. Some of the lads had never been to Old Trafford before; I was the local loser there, having played and lost three Grand Finals. I knew the place so well that I could have hung around and given the Japanese tourists guided tours!

As we boarded the coach to take us to the ground, Greg collapsed. It shocked us all.

I'd noticed throughout the year that he didn't have full use of his hands, and when he dropped a ball he'd joke about it with us. I just presumed he had arthritis but, when he collapsed, we all knew it was something more serious. He never talked about it, though. I think he was embarrassed that we were worried for him, while his focus was all on the team.

I was a nervous wreck in the days leading up to the Final,

because Stacey was pregnant with our first child, and her due date was the same day as the Grand Final. I went into the game trying to concentrate on the match, but really thinking about the baby. I spoke to Greg about it and he was great; he knew that if the baby came that day, I wanted to be at the hospital, and he agreed 100 per cent. As much as I love rugby league, it's only a game, and I wasn't going to miss seeing my first child being born. On game day, someone held my phone throughout the warm-up and the game, with instructions to tell Greg if Stacey phoned. I could have been withdrawn at any moment. Stacey actually came to the game to watch me. I thought, 'Here we go, she's going to have the baby right here at Old Trafford!'

We'd become the first side to reach a Grand Final from outside the top-two. Bradford were a good side that year but we'd been in great form, and we hadn't lost since Greg had taken charge. We made a good start, Danny Tickle putting us 6–0 up, but Bradford—to their credit—really gave it to us and we ran out of steam. This isn't an excuse, but the fact we'd lost Lammy a couple of weeks ago didn't help. That's not a criticism of his replacement, Luke Robinson, at all. Luke's a top player, but he'd only played one full game with the team and ideally he'd have had a longer run in the side. It wasn't to be. Bradford beat us 25–12.

I broke down in tears after the game. It was my fourth Grand Final in six years and my fourth Grand Final defeat. On top of that, there was all the emotion of Stacey's pregnancy and the stress of thinking she might go into labour at any minute. I poured my soul out right there on the pitch, and the photographers were only too happy to take my picture. I suppose people aren't used to seeing rugby players cry, but I wasn't bothered. It was only when my picture was splashed all over the front page of my local paper that I got a bit embarrassed. To make it worse, the picture was cut out and stuck to the wall in The Wheel! I went out with the boys afterwards for our traditional Mad Monday but I was on shandy. Stacey would have strung me up if I'd been drunk and she'd gone into labour. As it turned out, the baby didn't arrive until 10 days later. All the worrying was for nothing.

14

HIGH TACKLES AND TEST MATCHES

RUGBY PLAYERS don't do paternity leave. Not that I know of. Charley-Mia was born on 24 October, and I didn't spend very long at home with her and Stacey. I'd managed to end the season with no injuries—a first in five years—and was called into the Great Britain squad for the home Ashes series against the Aussies. The powers-that-be had already decided to switch to a Tri-Nations series the following year, so we knew it was going to be the last Ashes series for a while. It would certainly be the last during my playing career.

We warmed-up for that series with a match against New Zealand 'A'. I wasn't down to play, so the night before I volunteered to feed Charley-Mia during the night and let Stacey get some sleep. It was the least I could do, considering I was going to be sleeping away from home for the next few weeks. I only had about three-and-a-half hours sleep that night, then the following morning I got a phone call to say I'd been drafted into the team for the game later that night against the Kiwis!

Before the Aussies arrived on our shores, people were saying what a glorious chance we had to make history. We'd not beaten them in a series in three decades, but everyone just kept banging on about how many injuries the Aussies had.

What they failed to understand was that at any time, you could pick three or four Australian teams from the NRL and they'd still compete with Great Britain. That's how much strength in depth they have.

Sure, Andrew Johns missed that series, but who played instead? Brett Kimmorley. Hardly a weak option—if Kimmorley had been British we'd have built a team around him! I'm not saying we weren't confident, because we were. David Waite prepared us well. We went into the first Test at the JJB knowing it was going to be a tough game. What we didn't know was just how much tougher it would get after 12 seconds!

I was excited to be playing for GB in front of my home crowd in Wigan. I'd not played a Test in England for five years and I'd played that game down in Watford—hardly a hotbed of rugby league. My last match for my country had been the 64–10 loss in Sydney and all the anger and disappointment from that game was playing on my mind. We were all focussed on making an early impression so the Aussies realised we were up for it; that the past year's result had been a blip. The atmosphere was electric. We kicked off to the Aussies, and Moz flew out of the line. He was right next to me, and as Robbie Kearns brought the ball in, Moz put his arm out and caught the big prop with a beauty.

Kearns hit the floor like a bag of shit.

To Moz's defence, Kearns had a great little jink, which he puts on just a split-second before he collides with the defensive line. Moz turned to me and said, 'Was it high?'

I replied, 'Yeah but you'll be fine mate, it was just a lazy arm'. No sooner had I said that, Steve Ganson called his name and brought out a red card. I couldn't believe it! No-one gets sent off with the first tackle of the game.

I caught a glimpse of the big screen a couple of minutes

later and it showed Moz in the changing rooms, his head in his hands, and it really fired me up. I knew Moz must have been gutted. He hadn't gone out there to knock Kearns' head off—he'd caught him high, admittedly—but I didn't think he deserved a red card for it. I thought that was harsh to say the least.

Brian Carney scored two tries on his debut, he'd been awesome for Wigan that year, but with Moz off the pitch, the Aussies exploited their extra man in the pack and they really tired us out. Kimmorley kept on dropping A balls on our forwards—which is when the scrum-half will run flat across the line and drop-off one of their big guys, who has had time to gather up pace. Their plan worked a treat for them, as it made me, Barrie McDermott and Stuart Fielden work overtime in defence. They tired us out. The scores see-sawed all match until, right at the death, after Carney's second try put us ahead, Darren Lockyer spotted a gap in our defence and went over for the match-clincher. Craig Fitzgibbon converted and then hit a late penalty to make sure there was no way back for us.

We lost 22–18, but we'd done ourselves proud. We pushed the Aussies to within four points with 12 men, and salvaged some pride after the nightmare in Sydney the year before. We were always confident we could compete with the Aussies; that performance proved we were right to be confident.

During the match, I'd caught Fitzgibbon with a high shot. Luckily for me, the ref and the touch judges missed it, and I thought nothing more of it. After the game, though, the Aussies kicked up a real storm and said I'd only stayed on the pitch because Moz had been sent off. Well, that was a joke. I've never been shown any favouritism from referees—I'd argue it's been the opposite. The Aussies wouldn't let it lie, and said they were going to get video evidence to have me cited.

That really pissed me off. It was a Test match, not a game of tiddlywinks. I'd intended to put a big shot on Fitzgibbon, of course I had. I wanted to hurt him because he was their goal-kicker—and a bloody good one, too—and a very good player for them. The more hurt he was, the less damage he could cause. But I didn't deliberately hit him around the head!

Some people forget that Test matches are played at 100mph, and the difference between a great shot and a high shot is a split-second and about three inches—from the top of the chest to the neck. Players will be caught high—it's an inevitable occupational hazard. Fitzgibbon and the Aussie coach, Chris Anderson, both had a pop at me in the Sydney papers.

Anderson said I should have been banned for two weeks, while Fitzgibbon said: 'What happened to me, I really don't think that there is any need for it. It pisses me off that I have to miss so much of a game because of some crap like that.' But the best bit was when he was quoted as saying: 'What goes around comes around.'

Seriously, who says things like that?

He may as well have come out with 'It ain't over 'til it's over.' I don't know if he was planning to scare me, but when I read it, I burst out laughing. It always seems like the Aussies love a good whinge. The rest of the press jumped all over the quotes, and by the following Monday, when we had our regular media briefing at the GB team's hotel, I knew I would be in hot demand. I must have done a dozen interviews.

It's funny, all the journos were the same—they all started by asking nice questions. 'What are your thoughts about the next game? How do you rate your opposite number, Danny Buderus? What part can the fans play this weekend?' Then, at the end, they threw in a line like, 'That's great Terry, thanks.

Just one more question—what about Craig Fitzgibbon saying "what comes around, goes around"?'

I bit my tongue, and was careful not to give them anything they could use. After they'd finished, I did an interview with Peter Aspinall, who was the local hack at the *Wigan Evening Post*. I later did a column in the paper with Pete—he was a bloke I could talk to freely and I knew he wouldn't set me up for a fall. Halfway through the interview, Andy Wilson, from *The Guardian*, walked over and put his Dictaphone under my chin and started recording what I was saying. Pete asked me about the Fitzgibbon remarks and I recited the same, diplomatic response along the lines of, 'I'm a physical player, but it was accidental . . .'

Then at the end, Pete thanked me, put down his pen, and made a joke about how the whinging Aussies will still find something to moan about. I said to him, 'I know, let's hope I get away with some of the things I got caught with!' He laughed, I laughed and I didn't think any more of it, until the next morning, when my throw-away remark was quoted in *The Guardian*. Within hours, the Aussies were all over it, and then the Sydney papers were chasing Anderson and Fitzgibbon to get their reaction to it.

Andy Wilson's a good journalist and I'm not going to deny I said it, but I never thought I would be quoted on it. I suppose I was a bit naive. He did nothing wrong—I did say it—but in my mind the interview was over. It caused me a bit of bother with Brian Noble, who was David Waite's assistant. I explained what happened and he said it was fine. Afterwards, part of me was glad the quote had come out—at least that way, the Aussies knew I wasn't sorry. I knew Fitzgibbon must have been thinking, 'I'll get this bastard back', but I expected that. And you know what? If he had got me, I'd have still shaken him by the hand at the end of the game and said, 'Good luck next week'. But the thing about the Aussies is they're so easy to wind up, and they'll moan about anything.

If it had been the other way round, if someone had come out and whacked me high in the first Test, there's no way I'd have screamed like a girl about it in the press. I'd have kept it to myself, shrugged off any journalists' questions with the usual, 'It's nothing, what happens on the field stays on the field . . .' and let it be.

Then, the week after, I'd have gone and knocked his bloody head off.

As it turned out, in the second Test, Fitzgibbon didn't try to get even but I was still in agony at the end. We played the game in Hull and it was another nail-biter. I scored my first try for my country, courtesy of a sweet pass from Moz. We did everything right in the first-half and were 20–12 up at half-time. But we didn't score in the second-half and in the end, it was the same old story. Kimmorley and Lockyer were outstanding again. They won 23–20, and our hopes of winning an Ashes series went up in smoke. I was gutted.

We'd formed a good team. We were all from different clubs—just weeks earlier, we'd been knocking seven shades of shit out of each other—but we all got on great, and we played well together. The third Test, in Huddersfield, was a dead-rubber, and early in the game, Kearns was running the ball in. He did his jink, I stuck my arm out, caught him high and dropped him. I'll put my hands up—I was lucky not to be sent off. If anything, my challenge was worse than Moz's in the first Test! Poor Kearns probably wondered what he'd done wrong to keep getting chinned. I thought, 'Bloody hell, me and Moz, thick as thieves'. Fortunately I stayed on (I was later cited and got a two game ban and a £500 fine, thank you very much) and we ended up losing that Test, too. We were drawing 6–6 at half-time but yet again, they pulled away at the end and won 18–12.

We lost the series 3–0, every game by a score of six or less. I was happy with my form in that series and I felt like I was establishing myself at that level. I was so proud to play for Great Britain, but to keep losing was gut-wrenching. I was so demoralised after that series; the fact we'd pushed the Aussies close was only a crumb of comfort.

The series lost, we returned to the Worsley Marriot hotel and had a big drink to drown our sorrows. Moz, Baz and I drank straight through the night. The following morning, Barrie had to watch his little lad playing rugby at Shevington High School in Wigan, which is only a few miles from my house. We obviously couldn't drive, so I called Stacey and she picked us up. After dropping Baz off to watch his lad's junior game, I went home to shower and change, before picking Baz up for another session with most of the GB lads down at The Wheel. I'd missed the Mad Monday with the Wigan lads a month earlier because Stacey was pregnant—I made up for it that day. We drank the pub dry.

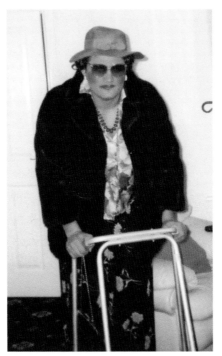

Haven't I aged? My fancy dress costume was so convincing, I ended up having a brew in a nursing home!

My uncle Paul Newton, granddad Alan Page Newton, uncle Alan Page, me and my dad before my uncle Alan's fight with Carl Froch

It doesn't get any better . . . winning the Challenge Cup with my hometown club. And beating St Helens in the process

Who's the chubby lad with the skinhead? Celebrating Wigan's Challenge Cup win in 2002

Who said rugby league players don't cry? I was gutted after the 2003 Grand Final—my fourth defeat at Old Trafford

I made the Super League Dreamteam in 2003 . . . one of my proudest moments

It's mine! Beating Danny McGuire to the ball for a try for Great Britain in 2004

For all their recent success, moving to Bradford was a step down from Wigan

Lesley Vainikolo, The Volcano, was a freak, and one of the best wingers I've ever come across

Having a minor disagreement with my good mate, Gaz Hock!

One of my best memories—beating the Aussies in their own backyard, in 2006

Tying the knot, Stacey and me after our 'first' wedding!

Me and Stacey with my mum, Val, and dad, Tony

My 'second' wedding to Stacey! With my rugby pals—from the left Gary Connolly, Mike Forshaw, Kris Radlinski, Danny Sculthorpe, Barrie McDermott, me, Paul Deacon, Adrian Morley, Brian Carney and Terry O'Connor

My last involvement in the international team—training with Great Britain in 2007. I played the first Test against the Kiwis but was then dropped ©RLphotos.com

With Charley-Mia welcoming Millie into the world

Now you see me . . . making one of my few appearances for Wakefield, before I was banned

©RLphotos.com

With boxing great Ricky Hatton at his home in 2009. What a top bloke

Moving on—with my father-in-law, Keith Holden, outside the pub we have bought together, the Ben Jonson in Wigan

My three princesses. Stacey and our two girls, Charley-Mia and Millie

15

LOSING LEANNE

I HAD A REPUTATION for being a hard-case growing up, but I knew someone who was two years younger—and a lot smaller—than me who could beat me up, no problem.

My sister.

Leanne and I never saw eye to eye as kids. Like typical brother and sister, we'd squabble about pretty much everything. She could easily sort me out; if she wanted the TV remote, she'd get it!

But I always looked out for her and, without ever telling her, I loved her to bits. We'd bicker and row, but if a mate fancied her I'd get all protective of her, like most brothers. Leanne was a cheeky sod, and a bit mischievous like me, but she was generally a good girl. When she started high school, the trouble started. She started messing around with the wrong crowd. I remember when she reached the third year of high school, I caught her smoking and I gave her a real bollocking but she wouldn't listen to me. It wasn't long before she started smoking pot, rather than cigarettes, as well as taking other recreational drugs.

When I signed for Leeds, I'd only see her on weekends and while I can't say I noticed a change in her, I saw a change in the way my parents were with her. They became increasingly worried about her. Leanne was living at home but you wouldn't know it, because she just detached herself. When I was playing at Wembley in '99 with Leeds, she didn't come, even though it was a massive thing for me. I wasn't all that surprised or too bothered about it, but I think my mum and dad were.

I had my rugby and from an early age, I'd had a bit of recognition and success. I'd captained England schoolboys and been in the paper with the Wigan town team. If Leanne was jealous of the attention I got as a kid, she didn't show it, but my mum and dad saw how rugby had given me something to do and got me away from drink, trouble and the idiots who were wasting their lives doing drugs.

My mum and dad tried everything to get Leanne away from it all. They even got her a horse. They didn't buy it, someone else owned it and Leanne looked after it for a year. That was just as well, because she lost interest in it quickly. She just didn't want to know.

I'm not blaming all Leanne's problems on the people she knocked about with because she had choices to make, and she chose that path. She gradually descended into a life of doing drugs, and as soon as she'd been gripped by heroin she didn't want to know anyone, or do anything. She became a shadow of herself. I never saw the drugs—to this day, I've never actually seen heroin—but I've seen how it can destroy a person. It was terrible to see.

I remember my dad telling me that Leanne was on heroin. It was bloody awful—I thought she was a pot-head who dabbled with harder drugs. I didn't know she was a full-blown addict. I didn't know what to do. At first, I ignored it, but I was so angry about it all. I considered going around and beating up the people she was getting the heroin from, but that would have just made her angrier and God knows what she'd have done. Probably stormed out and disappeared. My mum and dad were brilliant, they never gave up on her and they persuaded her to go into rehab.

She went in as a heroin addict, a junkie who I didn't recognise, and eight weeks later came out as a normal person. She cleaned herself up. I can't tell you how proud I was of her. I don't think anyone can truly know how hard it must be for someone to get off drugs without going through it themselves, but I can imagine. It used to kill me not going for a beer when everyone else was—God knows how hard it was to do that when you're hooked on a drug like heroin.

Things were going great for a while. I noticed a change in my mum and dad, too. They were happier, less worried. Within a year, Leanne was pregnant, and my mum and dad saw it as a chance for her to start afresh. They asked if I would buy a house for her, so she could make a life for herself. So I got her a nice, new-build semi-detached house in Worsley Mesnes, and in 2001 she gave birth to Callum. My mum and dad were so pleased for her—and they loved being grandparents. Leanne had everything set up. She had a nice home, a cracking little baby, and a great life to look forward to. Then she threw it away.

It felt like I'd only just got my sister back when she was snatched from me again. I'd been so proud of her for getting herself clean. Then she had Callum, a brilliant little lad, and everything seemed good, but there must have still been something inside her.

Heroin completely took its grip on her and changed her again. I'm struggling now to explain how much it ruled her. She was ill, I can see that now, but I didn't see it that way at the time. Deep down I loved her, but I couldn't stand what she was doing to herself. We all agreed it was in Callum's best interest if he stopped with my mum and dad while she cleaned herself up, but things got worse rather than better.

I was angry with her for what she was doing to herself. I couldn't stand her. Why would she throw everything away like that? How could she put my mum and dad through all that pain again? I couldn't understand it.

My mum and dad put everything on a plate for her. My dad went down to her place every day, making sure she had everything she needed, such as milk in the fridge and that bills were paid. They were always there for her, and she gave them nothing back.

I thought that she was taking the piss. I said to my dad, 'Leave her and let her stand on her own two feet'. Leanne deteriorated further and became a person I didn't know. She stole from me, as well as from mum and dad. It reached a point where we couldn't leave money or valuables around in case she pinched them. You can't imagine how awful it is, knowing you could walk into your parents' house and your sister might steal from you when you're not looking. When she was younger she would never have done anything like that. But Leanne knew she could get away with it because my mum and dad kept giving her second chances.

She became a person I didn't know, and didn't want to know. Heroin had taken her over and she was a mess. She was pretty when she was younger, she could have had her choice of boyfriends, but drugs changed her.

I cut myself off from her completely. I couldn't even look at her in the street. It's a sad thing to admit that once, driving to Asda, I saw her on the side of the street and I didn't acknowledge her. No wave, no beep of the horn. I just blanked her. I'm not proud of that, but I had so much anger inside me. Half of me couldn't stand her; the other half wanted my sister back. I've got plenty of mates with sisters and I've noticed that even though they were always bickering as kids, when they reached their 20s they became closer. I never had that. I had a sister I didn't recognise or even acknowledge. I was so pissed off with her, it was untrue. And it went on for years. Callum stayed with my mum and dad, they looked after him and raised him to be a great little kid. My mum and dad tried to get Leanne through rehab again but she didn't want to know.

And I still didn't want to know her. So much had happened in my life and Leanne had nothing to do with it. She wasn't there when I played in the Grand Finals, or for Great Britain, or when Charley-Mia was born. I cut her out completely.

At first, if anyone asked, I just told my mates that my sister was ill. But after a while, they stopped asking and I stopped talking about her. I was embarrassed about it. How do you tell your mates and team-mates that your sister is a heroin addict? I remember sitting in a group one day, and we were just talking shit. One of the lads mentioned a team-mate's sister, who he fancied, which prompted a chat about brothers and sisters and whether it's okay for team-mates to fancy them. It went on for a while.

'D'you have a sister, Tez?' one of them asked me.

I didn't even pause before responding. 'No,' I said, 'I don't.'

16

TACKLING THE VOLCANO

MY PLAN was simple. Wigan's first game of 2004 was against Bradford, and I was still angry that they'd beaten us in the Grand Final the previous October. Before the match, our coach Mike Gregory warned us about Lesley Vainikolo, Bradford's big Kiwi winger. Give him space and he'll punish us, Greg said.

So I decided to put a good shot on him early. It's not always easy for hookers to tackle wingers—we're usually in the middle of the pitch, while they prance about on the touchline—but I was determined to rattle Les. To me, anyone who had a nickname 'The Volcano' deserved to be hit.

After one of our kicks down field, Les did what all good wingers should do and went to dummy-half on the first tackle to take in a drive. I realised it was my chance to get him, so alongside Tez O'Connor and our new signing Danny Orr, I smashed him as hard as I could. Legally, mind. I just threw my arm at him and drove my shoulder into his ribs. I wanted him to know he was in for a hard game. For good measure, as I got up, I forced his head into the ground. I quickly pulled my hand back before the ref could see, but my fingers had become entangled in his hair and as I pulled, I ended up with some of Les' hair-braids in my hand! Les got up to play-the-ball, rubbed his head and eye-balled Tez O'Connor. I didn't know what to do with the braids, so I tucked them into my sock—I taped my sock halfway up, so they couldn't drop down into my boot.

My ploy didn't work. We lost the game, 34–6, and my efforts to rattle Les failed miserably—he went on to score five tries! After the match, I was chatting to Tez and he asked me if I'd hit Les high.

'No, why?' I asked.

'He eye-balled me like I'd got him high, but I hadn't. Was just wondering if you 'ad.'

That's when I remembered about the braids. I put my hand into my sock and got them out to show Tez.

'It was an accident, honest,' I said.

He started laughing, and said, 'You can't pull his hair just because you're scared of him.'

'I'm not scared of anyone.'

'Fine for you to say, but he's probably in there telling all his team-mates I'm a big girl who goes around pulling people's hair.'

'Fine then,' I said. 'I'll go and tell him it was me if you want.'

'Balls you will. You're too scared.'

I hate being called 'scared'. Terry knew that—he was winding me up, and succeeding. So after a quick shower, I left the Wigan dressing room and waited 10 yards down the corridor outside the Bradford room for Les to come out.

Tez stood by the Wigan room door, he couldn't believe I was going to apologise.

'Get lost, will you,' I said.

'No. I want to see it.'

The corridor under Odsal's main stand is quite narrow and with so much activity—kit men, stewards and lurking journalists are all jostling for space—I knew Tez wouldn't be able to hear me, even if he could see me.

When big Les finally came to the door, I handed him the braids and said, 'Here Les. These are yours.' I looked back at Tez, and then back to Les. 'Terry O'Connor pulled them out and he asked me to give them to you.'

Different players prefer different referees. I found some arrogant and cocky, and some plain useless. Others treated me harshly because of my reputation. Karl Kirkpatrick was always one of my favourites. He was down-to-earth, he showed me respect and he was always fair with me. I tested that once in a game against Huddersfield, when he happened to mention to me that Chris Thorman was giving him a bit of lip. I made a point of hitting Thorman with a good shot the next time he had the ball—I knew there was no way Karl would punish me for it, even if it might have been marginally high!

Generally, I tried not to cause him any bother, but I put him into an awkward position in our first derby against Saints that year. Our form had been mixed, to say the least. We won all three of our Challenge Cup games to book ourselves a place in the semi-finals, but in Super League we'd only won one from four and, once again, we went into our Good Friday derby as big underdogs.

For Wigan, and it's the same now, form means nothing when your next game is against Saints. Mike Greg was our coach and, as a Wiganer, he knew just what it meant to beat them. Tensions were high. We knew it was going to be a physical game. Everyone was on edge—it just needed that spark and it was going to kick-off. I was only too happy to provide that spark! After tackling Jon Wilkin, something must have happened or been said—I honestly can't remember what—because he pushed me and we ended up fighting.

I landed three sweet shots on him. Everyone ran in. The

fans went wild. The next thing I saw was Faz and Paul Sculthorpe going at each other—I thought, 'I'm glad I'm not between those two!' In a derby between Wigan and Saints, it doesn't matter if it's your brother or your best friend on the opposite side. If it kicks off, you go for them. The fact Faz and Scully, the Great Britain captain and vice-captain at the time, were fighting proved that—it was all heat of the moment stuff and when the dust settled, no harm was done.

I'd started the brawl. Players had been sent off for less. But Kirkpatrick was refereeing the game so I fancied my chances of staying on the pitch. When the fight had calmed down, and the last of the brawling players were separated, someone ran over and jabbed me on the side of my face. Credit to him, it was a good shot, too! I looked around to see who'd done it but no-one was near me—he'd obviously run in, hit me and run out.

I turned to Kirkpatrick. I thought it was a bit much of me to ask the ref who'd hit me, but Karl stunned me when he pointed into the Saints line and shouted, 'Scott Moore'. He dragged him out for a bollocking and—in turn—told me which cheeky sod had run over and whacked me!

My luck ran out, though. He then hauled me and Wilkin in and sin-binned us both, which was to be expected. We drew that game 21–21. I know what you're thinking, did I get Moore back? No. I calmed down during my time in the sin-bin, so I didn't chance my luck. I'd already caused one brawl—I'd have done my team no favours had I gone seeking revenge and been shown a red card.

Ian Millward, who was coaching Saints, had a pop in the press conference afterwards for what I'd done to Jon. I don't know why he did it—maybe he was trying to pressure the RFL into citing me. Jon was like me—what happens on the field, stays there. I can't count the times we've had ding-dongs—

he's hit me, I've hit him—but we're always fine afterwards. He even went on TV a couple of days later and said, 'It's the very nature of the sport, things like that happen. I'm pretty sure Terry hadn't intended to do it.'

It was an epic derby. And that performance gave us so much confidence that we won our next five games—including a Cup semi-final against Warrington, when good ol' Brett Dallas scored a hat-trick—before our next meeting with Saints in the Challenge Cup Final.

With Wembley still not complete, this time the final was at the Millennium Stadium in Cardiff. As usual, we travelled down a couple of days early and stayed in a nice hotel down in the Welsh capital. A few of the lads were lounging around the lobby, killing time and playing cards. I was a spectator—I'm not a card player—when in walked this pretty girl.

Danny Tickle laid eyes on her and said to me, 'You know who that is, don't you?'

'No.'

'It's Jennifer Love-Hewitt.'

'Who's that?' I asked. I've never been one to keep up with all the celebrity stuff.

'She's a film star, you idiot.'

I'd never heard of her. Other lads were far more impressed. They were bouncing around like little kids on Christmas Day. For some reason, she came over and sat with us, and asked who we were and what we were doing. Brian Carney tried his luck and failed—no shock there, then—and I spent the next hour or so laughing my head off, as I watched some of my team-mates try their best to pull a Hollywood actress.

Challenge Cup Finals are often played on nice, sunny days and that one was no different—it was scorching inside the Millennium Stadium.

By that point, we all knew it was going to be Greg's last

game in charge, even if he never talked about it with the lads. He was heading to America after the match for treatment for his debilitating disease. We went on the pitch before the game. I stood next to Greg. I'm not normally one for showing my feelings and emotions, but on that occasion I wanted to let him know how much we all respected him. I said to Greg, 'Look, whatever happens today, there's going to be 17 blokes giving their all for you. We all love you.'

It brought a tear to his eye. Part of me wished I hadn't said it because it made me emotional too!

Saints scored the first try—even though Jason Hooper was a mile offside when he tackled Rads, forcing the ball loose— and then when I crossed, I had a try ruled out. I thought, 'It's going to be a long day'. The video ref said Faz had knocked on, even though Paul Sculthorpe had dislodged the ball. We didn't disgrace ourselves but it was Saints' day, they played well and won 32–16. It hurt that it was Greg's last game in charge. He never wanted us worrying or thinking about his illness, but we cared so much for him, it was impossible not to. We wanted to make it a special send-off, but it wasn't to be. The fact we lost to Saints just rubbed salt into the wound. Had it been another team, it wouldn't have hurt half as much.

Greg never returned to Wigan, and it was sad to see his fight with Maurice Lindsay and Dave Whelan turn messy. The club really could have handled it better. As players, we made sure Greg knew we were supporting him, not the club. We leant our support to any of the fundraising events that were organised by his army of friends and family members. We wanted to show him how much we thought about him.

His condition was gradually worsening, but Greg was a great coach and the lads responded to him. We all loved playing for him. He worked well with Denis Betts, his assistant. Denis did the technical stuff and Greg got us hyped up for games—they complemented each other.

Greg really got us playing for the Wigan club. He was the old style coach who wanted us playing with passion, and I loved that style. It also helped that he'd been such a respected player, because when you're listening to someone like Greg, who'd been there and captained his country, you knew he wouldn't ask us to do something he wouldn't have done himself.

Denis was promoted to the top role in Greg's absence, and he was smart enough not to change anything—not that he would have wanted to, other than a couple of little subtle ideas. Denis just carried on the same way it had been with Mike, and for a spell it worked. But it felt a little awkward. Personally, I'm not a fan of being coached by someone I used to play with. That wasn't Denis' fault, it was the situation he found himself in. One minute he was my mate, the next he was telling me what to do—it felt weird. It was hard to break that barrier, and start treating him as a coach rather than a mate. It must have been strange for him, too, talking to us and telling us what we'd done right and wrong.

I've got to stress, though, that it wasn't Denis' fault. It was tough for him on his own, and he did a good job. As a coach he's very talented, but because of the circumstances it was probably a case of too much too soon.

17

'BRING BACK THE BIFF': THOUGHTS ON THE GAME

I PLAYED AT the top level in England for a decade-and-a-half. Rugby league gave me a great living and I'd like to think that, despite the disappointing end, I gave a fair bit back, too. I love the game; always have, always will. And at first I didn't want to have a pop at the administrators because I didn't want anyone accusing me of being bitter about the two-year ban. Not to mention all my other disciplinary suspensions!

But then I thought, 'Sod it. It's my book, I'll say what I want . . .' So here are my thoughts on the game, on how it could be improved, and why I think the people who run rugby league are selling it short . . .

My old team-mate, Matty Johns, used to have an alter-ego on Australian TV's *Footy Show* named Reg Reagan. It was absolutely hysterical, and Reg would always bitch about the game being too clean. 'Bring back the biff,' he used to say.

While I'm not saying players should have a green light to clean everyone out like Les Boyd used to do, the RFL need to realise that one of the best parts of the game are the scraps. We can all pretend we don't like the fisticuffs, but we'd be bullshitting ourselves.

No-one ever gets seriously injured. When the dust has settled, players are all mates, everyone shakes hands.

But the introduction of the 'On Report' system, as well as the increased video scrutiny, has changed that. Now, players involved in a scuffle might be banned for three matches and stung in the wallet, too. It's wrong.

The opposition team doesn't benefit—a rival team does, while the player is banned—but also the punishment doesn't fit the crime. I'm not saying the refs should let it go, but what they need to do is sin-bin players instead. That way, the brawling player gets punished, he gets time to cool-down and the other side gets rewarded with an extra man for 10 minutes.

Unfortunately, the 'On Report' system gives referees an easy cop-out when really, they need to have the balls to produce a yellow card and deal with it at the time.

This isn't a pop at the refs because they have a hard enough job as it is. I feel sorry for them sometimes; the RFL don't help them by bringing out new bloody rules every year! At the start of 2009, they told the players that if a ball-carrier has one leg lifted off the ground it's classed as 'held'. Who thought of that daft idea? I'd be shocked if players were consulted about that one. Players have a hard enough job concentrating on their own game, without having to worry about new rules. Then the players end up bitching among themselves about the rules and it just creates friction between them, and the people running the game.

In the middle of this are the refs, trying to make sense of it all. Luckily, in our great game, players don't gang up on the referees like they do in football—and that's something rugby league should be proud of.

Honestly, I watch football and I think it's embarrassing the way the players bully the refs when they don't like a decision.

It's a joke. I can't understand why they do it. Refs make cock-ups—as do players—but they're never going to change their mind, are they? I always tried to bite my lip. If I was going to give a penalty away, it'd be for holding down or a high shot, not for calling the ref a tosser!

Many footballers are so soft. Refs make mistakes, of course they do. But they don't cheat—and that's what footballers do when they dive on the floor and roll around like someone's chopped their bloody leg off. That's another good thing about our game, players will never lie down and play for a penalty. Every time I was put down, I'd get up—and it's not just because I didn't want the opponent knowing they'd hurt me, but because I wouldn't stay down to try to get someone sent off. Personally, I wanted them to stay on the pitch, then I could punish them myself!

I just hope the game's officials read this and think, 'Next time we want to change a rule, let's run it past some players first'. Maybe even try it out in the pre-season friendlies. Because if they did, the players would be honest with them. The 40/20, for example, is a rule change that I think most players like. The problem comes when they introduce little rules that are hard to remember in the heat of the battle. And then what happens? Refs end up blowing the whistle and dishing out penalties, the games become stop-start and suddenly our great game ends up looking like rugby union! Have you seen rugby union? Fuck me, it's boring. How on earth people prefer that to league I'll never know. Union is kick, clap, kick, clap. One thing they've got, though, is a good organisation.

I can't tell you how frustrating it is for a league player to see the way union is handled, because they do things far more professionally. They make their international game the focal point. In league, it's almost an after-thought. It must be—why else would they allow the Super League to kick-off two entire months before the NRL? The Super League players play far more games than the Aussies and the Kiwis, and then at the end of the year the RFL expect them to go out there and beat 'em! It's a joke.

If they want England (we're not Great Britain any more—another decision that players should have been consulted about) to beat the Aussies they've got to keep the top players fresh. By overloading the players, they play right into the Aussies' hands.

The Aussies already have the advantage because of their better climate—training in the sunshine is a lot better than training when it's pissing down—and they've also got the strength in depth because they've so many more players to choose from. We can pick 17 to compete with Australia—I truly believe that—but they could pick seven or eight teams to compete with us.

Fortunately, the game over here is gradually closing down on the number of imports allowed in Super League, which will hopefully make the clubs more cautious about the Aussies and Kiwis they sign. For too long, we've had numerous crap overseas players in the competition. And they take places that could go to young English players giving the national coach some more options when it comes to the international matches. Instead, the young players are left to rot in an Under-20s competition that is nowhere near as competitive as it should be. When I started out, the reserves comp had open age players—I remember facing Les Davidson at Halifax once—and bloody hell, that's what toughens young players up. These days, they don't face that standard and unless they go out on loan to other clubs, it's hard to force their way into the side.

One position that we've really lacked over the last decade

or so is an outstanding No. 6. Ever since the likes of Garry Schofield and Shaun Edwards retired, we've not really had a play-maker to fill that role. They've tried Andy Farrell, Paul Sculthorpe and Kevin Sinfield in that role—and even played half-backs like Longy there—and it's just not worked. All of those were, or are, great players in their own right, but they're not stand-offs. The Aussies, by contrast, always had a production line of great stand-offs during my international career. If it wasn't Brad Fittler it was Trent Barrett or Darren Lockyer.

One solution shouldn't be giving England shirts to people who aren't English. I couldn't believe it when I played for Great Britain in 2007 and Maurie Fa'asavalu was one of my team-mates. What the hell was that about? It makes a mockery of our game. The Aussies wouldn't pick an Englishman—it makes us look like a bunch of amateurs. I realise some players have loyalties to two countries—Pat Richards at Wigan, for example, is an Australian with Irish parents—but those cases are the exception. Far too often, players are taking the piss with the way they switch allegiances.

It's another example of why I think rugby league is run poorly. What really annoyed me was the way they fast-tracked Celtic Crusaders into Super League. It was just wrong. It was a complete disaster in an area that didn't care for rugby league, and what happened? They moved 130 miles away to Wrexham the following year! It's embarrassing, especially when there are great clubs like Widnes who would be desperate to play in Super League.

Before they look at expanding rugby league into London and Wales, I think the RFL would be better served making the stronghold stronger. Bringing in Catalans was a smart move—because fans down there love their rugby league. But why give places to Wales and London when you've got clubs like Widnes who would pack out the terraces and bring in money through sponsorship and hospitality. And what about Cumbria? They love rugby league up there. I get recognised as much there as I do in Yorkshire—it's a genuine hot-bed for our game. I'd love to see a Cumbrian side brought into Super League, with the current three clubs up there—Whitehaven, Barrow and Workington—acting as feeder clubs. I'm convinced the fans up there would get behind it.

It's not rocket science or brain surgery (if it was, I wouldn't have stood a chance!) Believe me when I say I'm not having a pop because of any bitterness at the RFL, but because I love rugby league, and it annoys me when I see the way it is run. It's a great game but it could be so much better, and watched by so many more people.

18

BOXING CLEVER!

I'LL ALWAYS remember Palma Nova as the place where I got engaged. It was also the place where I got recognised by someone I definitely should have recognised myself!

During the '04 season, we were given a few days off, so Stacey and I took Charlie-Mia on her first overseas holiday. We went back to Palma Nova—where I'd proposed to Stacey.

I was pushing the pram with Stacey next to me, when a big, black Escalade—a huge SUV car—came down the road. It slowed down as it approached me, the tinted window went down, and there was a huge black guy driving it.

'Hi Terry,' he said, and then drove off.

I was stunned. I turned to Stacey and said, 'Who the hell was that?'

She was about to ask the same thing of me. We watched the car as it made a U-turn a little further down the road, and headed back towards us. It pulled over, and the guy yelled out, 'Terry how you doin'?'

I went over to talk to him, and we made small chat about Wigan and rugby and the holiday destination, but I got a feeling he wasn't your bog-standard, typical Wigan fan. The fact he was driving a car that cost a frickin' fortune gave it away.

His face looked familiar, but I didn't have a clue who he was. Then, after about two minutes, it clicked—it was Nigel Benn. I was embarrassed I hadn't recognised him straight away. I follow boxing, and I should have recognised one of Britain's greatest ever fighters! I decided to play it cool and not give myself away. I switched from 'I know what you mean, mate' to 'I know what you mean, Nigel'.

I pulled it off pretty smoothly, too, I thought. After a few minutes of chatting, we went our separate ways. As he pulled away in his car, I waved and said, 'See ya, Nige'—which earned me a slap on the back of my head from Stacey!

I thought afterwards, 'Bloody hell, it's nice that someone like him follows his rugby league'.

My uncle Alan Page was a boxer, who made it into the pro' ranks. He's my dad's half-brother and he's only three years older than me. All the family went to watch him fight Carl Froch once down at Derby Ice Rink, for the English Super Middleweight title. He did well but Froch was a bit too strong for him, and he retired after that defeat.

I'm a fan of boxing—a signed Mike Tyson glove is one of my prized possessions—but I never fancied doing it myself. The fighting wouldn't be too bad, but their training schedules are ridiculous and the money only goes to those who make it to the very top. Everyone else is left to scrap for peanuts.

I did come close to stepping into the ring once during my Wigan career. I was asked to fight Trevor Leota, the giant Wasps hooker, in a charity boxing match. I think Joe Lydon got in touch and asked if I would be willing to do it. The fight was being sold as a battle of the two codes.

I thought it'd be fun and I'm all for helping good causes, so I agreed. I spoke to my uncle, though, and after he discovered Leota was about 20 stone, he told me I was in for a battering! 'Great', I thought. 'I can't pull out now, I'll look stupid.'

I started to get a little worried about it, until I broke my thumb playing against London Broncos leading up to the fight, and Maurice Lindsay pulled me out of the contest. It was a Godsend—I saved face without having to get in the ring. When I told people I'd had to pull out I pretended to be upset, I might have even cursed Maurice for preventing me fighting, but deep down I was made up!

Rugby league players are a tough breed, even the soft ones, and boxers are the same. If you're not tough, you don't make it.

When we got back from that break in Palma Nova, Andy Farrell typified how tough rugby league players are during a game with Leeds. He broke his nose and had to leave the pitch, but a few minutes later he was back on, with a bandage covering his hooter. He looked stupid, but it showed how tough our sport is. If a footballer did that, I'd show my arse in Wigan. It just wouldn't happen.

Everyone knew Faz must have been in pain that day, but all players regularly play with injuries that your average person in the street would be moaning about. Even in that game, I needed oxygen at half-time and a pain-killing injection because I had a bad sternum problem. But it didn't stop me from going out for the second-half. That's not a boast; you'll see similar examples in every dressing room in every rugby league club. And it makes it worthwhile when, like in the Leeds game, we won 26–22. That was only Leeds' second defeat all season—when you pull off a win like that, you don't care how much pain you're in. Trust me, the pain of crying off with an injury and seeing your team lose is far greater.

We were unbeaten in eight and finished the season in fourth place. I was happy with my form—I'd even scored four tries at Widnes. We'd made the Grand Final the previous year from third, but that season it proved a hurdle too far. We beat Saints and Wakefield in the play-offs but at Headingley, we ran out of steam, and lost 40–12.

Lammy was in tears afterwards. I was gutted for him—it was his final game for Wigan, and there were a few other lads leaving, too, such as Tez O'Connor, Mick Cassidy and Gary Connolly.

I picked myself up for the Tri-Nations at the end of the year. It was a great concept; two Tests each against New Zealand and Australia, with the top two sides meeting in the final. And it was on home soil, meaning I wasn't too far away from Stacey and Charley-Mia.

Brian Noble had taken over from David Waite as coach, which I was more than happy about. Nobby had always been a fan of mine and, as a former hooker himself, I liked his coaching approach. I've got a lot of time for him. Other players may say other things—they are entitled to their opinions—but I liked him.

He brought in a couple of new team-bonding ideas to encourage us to gel together. We had to walk over hot-coals, and then a karate expert came in and showed us how to chop pieces of wood in half with our hands! It was good fun, and I was good at it. I called Stacey that afternoon. 'I've been walking bare foot on hot coals and smashing up pieces of wood with my hands,' I informed her, proudly.

'Oh my God,' she said. 'I can't believe you're pissed up already.'

We lost to the Aussies (again). It was a narrow defeat (again) that was only settled right at the death (again), and we hardly made a dream start against the Kiwis at Huddersfield in our next match. We were 12–2 down at half-time, but straight from the restart I scored a try that brought us back into it. From dummy-half, I dummied, I ducked and I scored—Scully kicked the goal and it was 12–8. Game on. The Kiwi boys are good at smashing players and when they want to they really can play. But when things aren't going their way, their discipline goes to shit, and that's what happened that day. We won 22–12.

Our next game was against the Aussies and I hardly had the best record against them. Played five, lost five. It was annoying that I couldn't beat them. In the past four matches they'd won by less than six points. In our first match in that Tri-Nations, we were drawing 8–8 when they scored a try with 35 seconds left. It was ridiculous—the UN should have sanctioned them for torture!

I started at hooker and again scored our first try—who'd have thought it, Terry Newton the Test match try-machine! That put me joint top of our try-scoring chart for all of three minutes, until Stu Reardon crossed—he'd bagged two against the Kiwis the previous week. It was a great, flowing try that started in our half—the kind of try the Aussies usually score. We were 18–6 up at half-time. But the thing we all knew about the Aussies was they played until the final whistle—that had been the difference in our past four meetings—and none of us were getting carried away. Nobby drilled home to us at half-time not to switch off.

Sure enough, Kimmorley carved open a try for Mark O'Meley and added the conversion early in the second-half but for the rest of the game, our defence was awesome and we never felt in trouble. We were in control, we were commanding the game—we beat them 24–12 and it felt like it could easily have been by more.

Beating the Aussies that day was unreal. It was one of my lifetime goals ticked off. Wembley, tick. Challenge Cup with Wigan, tick. Playing for my country, tick. Beating the Aussies, tick. And to do it in front of my own fans in Wigan, made it even sweeter.

I'd injured myself in the match against the Aussies, and my Wigan team-mate Sean O'Loughlin had to come on for his Test debut at hooker, even though he'd never played there before!

I missed the following week's game, when we beat the Kiwis for a second time to finish on top of the pile, but I was back for the final and some people thought we were favourites in that match. We'd beaten the Kiwis twice and the Aussies in our last meeting—we were in good form.

But that day, like in Sydney two years earlier, we just didn't turn up and the Aussies were awesome. They hammered us 44–4, it was a case of men against boys and Darren Lockyer and Kimmorley were, again, exceptional.

19

MORE HIGH TACKLES AND A RECORD BAN

HE'D NOT been at the club a week, when Dennis Moran came to see me.

'I'm looking for a car,' he said. Someone must have told him I'm a second hand car dealer, which I'm not, by the way. But I know a few people.

'What are you after?' I asked.

'Something stylish.'

'Okay.'

'Quick, reliable.'

'Alright, leave it with . . .'

'It's got to have 12 months MOT. And tax. I want a car that's taxed.'

Bloody hell, I half expected him to say he wanted tinted windows and a built-in DVD player as well.

'How much d'you want to pay?' I asked.

'I'm pretty easy,' he replied. 'But definitely no more than £500.'

Yep, I thought. Mick Cassidy might have gone, but Wigan had definitely found a replacement for the tightest player around!

We were disappointed not to make the Grand Final the year before, so Denis Betts hit on the idea of going to Florida for our pre-season training. Denis didn't want to leave any stone unturned, and he told us Florida had the best training facilities.

I was excited because I'd never been to America before. We had a team meeting a few weeks earlier and Denis explained that, since the 9/11 attacks, America had really clamped down on security and that they, as a club, weren't taking any chances of players being turned away at customs. He asked us all if anyone had any driving convictions.

Gaz Hock's hand shot up.

'Don't worry about it Gaz,' Denis said. 'You'll still be able to come, but we'll just have to check whether you need a visa or not.'

Gaz looked puzzled.

'I don't need a visa,' he said. 'I'm not going to do any shopping.'

I'd never seen so many men cry with laughter before!

Gaz is always brilliant for a laugh. I remember once going to a training session down in Wales, at Bangor University. Some tight sods told Gaz he needed to take his passport because Wales was a different country, and he did!

When we all calmed down from his 'visa' gaffe, Denis asked if anyone had ever been in trouble with the law. Sheepishly, I put my arm in the air—everyone knew anyway—and he told me I'd need to go down to the American Embassy in London.

It was a pain I could have done without. After catching the train to London and eventually finding the building I needed, I spent an hour with a Yank who asked me every possible detail about my past. 'Do you regret what you've done? Do you consider yourself a threat to the American people?'

I'm surprised he didn't ask if I was a suicide bomber.

It was a real interrogation, and for a while I thought he wasn't going to let me go, until I finally convinced him that I was just plain old Terry Newton from Wigan, and not a terrorist, and he gave me the paperwork I needed.

When we got to Florida, the squad was divided into different chalets. I was with Andy Farrell, Danny Tickle, Luke Davico and Jerry Seuseu. In the chalet nearest to us were Wayne Godwin—who'd joined that year from Castleford—Martin Aspinwall, Brian Carney and Kris Rads. All the nutters, basically, with the exception of Mr Sensible Rads.

We walked to their place every morning to go for breakfast together and for some reason, Wagga was always walking around completely naked! He'd make everyone a brew, then sit with us completely in the nude—I wondered who Wigan had signed. He only got dressed when it was time to leave the chalet. Wagga's a real athlete, there's no fat on his body and he's not shy to show it off. When your face looks like a leather sofa, I suppose you've got to make the most of what you've got (only joking, Wagga)!

I also discovered Aspy's strange eating habits: instead of putting milk on his cereal, he'd put Powerade on. Mind you, he's ripped to the bone, one of the fittest players I've ever seen, so he must be doing something right.

It was a tough camp and training was intense. Faz and I both had knee injuries so we spent a lot of time together doing upper-body work as well as rehab. It was at a time when Faz was attracting interest from rugby union clubs, but he never talked about it. We had mini-buses to go to training sessions, and Faz was our nominated driver. On the way back from training, Danny would always beg to call in at Dunkin Donuts but Faz never allowed it!

About halfway through that camp, both Faz and Danny flew home early. Danny's wife was expecting twins and had gone into labour, while Faz's knee wasn't responding to treatment. As I was left sharing with two new blokes, it meant I had the rule of the house!

Aspy tried to sneak in to get out of their mad-house, but I wasn't having any of it. We didn't get much social time, but I saw on our schedule a block that had been left free and I thought, 'Great, we've got a few hours off. We can go for some beers'.

Instead, they took us to bloody Disneyland! I wasn't impressed at the prospect, but it was actually quite good fun. It was certainly a lot more interesting than the basketball game we watched that night. Talk about dull.

That off-season had seen the biggest turn-over of Wigan players I'd known. It was becoming obvious that Faz would be leaving to go to union; we'd already lost Adrian Lam, Quentin Pongia, Craig Smith, Terry O'Connor, Mick Cassidy, Gary Connolly, Luke Robinson and Mark Smith.

That was a massive chunk of our side. Between them, those players had racked up hundreds of games for Wigan. But more importantly, they all knew about the culture of the club. It wasn't just the quality of the players we were losing that stung us, but the quantity: it was a mistake to let them all go at the same time. One thing I have to praise St Helens for is the way they've tried to make changes to their key players gradually— first Paul Sculthorpe went, then Sean Long and next it will be Keiron Cunningham. Wigan didn't do that.

To replace the great players we lost, Maurice signed Luke Davico, Jerry Seuseu, David Vaealiki and Dennis Moran. No disrespect to them, but they weren't the same class.

Vaealiki was returning from major surgery, Davico had a major chest injury, Jerry—who'd been a very good player in his day—was by then running on one good knee. It wasn't their fault—they tried their best. It was Wigan's fault for signing them. One signing I was excited about was Moran. When I'd played against him at London he'd annihilated us, and I'm not sure if he was overawed or he felt under pressure, but he was never the same player at Wigan. Perhaps, had Faz stayed on, he may have been better, because Dennis was a free spirit—not a chief organiser—and a large part of his success in London had been while playing alongside Jim Dymock, who was a great organiser.

There were a lot of expectations on Dennis. He was replacing Lammy and the fans were excited about what he might do. When he didn't perform, they got on his back and his confidence melted. I'll never slag off the Wigan fans. They only criticise players because they care about the team, but sometimes I don't think they realise how some players can struggle with their criticism. Personally, I used to love it when I got stick—I buzzed off the Saints fans jeering me—but others struggled with it.

Luke Davico was a good player and a good bloke, too, but he suffered a recurrence of a nasty pectoral injury in our first friendly against Salford—a game I remember best for Brian Carney attempting to charge down a conversion! What he was thinking, I have no idea.

It felt like we were jinxed. I was injured at the start of the year, so was Rads and every player we signed was crocked aside from Dennis, who was struggling for form.

When Terry O'Connor left, I took over his newspaper column in the *Wigan Evening Post* and I had some fun with it. I never crossed the line—at least, not that I was aware—though Gaz Hock got annoyed that every time he failed his theory driving test, I put it in the paper. When he finally passed it at the sixth attempt, he was more than relieved. It was strange. I felt like a bit of a journalist, snooping around for gossip! Every time a lad did something silly they'd hope I'd not find out about it to keep it out of my column. When Kev Brown put petrol into his diesel car, he never lived it down.

While I was playing journalist, some of the real journalists were writing that I was attracting interest from a few other Super League clubs including Bradford, who were coached by my old GB boss Brian Noble. 'He's the best hooker in this country,' Maurice Lindsay was quoted as saying in the press. 'I don't care if someone offered me a quarter of a million pounds, they wouldn't get Terry Newton.'

Deep down, I sensed Denis Betts was on borrowed time. I'm not sure Maurice saw Denis as a head coach so soon in his career. I'm sure he respected him, but Maurice likes big-name coaches and Denis only got the job by default because of Greg's illness. We lost as many games as we won in the opening three months of the season. When you look at the players who had left Wigan before the season started, Denis did a good job. Maurice's signings were the problem rather than Denis' work as a coach. Then Faz and Davico left before a ball had been kicked and Lockers and Gaz Hock suffered season-ending injuries. Again, hardly Denis' fault. He did as well as he could have been expected to do, with the players he had. But Maurice was desperate for success and he was convinced he'd signed some good players.

We even beat Saints on Good Friday and, three days later, we had a great win at Hull with Wagga and Chris Melling playing at half-back and a load of kids on the bench. But when we lost five of our six in Super League leading to May, Maurice decided to act and appointed Ian 'Basil' Millward as our new head coach. I got a load of text messages from mates and family members asking me why I hadn't told them. But I was the last to find out about it!

You may not believe this, but I've always had problems with my weight. Honestly—this six pack is not natural! I'm an early bird by nature, and I've always turned up early for training. I was in the gym under the stand at the JJB Stadium, on my own.

It was about 8am, and I was on a treadmill when I heard an Aussie voice yell out, 'Hi Tez'. I turned to see who it was and saw Basil wearing a Wigan top. I nearly fell off the bloody treadmill. That was the first I knew about it!

He'd been Saints' coach for so long, just seeing him wearing the Wigan crest looked wrong. I hadn't been the No.1 fan of him as a bloke—there was just something about him that niggled me—but I must admit my first reaction was, 'If he makes us as successful as Saints, fair enough'. Denis stayed on as his assistant.

He'd done a good job at St Helens—no question—and some of his coaching techniques were good. I still say that some of the best drills I've ever done have been under Basil. I saw one session when I was out injured where Basil made all the lads train in dark sunglasses. The idea was that they had to bend forward to look over the top of the frame—and it worked. Lads stopped standing upright in defence, and started bending their backs more. It was genius. When Kris Rads was out injured, Basil called me into his office and said, 'I respect you as a player, I'm going to make you captain'. I was walking around like a dog with three dicks. Captain of my hometown club.

Basil realised we needed some reinforcements and signed Liam Botham, son of England cricket legend Ian. We never saw his dad but I remember we were all pestering him for signed cricket bats! I never got one, mind.

My problem with Basil wasn't his coaching, but the way he handled players. I didn't like it.

He was all right with me, but I didn't like the way he was with some of the younger lads. For example, if Wayne Godwin did something wrong he would get hammered for it. But if I made the same mistake, Basil wouldn't say anything.

We made a winning start at Salford, which was to be expected anyway. In our next two matches, against Hull and

London, we lost them both by four points. For those games, we were still playing to Denis Betts' plan, but then for our next match, against Leeds, Basil decided to change our game plan completely. It was too much. He did it all at once against a good side, and Leeds absolutely slaughtered us that day, winning by a Super League record 70–0.

There we were, with the coach who was supposed to transform Wigan's fortunes, and we were run ragged. Sure, we had loads of injuries, and we were desperately lacking the quality of the players who had left the previous season, but had we stayed under Denis I'm sure we wouldn't have lost by such a cricket score. I put it down to Basil's tactics. It wasn't that they were wrong, it's just he tried to change too much, too soon. The following week we had a week off from Super League; we had a Challenge Cup game against St Helens at Knowsley Road. I thought, 'Surely it can't get worse than 70–0'.

I was wrong.

Basil gave me the game plan to attack the markers, then give short balls to the forwards running between the back marker and the A defender—which is the opponent positioned in the defensive line, closest to the play-the-ball. I remember after the first set thinking to myself, 'This isn't going to work'.

I told him at half-time that the game plan was getting us battered, but he told me to stick with it. We got blown apart. The forwards must have looked at me and wondered what I'd done—I'd put them under so much pressure. My job was to run out and engage the marker before passing. Basil said Saints couldn't defend against that and, given his insider knowledge, I trusted him. I'm not shirking the blame here, but I had to stick to the coach's game plan. If I hadn't, what would have happened then? He may have subbed me. He may not have played me again for ignoring his tactics.

Again, with the players we had, the defeat itself can't just be put down to Basil. He didn't take to the field, he didn't miss those tackles or drop those balls. But he was the one who picked the players, picked the tactics and he was responsible for creating the mood in the team.

That was the worst defeat of my life. I can't remember clapping our fans—if I did, I was on autopilot. I was so embarrassed, I just wanted to go home. I couldn't speak to anyone, I couldn't look at anyone. I hated it, and I hated playing for Basil. He had come in and everyone expected him to turn our season around. Well, he certainly did that, only he turned it the wrong way. We'd beaten Saints earlier in the year under Denis Betts and just a few months later, under Basil, we were losing by a record scoreline that brought our fans a lifetime of torment from Saints' fans.

I considered telling Maurice how I felt. But Maurice wasn't stupid. A 75–0 scoreline against Saints—it was blatantly obvious we weren't playing for him.

The following day, the club invited us for dinner at Frankie and Benny's to try to raise morale. Everyone was fed up, no-one wanted to be there. To make matters worse, they made all the lads pay for the meal at the end! It was hardly the best way of lifting morale. Young lads were blowing up, they didn't have much money and they didn't have a choice—they had to attend. It was horrible being around the club at that time.

As much as I loved Wigan at that time, I hated going to training, and I hated playing for Basil. I talked with other lads about him behind his back, and that would never have happened under Frank, Mike Greg or Denis.

I wasn't the only one who felt like that. Kris Rads announced his retirement. He wasn't happy playing for Basil. When a guy like Kris Rads, who has spilt blood and broken bones playing for Wigan for so many years, was getting fed up with it all, I knew something wasn't right. If anyone loved Wigan more than me, it was Radders.

He's a champion fella, and one of my best mates. It's funny how, looking back on those friendships, it's not the big belly-laugh incidents that stand out but the little, childish things. A group of us used to go to Blackpool quite a bit on the train and we devised a game where we'd all pretend to be asleep when the conductor came. Whoever was the first to crack would have to pay for all the tickets. I'm not joking, if you see Radders in a pub or a coffee house, buy him a drink—he must be broke from the number of train tickets he's forked out for over the years! He was always the first to crack. Every single time.

Wigan felt wrong without him there.

Despite his loss, we managed to pick up a couple of wins. As our season reached its close with a home match against Saints, Basil summoned me into his office and said he had an opportunity to sign Micky Higham from St Helens, and that he didn't think I had a future at the club.

I was stunned.

I had a year left on my contract, and I'd not even thought of going anywhere else. Basil said he admired what I'd done for the club but he thought it was time for us to part. While I was still digesting what he had told me, he said Bradford were interested in signing me.

I said, 'It's the first I've heard of it'.

'I'll leave it with you.'

It was a bombshell. I couldn't believe it.

I thought, 'I can't go, people will think I'm deserting them'. But what choice did I have? I had Bradford—the most successful club of the time—chasing me, and I didn't like playing under Millward. The mood around the place wasn't like the Wigan I signed for—it wasn't the Wigan that Andy Farrell had played at, or Terry O'Connor or Adrian Lam. The club was dying. I had a coach who didn't want me, and who obviously wasn't going to keep me on when my contract expired. At the time, Kris Rads, Sean O'Loughlin and Gaz Hock were all out with long-term injury problems and I thought, 'What if I stay and get a nasty injury like that? What then?'

I had to think of my family and my future. Of course, no-one likes to be told they're not wanted, and I couldn't understand why Basil wanted to get rid of me. I'd given everything for Wigan. I trained hard, I played as hard as I could. Micky Higham is a very good player, no doubt, and every coach should have the choice of picking their players. But a few months earlier Maurice had called me 'the best hooker in the country' and I couldn't have been that bad if Bradford wanted me.

After a few days, we met again and Basil told me he had the opportunity to do a deal in which Bradford would sign Micky Higham, and then they'd swap him for me.

'What if I don't want to go?' I asked.

He advised me to think of my future, because there'd be nothing on the table after 12 months. We went to see Maurice, and he told me he wanted to keep me, but that Ian was calling the shots.

'I took a lot of persuading by Ian, but I did as I have always done and backed the coach,' Maurice later said in the press.

I knew Maurice was gutted. We'd always got on and I think he knew how much playing for Wigan meant to me. While I hated Basil for his decision, there's a part of me—a small part—that admired him for having the balls to tell me to my face. But I couldn't work out why only weeks earlier he had told me he wanted to build the club around me and made me captain.

In hindsight, I wish I'd backed myself. Maybe I should have said to him, 'I'm staying, I'm going to be here longer than you'. It was obvious by the way we were playing, and from the mood in the team, that he wasn't going to last long. But I couldn't risk getting injured in my final year—with a little baby girl, I had to take the security.

I met with Bradford's coach, Brian Noble, and he sold the club to me. Not that they needed much selling—they were awesome at the time. Reaching a Grand Final every year was a given for them. They were beating Saints and Leeds in finals, not being battered by 70 points by them.

I agreed to the move. I didn't feel like I had much choice. It was all kept under wraps, and I was happy with that—I was still coming to terms with it myself, the last thing I needed was fans and team-mates asking me about it.

I went into our game against Saints—our penultimate match of the season—in the mindset that it was my last game in front of my hometown fans as a Wigan player. It was also my last Wigan-Saints derby. Basil even said to me, 'Be a leader out there and show us what we're going to miss'. I was so hyped up to make a lasting impression, and I did—though not in the way I intended. I made headlines for all the wrong reasons for my challenges on Lee Gilmour and Sean Long.

Gilly is a good lad off the field, but we always had a bit of a ding-dong together when we played. He's fast and strong and causes teams all sorts of problems. Early in the game, I saw him bringing the ball in and I thought, 'I'm going to whack him here'. I swung my arm, he ducked into me and I knocked him clean out. I went in to hurt him, no doubt. But I never intended to knock him out. As the medical team dealt with Gilly on the floor and moved him onto a stretcher, I thought, 'I'm off here'. But either the ref didn't see it clearly or didn't think it was malicious—which it wasn't—and I stayed on the pitch.

The Saints lads were furious, and in the next few tackles I was involved in, they gave it to me, saying things like, 'It's your turn next'. Sledging is part of the game. I've been called every name under the sun in tackles and it's never bothered me. I've never really got involved in it—I'm usually too knackered to talk in tackles!

I knew I had a target on my head but it wasn't my turn next. It was Longy's.

I have a few regrets from my career and my tackle on Longy in that match is certainly one of them.

We were defending our line and I saw Longy talking to Maurie Fa'asavalu, a big Samoan forward who somehow played for England a couple of years later. I read the play perfectly. I knew what was coming. Longy was going to receive the ball at first-receiver and arc across our line, away from the play-the-ball, and drop an A ball—an inside pass—back to Fa'asavalu. I saw him organising it.

I knew that if I timed it right, I could smash Longy into Fa'asavalu—get two for the price of one, so to speak. I flew out the line, I saw Longy run and then twist to pass the ball, and I tried to shoulder-charge him into Fa'asavalu. They rattled into each other and I thought, 'Bingo, job done'. Longy went down, and stayed there for an eternity.

He was hurt—I thought he'd injured himself in the collision with his own team-mate, which is not unusual: I've suffered loads of injuries in collisions with players from my own team.

After the game, one of the Saints lads said to me, 'That was well out of order, Tez.'

At that time, I didn't think it was a bad challenge. A bit high, maybe, but I was quite proud of myself for reading the play and getting them both. When I got into our changing room, I asked someone whether it was high and one of the lads said, 'Yeah, you dickhead. You got him with your elbow'.

I was devastated.

It crossed my mind to go into the Saints dressing room to check on him, but after something so bad, his team-mates would probably have strung me up and killed me. Much safer, I thought, to call him, so after I'd showered and changed I phoned Longy to check how he was and apologise.

There was no answer.

I avoided the players' bar afterwards and headed straight home to watch it on TV. When I saw it, I thought, 'Shit. That looks bad'. It was obvious that I'd caused Longy a serious injury, and I wouldn't wish that on anyone. Certainly not a mate.

To this day I feel bad about it. In his autobiography he wrote that I'd claimed to the press I'd apologised when I hadn't, but what I remember saying was that I'd tried to call him to say sorry—which I had. To make it worse, it seemed half of Wigan was talking about it. Longy has a habit of upsetting and annoying opposition fans—he loves that kind of controversy—and many fans in Wigan seemed glad that I'd done it.

Some fans slapped me on the back as if I was a hero, but I was embarrassed and mortified. Sometimes I've done things, intentionally, in the heat of the moment and regretted them afterwards—but this wasn't one of those times. I regretted it, sure, but it was never intentional. If I could have undone it, I would have.

When I got to training on the following Monday I wasn't shocked to discover I'd been cited for both incidents. I went to the RFL's head-quarters, Red Hall—I practically have my own parking bay there—and pleaded guilty to the challenge on Gilly. It was mis-timed, but when you intentionally put on a big shot like that and miss, you deserve a ban.

For the Longy one, I tried to argue my case because it had been an accident. But they played it on the TV screen in slow-motion and there is a frame showing my elbow connecting with his cheekbone. As soon as I saw that I said to myself, 'I'm screwed'.

I was banned for 10 matches—seven for the tackle on

Longy, three for the one on Gilly—and fined £600.

It was a record Super League ban.

I appealed the Longy ban straight away. There was already plenty of speculation about me joining Bradford. Basil was quoted as saying, 'I think we'll see Terry Newton in a cherry and white shirt again.' That was bullshit. Basil did at least back me on the ban and said that seven weeks was harsh. Or maybe he just didn't want my swap with Micky Higham to fall through.

I'd already told Nobby that I probably wouldn't be able to play in the Tri-Nations that year. I had a few niggling injuries that needed sorting out. But I hadn't actually officially pulled out of the Great Britain squad, so I thought, 'Even if the ban is held up, I can use four games from the Tri-Nations.'

I couldn't believe what the judiciary did on my appeal. They must have pre-empted what I was going to do with GB, and changed the ban from a set number of games to a length of time, banning me from playing until 15 April the following year. A seven month ban! That took in an extra two club games, plus the Tri-Nations. Given that players can use a friendly as one game of a suspension, it, in effect, changed a 10-match ban into a 17-match ban.

I spoke to Nobby and he said he was still desperate for me to join Bradford, and that the ban wouldn't affect my transfer. A few days later, the swap deal was confirmed in a press release by the club.

My Wigan career was over.

Sean Long
Former Great Britain team-mate

TEZ AND ME *have been mates since we were six, and he was a tough bugger back then.*

We grew up on the same streets in Worsley Mesnes, outside Wigan, and it was rough. It made the estate on Shameless *look like Beverly Hills!*

It was full of dodgy people and scumbags. It was the kind of place where older lads used to walk around with their airguns and bully younger kids. Before I'd turned five I'd been in trouble for smoking and bunking off school. When I was shot in the back when I was seven, my mum and dad decided enough was enough and moved house, but Tez spent his teen years on those streets and that's why I have a ton of respect for what he's done.

I know how tough it was where he lived. Like me, he got hooked on rugby league down at Wigan St Jude's amateur club and full credit to him, he stayed focused on rugby and wasn't led astray by what everyone else was doing. He always knew what he wanted to do and he was always dedicated, and that's why he was such a success.

When we both made it into the Great Britain squad in '98, we were as thick as thieves. We really bonded—we called ourselves the bomb squad. We didn't play in the first two Tests and so, with Harvey Howard, we used to go to the Love Train—a 70s themed night—for a few bevvies at Leeds' Town and Country Club, and then we'd sneak back in to the hotel at 3am, wearing afro wigs, trying to be quiet but probably making a racket!

They lost the first two Tests so they called on the bomb squad—me and Tez—for the third Test, and we drew the game. We were both making our Test debuts, against one of the greatest Kiwi teams I've ever seen. Their line-up was bloody awesome. Jarrod McCracken, Joe Vagana, Craig Smith, Quentin Pongia, Tony Puletua, Ruben Wiki—it was a fierce side. I watched them do the Haka and I thought, 'Bloody hell, I wouldn't like to mess with that lot'. Then the game kicked-off, Tez spear-tackled huge Joe Vagana and a big brawl erupted with me smack bang in the middle of it! So cheers Tez, thanks for that!

Tez was always a handy bloke to have on your side. He played rough, tackled hard and he was a nasty bastard with it. That was his game—and it helped make him one of the best players of his generation. He was hard to defend against, because he took the line on and popped up great short balls for the forwards. I'm lucky that I spent most of my career with Keiron Cunningham as my hooker at St Helens, and Tez was another top-class No.9. He could fire a ball from the ground and it was always on the button, left side and right, and as first-receiver that allowed you to stand a lot further away from him. With other hookers, you find yourself having to stand a lot closer to the play-the-ball because they can't pass as far, and of course that has a big knock-on effect. That's the kind of thing that fans probably didn't notice about Tez, but all the players on the pitch noticed it. His skill level was very good.

He's great company, Tez. A real wind-up merchant. He's never got me with any of his prank phone calls but he's always terrorising team-mates. He's a real laugh and he used to liven up the GB camps.

But no matter how well he knows you, if you're on the opposite side he treats you like an enemy. As I discovered when he nearly removed my head with his elbow during a Wigan-Saints derby in 2005. He'd already cleaned out Lee Gilmour, and then he did me, fracturing my cheekbone and eye socket.

I think something short-circuited in his head that day. I can *see now that he accidentally caught me with his elbow, but at the time I would have loved to punch him in the face. Of course, if I'd done that I doubt I'd have walked away afterwards!*

If it had been anyone else who'd done that, I'd have found it hard to forgive them. But Tez is Tez, he's as daft as a brush and I certainly don't hold a grudge. As I said earlier, knowing the area he grew up in, I take my hat off to him for carving out such a successful career and life for himself. He's happily married, he's got two kids and he's a nice bloke.

A bloody aggressive player, but a nice bloke!

20

RUNNING WITH THE BULLS

IT'S A WEIRD feeling turning up at a new club, fully fit, and unable to play. I'd been all over the papers for smashing Gilly and Longy and getting a record ban and I didn't know most of the Bradford fellas—God knows what they thought of me. When you join a new club the easiest way of getting the lads to like you is by playing well. But because I was banned, I couldn't do that and I was worried that they'd see me as a liability, and that they'd be pissed off with me because I couldn't play.

One of my first tasks with Bradford was travelling to Lanzarote for a pre-season training camp. Nobby stunned me on the first day when he approached me and said, 'We know the situation you're in with your suspension, so I want you to stand up in front of the team and talk about discipline'. I didn't know what to say. I'd never met half the players, I was serving a suspension that had made national headlines and I had to do a 15-minute speech about discipline.

I called Kris Radlinski for advice and he said, 'Just tell them your thoughts about it'. That evening, Nobby told the players I had something I wanted to say. The first thing I did was apologise about what had happened with the ban, and I told them that I would train the house down for 14 weeks so that, when I got back, I'd be able to help them out. They seemed to accept me, which was important because I didn't want them thinking, 'Why've we signed him when he's got such a big ban?'

My first game for Bradford would have been the World Club Challenge—I was gutted at first, but to be honest I wasn't a part of the Bradford side that qualified by winning the Grand Final the year before and the more I thought about it, the more I felt glad I wasn't involved. It wouldn't have seemed right to come into a new side and, in my first game, win a World Club Challenge. I watched the lads beat Wests Tigers and I was made up for them, but I didn't feel part of that.

I quickly settled into a routine of crossing the Pennines from Wigan to Bradford. The daily journeys weren't as bad as I imagined, with Paul Deacon and Paul Johnson—lads who I'd played with and against since I could remember—in the car too. It was frustrating not being able to play but Bradford's conditioner Martin Clawson really helped me out. I effectively did two pre-seasons—one with all the players in December and January, and then another in February, March and April while the rest of the lads were playing. Sam Burgess was just coming onto the scene then. Bradford had big expectations of him but he wasn't quite ready for the first-team, so they hit on the idea of having him train with me for the duration of my ban. Under Martin's watchful eye, we trained together every day and got on well.

He was only 16, but he was already incredibly strong, and it was obvious he was going to be something special. In our first wrestling session, Sam threw me around everywhere. After that we had a five-minute sparring session, and he could box too. We were supposed to keep it to body shots, but it got a bit heated and he clocked me around the head.

I thought, 'I'll show the cheeky sod', and swung at him. He smartly ducked down, but I managed to get him with a good uppercut. Splat! Sam's nose just exploded. There was blood everywhere and Sam fell to the floor. Martin started panicking, and shouted, 'Stop what you're doing, stop what you're doing!' I think he was worried he'd get in trouble. Sam took it in good spirits, and nicknamed me 'bully' from then on. I hope he never decides to get me back—he'd knock my head off now!

The Bradford lads were all a great bunch, and they quickly helped me to feel settled. Stanley Gene, the ageless Papua New Guinea veteran, was at the club and he was a real character. We had a drink at Christmas time, and he started calling me 'Cuz'—a nickname that I preferred more than 'Bully'. He said, 'You know what Cuz, I used to despise you. Now I know you, I like you'. I thought that was nice—his opinion of me had changed in the same way my opinion of Neil Cowie had changed once I'd become his team-mate.

We were given a meal after every session, and Stan always said, 'Free food, good food'. That's all he'd say. 'Free food, good food.' Stan's eating habits are nearly as infamous as his age, and for good reason. Once, we were served king prawns and he ate everything—shells, heads, tails, you name it. After that, he leaned over and grabbed the discarded shells from my plate!

I said, 'Stan, you're not supposed to eat those.'

He smiled and said, 'Cuz, what my body doesn't like, I'll shit out'. He took the leftovers back home to Hull in doggy bags.

Bradford made a decent start to the season, which only made me angrier—I wanted to be out there with them. What pissed me off even more was when Wigan sacked Ian Millward. I was pleased about it because I didn't like him, but I thought, 'I bloody knew I should have stayed and dug my heels in!' My suspension finally ended and I made my debut against Huddersfield. We strolled to a win and I did well—I scored a try with practically my first touch and then set up two more! It was one of the sweetest wins I'd had. It was my only game for Bradford with Nobby as coach—he left to take over Wigan the following day. I was stunned when he told us.

Nobby had tried so hard for so long to bring me to Bradford, even swapping me with Wigan for Micky Higham. Now he was going to Wigan himself! The day he left, I phoned him and asked if I could go as well. He said he'd do everything in his power to sign me, but it didn't come off. I was gutted. I was happy at Bradford—but it wasn't Wigan.

Nobby signed the best player at the time, Stuart Fielden, and he helped keep them up that year. I wanted to be there with them. Nobby sometimes phoned me to see how I was— just polite chats, really—but it kept my hopes alive that I could return to Wigan.

Steve McNamara was promoted to head coach and his first game was away at Warrington, which we won—but that's not why I remember it! Brett Ferres tackled someone off the ball, I was standing yards away and the ref shouted me over and sent me to the sin-bin! I couldn't believe it. I don't know if it was a case of mistaken identity—Brett and I are hardly identical bloody twins—but when he showed me the yellow card, I didn't know what to do. I was about to protest my innocence but I couldn't blame a team-mate, could I? So I took it on the chin.

We played Saints and I'd still not spoken to Longy since breaking his jaw a year earlier. Even though I was now at Bradford, people continued to talk about it. It was even mentioned on TV in a programme about the 100 worst incidents in sport. I think I was number 11—I was pissed off I didn't make the top 10! I did an interview in Manchester to try to give my side of the incident and clear the air, but looking back, what I should have done was apologise to Longy. I still felt a bit embarrassed about what happened, and when I saw him at that Saints game, there was a real atmosphere. I avoided him. As soon as the final whistle went, I headed down the tunnel to get changed, and straight onto the team coach.

A few weeks later, Great Britain had a mid-season Test against New Zealand. It was a real Test but it didn't feel like one, because the Kiwi side was drawn almost entirely from Super League players. My form for Bradford had been good, Nobby was still the coach and I wasn't shocked to get selected. I wasn't shocked that Longy was picked, either. To make matters worse, the match was at Knowsley Road—St Helens' home ground.

'Brilliant,' I thought. 'I'm going to be the only bloody Great Britain player in history to get booed by the home crowd.' The game was on a Tuesday night so we were only together for a day or two. In training for that game, I kept looking for an opening—a chance to go over to Longy and say, 'Sorry', but there never seemed to be a good time. I avoided him, and there was an atmosphere in that game because I hadn't broken the ice. Looking back, I wish I'd been the bigger man, but I'm rubbish at doing things like that and instead I took the easy option. He must have been pissed off with me, I wouldn't have blamed him; but incredibly, some of the Saints fans seemed to have forgiven me. Maybe it was because I no longer played for Wigan, or maybe because I was in Great Britain's colours that day, but during a quiet spell in that Test—we won comfortably—I heard the chant, 'Newton give us a wave . . .' I looked over at the section of the crowd and they were all Saints fans! I didn't know whether they were taking the piss or what, but I waved and they cheered—it was one of the weirdest moments of my life, having Saints fans cheering me, especially after what I'd done to one of their best players a few months earlier.

Bradford finished the season strongly but we just missed out on the Grand Final—Hull beat us 19–12 to qualify for Old Trafford instead. I was pissed off, because Bradford had been to the previous five Grand Finals and as soon as I joined they missed out. It felt like I'd cursed them!

Great Britain had another Tri-Nations series down under later that year.

Keiron Cunningham announced he was retiring from international rugby, and it crossed my mind to do the same. I was getting married to Stacey that autumn, plus I knew it would be Charley-Mia's third birthday while I was away on tour, and missing that would kill me. I spoke to Stacey about it and she convinced me to go on tour. She said I had a great chance and encouraged me. I think she also wanted to organise our wedding without me being there to stuff something up!

She was right, though. We did have a great chance—we had some great players like Moz, Peacock, Stu Fielden, plus a few young lads like Sean O'Loughlin, James Roby and Gaz Hock. I genuinely fancied our chances, and since I'd not been to Australia since the record 64–10 defeat four years earlier, I was keen to show that we could do better than that on Australian soil. Half the squad flew out as an advanced party, with the lads from Saints and Hull joining us a week later after they'd played in the Grand Final.

We were staying in the Manly Pacific Hotel, a cracking hotel, and when the Hull and Saints lads arrived, Nobby told us all to go to the lobby to meet them. But I still hadn't spoken to Longy and as they were coming in I thought, 'What am I going to say to him?' I knew I'd have to say something—I managed to avoid him in the one-off Test in June, but we were on tour for six weeks! Anyway, before I could say anything, he walked straight up to me and shook my hand.

I said to him, 'Look Sean, I meant to do Gilly but I honestly didn't mean to hurt you'.

I think he believed me. 'Don't worry about it,' he said. I was glad he broke the ice by coming over to me, because I didn't want any atmosphere in the GB camp. Later in that tour, we spoke about it a bit more and I apologised fully, which was good because—just like after I'd punched Barrie Mac back in my Leeds days—I hated the fact that my own stupidity had upset a mate.

During that tour I noticed just how cut-throat the Aussie press is. Man, they're awful. In England, we'll have a laugh and a joke with the local newspaper journalists after games and during the week, and occasionally writers from the two rugby papers will call, angling for a story. We rarely speak to the journalists for the national newspapers—they hardly ever hang around outside the dressing rooms after matches. In Australia, though, it's totally different. Along the Eastern coast, rugby league is massive—and the coverage on TV, radio and in the papers is like Premier League football over here. It was a real eye-opener. Reporters were in our hotel lobby every day. On one occasion, Moz got off the team coach and there was an attractive girl dressed up to the nines in a short dress and high heels.

She started talking to Moz, and so we just assumed she was a Roosters fan, because Moz was a bit of a cult hero after the impact he'd made in the NRL. Moz, being the polite bloke he is, stopped to talk to her. A few minutes later, I was chatting to Moz in the hotel when our team manager, Abi Ekoku, came over and told Moz she was an Australian news reporter looking for stories! I couldn't believe it.

I was glad I'd seen that, because I was on my guard for the rest of the tour. One of the papers tried to set me and Stu Fielden up. Abi warned us that they were trying to add fuel to the fire before our Test against the Aussies, so we straight-batted every question. They kept niggling away, trying to get us to say something stupid.

'Have you got a message for the Aussie forwards? Are you scared of their formidable pack?'

When it was done, we posed for a few pictures, job done. The following day, we were labelled, 'The enforcers coming to smash the Aussies'! We didn't say anything at all like that, but they put it anyway. It probably did a great job to sell tickets and promote the Tri-Nations, but it put a target on our head that you could see from space! On top of that, I thought, 'Brilliant, the ref 'll be looking out for us'.

I'd always spoken to journalists, even after the most painful of defeats. At the end of the day, as a player, I had a duty to help promote the game, and newspapers do that. But the way the Aussie press acted put me off speaking to them. Leon Pryce was brilliant—he was doing an online tour diary for the BBC, and he wrote that he preferred Blackpool over Bondi. It was hilarious. I'm convinced he knew it would cause a real shit-storm and it did. The Aussies hated it, and everywhere Leon went for the next few days, he had a posse of reporters and photographers following him! Leon had a point, too. If you ever get a chance to go to Bondi, don't bother. It's crap. It's full of rubbish and graffiti. You're better off at Blackpool Pleasure Beach, but the Aussies wouldn't have any of that.

The lads bonded pretty closely on that tour but our preparations weren't great. We did far too much fitness work. Press ups, sit ups, shuttle runs—we got flogged. We'd all just finished a tough season and were fit, we didn't need to be beasted like Army recruits. I did some of the toughest gym sessions ever on that tour, and by the end of the week I wasn't ready to play, I was ready to sleep! They'd have been better off trying to keep us fresh, and concentrate on ball sessions rather than have us do wrestling practice and lift weights. I was ready for bed at 7pm each night—luckily I was rooming with Sean O'Loughlin, who's not only tidy, he turned the TV off without complaining and even made me a brew in the morning!

We were based in Australia and flew out to New Zealand for our two Tests against them. I wish it had been the other way around—it would have been better staying in New Zealand, the people are a lot friendlier. There's none of the 'Pommie this, Pommie that' you get in Australia.

We lost our opening Test against the Kiwis, 18–14, but because they'd fielded an ineligible player, they had the two competition points wiped off.

Next up was a game against the Aussies, and after all the press build-up, we knew it would be a fiery affair. We knew that if we could get among them we could beat them. Nobby's big strength is motivating players for big games. He'd captained Great Britain in '84 when they'd lost every game against the Aussies and Kiwis, and he told us that he didn't want us to feel that pain.

The Aussies knew that our strength was our pack, so they used shit-house tactics to try and knock us off our stride. Early on, Willie Mason hit Stu Fielden and it was on—Longy ran in and then JP. Poor Stuey got dropped and people still remember that punch, but Mason just caught him with a fluke—he'd have dropped me with a lucky punch like that. Believe me, I've seen Stu fight and he's a tough bastard. I once saw him and Hull's Jason Smith going at it, and I'd never seen a bloke throw as many clean punches as Stu did, he annihilated him.

I can't believe Mason didn't get sent off. As soon as he knew he could get away with shit like that, he cleaned out Longy with an elbow and still stayed on the pitch. Longy got his revenge in the best way—he was outstanding that game. But the one who really stood out for me was Gaz Hock. A few fans may have raised their eyebrows when Nobby picked him but he absolutely tormented the Aussies, every one of them was terrified of him on the left side—they just couldn't handle him. The game was nip and tuck for a while and when we couldn't kill them off I thought, 'Here we go—the Aussies will do us again at the end'. But Longy and I helped set up a great try for Gaz Raynor and when Longy kicked a drop-goal, the score was 23–12.

That was one of the highlights of my career. You think about playing the Aussies and winning, and then to do it on their own turf—it's a feeling I can't really describe. The Aussies were being talked up so to go out there and beat them was brilliant. They were 12–1 on to win that game, and for good reason—Britain hadn't won in Australia since 1992.

It gave us the confidence to go on and reach the final. We had to play the Kiwis and the Aussies again. Brian Carney injured himself during our win against the Aussies, but rather than replace him with another winger—Martin Aspinwall was in the squad, chomping at the bit—Nobby decided to move Leon from stand-off to the wing, and bring in Danny McGuire at six. I'm not one to pick a team but I couldn't understand his logic. Why take a good winger like Aspy on tour and not use him? Little wonder he was pissed off about it. And it wasn't just him—Longy and Leon were furious about it. That isn't a criticism of Danny McGuire at all, because Danny's a great player, but it's inevitable two club half-backs will work better together. Had it been Rob Burrow at half-back, he would no doubt prefer Danny to Leon as his No. 6. Our preparation was crap for that match—our training pitch was bloody awful—

and we got hammered 34–6.

Afterwards Longy called a meeting for a group of senior players. He said, 'Look, we've got a great opportunity here, we need to beat the Aussies next week and we're in the final— I don't think anyone should drink.' Moz and JP nodded their heads enthusiastically; it seemed like a good idea. That night, though, he ended up ordering wine from room service and coming around to my room and we got smashed!

In the airport the following day, I saw Longy with a protein shaker, drinking what I thought was chocolate protein. He was acting giddy, which is not too unlike Longy—he's got that hyperactive personality. On the plane, Longy sat in front of me and it soon dawned on me that he'd filled up his protein shaker with Bailey's. He wasn't being particularly rowdy, but he was talking loudly and singing and it was enough to piss off a load of German tourists sat nearby! Nobby gave him a bit of a bollocking for it and a day later, Longy told Nobby that he wanted to go home. It wasn't because of what had happened on the plane—he was missing his missus. Longy's departure was a huge loss. We needed to beat the Aussies up at Lang Park in Brisbane to reach the Final, we were already up against it. We put in a ton of effort and didn't play that badly, but sometimes you've just got to take your hat off and admit you're not good enough. The Aussies won 33–10.

I flew home, depressed but desperate to see my family. Being away from them had killed me. I didn't watch the Tri-Nations Final between the Aussies and the Kiwis—I'm not one for watching big games that I've missed out on—but I'm told the Kiwis went close until Darren Lockyer settled it right at the death.

I sure knew what that felt like.

21

DREAMTEAM

I PLAYED with some of the game's true greats during my 15 years in Super League and one of the questions I get asked a lot is who was the best. It's tough to choose one, but I can't look further than my former Wigan team-mate, Adrian Lam. He had a massive influence on my career and he taught me so much. My happiest memories are of playing at Wigan with him at half-back. Lammy knew the game better than anyone I've ever known. Some half-backs are good at reacting to what happens—Lammy saw things two tackles *before* they happened. He was that good. He had all the skills and the mental toughness of a top player, but more than that, he improved the players around him. When Lammy played, he wasn't just bothered about himself performing—everyone around him played well, too. For that reason, I regard him as my best ever team-mate. But as I said, it was a tough choice—as was picking out my Dreamteam of my former team-mates. Imagine this lot in their prime in one team. They'd murder everyone!

Full-back: Kris Radlinski
Rads was exceptional. He was professional and mentally tough. He loved Wigan as much as anyone, and he became the player he was through a ton of hard work. In defence, he was dependable. If someone broke the line, Rads was there. If

someone put a kick in the air or through the line, Rads was there. He also bagged a lot of tries and people said he was 'in the right place at the right time', but that wasn't luck. One thing I learned from watching Shaun Edwards was about being a good support player, and I tried to take that into my game. There are two secrets to support play—fitness and anticipation. It's about expecting the break, and having the legs to get there for a return pass. I scored a few myself from support play but if ever I was tackled, or had the full-back closing down on me, I knew without looking that Rads would be on my shoulder. He was the king of that.

Winger: Jason Robinson
I only spent a season with him before he switched codes, but Jason was awesome. His acceleration off the mark, and his foot-work, were out of this world. It was like he had jet engines on his boots. He was the first to go to rugby union and at the time, there were loads of people lining up to say he'd never make it, but I knew he'd be a mega-star. Jason was also the toughest person I've ever played against. He could dance around so quickly, you'd end up on your arse without laying a finger on him.

Centre: Steve Renouf
I spent two years with him at Wigan and it's a shame he didn't play at the club longer, because he was still in awesome form when he retired. Pearl certainly wasn't the best trainer in the world. He had diabetes and I think he probably played on it a bit—every time training got tough, he'd pull up, eat a Mars bar and blame the diabetes! But the thing about Pearl was he knew when to hit top gear and when it came to game day, when we needed him to explode, he did. He was an awesome attacking centre. He could score tries and he could create

them as well with his brilliant, balanced running style. He was a champion bloke, too.

Centre: Gary Connolly

Gary's a freak of nature. When he snapped his cruciate ligament in his knee, he continued playing for 12 months. How he did that, I'll never know. His defence was incredible—he had so much upper-body strength, his one-on-one tackling was the best I've ever seen. He's probably not the strongest bloke in the gym but his natural strength is unreal—one of the legends about Gary is he beat the country's third best arm-wrestler, and I wouldn't be surprised if it was true. One of the legends about him that I definitely know to be true is his drinking ability. Get him on the beer and the man's a monster! But what many people don't realise about him is that his diet was phenomenal. Still is. Everything is fresh and steamed— you'll find no McDonalds' wrappers in his car.

Winger: Lesley Vainikolo

It pained me to leave Brett Dallas and Brian Carney out of my Dreamteam, but Les was phenomenal. He wasn't the best trainer and he wasn't the fittest guy in the world, but he could score tries that no other player could score. He was big, powerful, fast, and at his peak, unstoppable.

Stand-off: Iestyn Harris

When Graham Murray joined Leeds—in '98—Iestyn practically carried us to the Grand Final. He was outstanding. He wasn't an organiser, he was a freak. He had a stunning left-foot step and while defenders knew to expect it, they couldn't stop it. He'd lost a yard of pace when he joined Bradford from union—don't get me wrong, he was still a decent player—but he's in my Dreamteam on the basis of his form for Leeds.

Scrum-half: Adrian Lam

I learned more about the game from Lammy than from any coach I've ever had. The partnership between me, Lammy, Faz and Rads was the backbone of Wigan during the early 2000s and how we didn't win a Grand Final, I'll never know. Lammy was also hard as nails, and Wigan fans loved him because they saw how passionate he was about the cherry and white—he absolutely hated Saints! I'd love to see Lammy coaching in Super League.

Prop: Quentin Pongia

I was torn between my heart and my head here, because Barrie Mac and Terry O'Connor are mates of mine and were great players in their own right. They'll probably knock my head off for leaving them out, but I've had to go with Q and Craig Smith as my Dreamteam props. I knew about Q but when he signed for Wigan in 2003, and I'll be honest, I thought he may have been past it. He was playing in France at the time and when he arrived, he had grey hair! Q was probably the toughest guy I've ever known. Everything was 100 per cent. No-one drove him backwards. He did little things that players noticed. For example, when we were on the ropes on our own 10m line and the opposition smelled blood, Q was the first one there to take the drive in and he'd *demand* the ball. A true warrior.

Hooker: Easy—me!

Prop: Craig Smith

He came to Wigan with a big reputation and he showed the young lads how to train. He always did extra work. Once he settled in, he was a colossus for Wigan and his go-forward and engine were incredible. I have to say, though, that I loved playing with Jamie Peacock for my country and had I played more games with him, he'd definitely have been in contention because he's another prop I have a lot of respect for.

Second-row: Adrian Morley

I grew up with Moz and I know he's a prop now, but he was a brilliant second-rower when he was starting his career. I remember the '97 series against the Aussies when he was only a kid, and he went head-to-head with Gordon Tallis and came out of it with a bigger reputation.

Second-row: Gareth Hock

I saw him come through the system at Wigan and he was a freak. An absolute freak. He is the second-row equivalent of Jason Robinson, in that he does things that I don't think he knows he is going to do! His handling skills, his ability to offload, his change of direction and speed . . . he has it all. He attracts so many defenders to him that it creates gaps elsewhere. The biggest compliment I can play Gaz is that I saw him play against the Aussies and they were absolutely petrified of him. He ripped them to pieces. I also need to mention Glenn Morrison and Dave Furner; two great players who I'd have loved to have played alongside when they were younger.

Loose forward: Andy Farrell

It goes without saying. He led by example on and off the field. He was Wigan. He'd look out for you, he was our leader and he played with his heart. He also had so much skill—he was awesome at stand-off, or prop, or second-row. Then when he went to union he played centre. If any youngster wants lessons on how to make it in the game I wish they could have seen how much work Faz put in—he was the most professional player I've ever seen. I was made up when he won the Golden Boot as the world's best player. As soon as he left Wigan, the club went down-hill. It wasn't a coincidence.

Coach: Graham Murray

I've had some odd-ball coaches and some great coaches. I've a lot of respect for Dean Bell for making me a hooker. Other coaches had different strengths that I really admired—Mike Gregory had the passion, David Waite had superb tactical awareness, but I've got to go with Muzza. He transformed Leeds when he came in and took us to a Grand Final, and then the year after we won at Wembley. His man-management and his approach were brilliant. He was the first to introduce two hookers to Super League. At the time, I didn't like it, but now every team does it. That alone showed just how far ahead he was when he joined Leeds.

22

MORE BANS AND BRUSHES WITH THE LAW

EARLY INTO my second season with Bradford, I was in trouble with the law again. Arrested, handcuffed, embarrassed . . . only this time I'd done absolutely nothing wrong.

It was April, we'd made a great start to the season, winning six of our eight matches (though I was banned for two of those by my good mates, the RFL disciplinary, for a high shot on Jon Wilkin . . . what is it with those St Helens players!) Our big test was against Leeds, our derby rivals. After night matches, it's not unusual for club doctors to give players sleeping tablets. I've always struggled to sleep because of the adrenaline. During the week ahead of our match with Leeds, the club doctor—a great fella named Roger Brown—gave me a prescription for some sleeping tablets, and some anti-inflammatory tablets.

On the day of the game, I nipped into my local chemist in Orrell on the main road. I handed the prescription in and, as there were a few people waiting for their medications, I said to the lady behind the counter, 'I'll nip back in half an hour to collect it'. I left, went to my mum's around the corner for a quick brew, and then drove back.

I walked into the chemist, towards to the counter and the lady said—as they do—'Prescription for Newton'.

'Yep,' I replied, and stepped forward to collect it from her. As I did, a copper came from around the corner. It startled me at first—I thought, 'What's he doing?'

'You're under arrest,' he said. I did a double-take—I looked over my shoulder to check he was definitely talking to me. When I realised he was, my next thought—stupid as it sounds—was that it was one of those piss-take TV shows.

'What for?' I asked him.

'Forging a prescription.'

'Are you taking the piss?'

But he repeated quite forcefully, 'You're under arrest'. He then grabbed my arms, ordered me to the floor and handcuffed me. And they weren't the type of handcuffs with a chain-link—they were the new, solid type. Believe me, they're not comfortable!

I wasn't worried. I knew I'd done nothing wrong. I thought the doctor mustn't have signed the prescription or something like that, but I was really embarrassed: I was lying down in the middle of my local chemist—most people in the area know who I am—and anyone walking past would have thought I'd tried an armed robbery or something!

I told the copper I'd done nothing wrong, but he wouldn't listen to me. I tried again, but he was having none of it. The more he ignored me, the more I began to worry that I'd miss one of our biggest games of the season. How was I going to explain this to my coach?

'Hi Steve, sorry I won't be able to play in tonight's vital televised Super League game. I've been arrested for getting a sleeping tablet . . .'

By this point a few more customers had arrived in the shop and, for those who didn't know who I was, I could hear the others informing them, 'That's Terry Newton, the rugby player'.

I was getting really pissed off. 'Listen mate, you've made a mistake,' I said to the copper.

He told me to be quiet, again, and reminded me I was under arrest, but when I protested again he told me that I wasn't registered at the surgery.

I knew I wasn't registered at the doctor's surgery—our doc had given me the prescription as the club doctor, not as a GP. I thought I was off to the police station, but as a last, desperate plea I asked the copper whether I could call Dr Roger Brown.

'He'll explain everything,' I said.

I realised then why the pharmacist had called the police. They must have thought it was a bit suspicious for someone to come in with a prescription from Yorkshire, and then not even hang around to pick it up, and so called the doctor's surgery to check whether I was registered there. Obviously I wasn't, which is why they'd called the police. Luckily, Dr Brown explained everything, the copper released me from my handcuffs and it was all cleared up.

The pharmacist was really apologetic afterwards. The copper wasn't—he left without saying sorry. I don't know how, but Dr Chris Brookes—the Wigan and GB doctor—got wind of the incident and when I saw him next, a few weeks later, he joked, 'Terry, if the copper had phoned me, I'd have said I don't know you!'

As it turned out, we lost that game 18–14, but we played pretty well and we went on to win our next four matches before we faced Leeds again, in the first Millennium Magic.

It was a brave call by the RFL to add a full round of fixtures to the schedule and play all the games at one stadium, over the one weekend. Some didn't like it, but I thought it was a great concept.

It'd be easy for the Test players to be selfish and moan that they already had plenty of games to play without an extra fixture, but they need to realise that there are plenty of good players at teams like Salford and Castleford who have never had a chance to play at the big stadiums. I've been fortunate to play on the big stage, but they'd not, and the Magic weekend at Cardiff's Millennium Stadium allowed them to do that.

It was also great to see fans from the different Super League, National League and amateur clubs all mingling together at the same ground. There'd be Wigan fans and St Helens fans sat next to each other with their kids, enjoying a drink and a laugh, which was great. Football would kill to have fans who behaved like that—we're right to celebrate it and make the most of it.

Our game was the last one on the Sunday, so the pitch was slippery and cut up from staging five games in the past two days. It was a crazy game which we lost, 38–42. We should have won it—any time you score 38 points, you should win. But our defence was shocking that day and, on top of that, we had Steve Ganson as referee!

We were leading 38–36 with a few seconds to go when Leeds were awarded a penalty for offside—even though I'm convinced we were all onside. Kevin Sinfield tried to kick the goal, which would have drawn the scores level, but the ball rebounded off the upright and Jordan Tansey, the Leeds winger, was on the spot to pick it up and go over for a match-winning try.

Tansey was blatantly offside, so at first I wasn't worried because I knew the video referee would rule it out. Ganson had called on the video ref eight times during the match, but for some reason—and for the life of me, I don't know what he was thinking—he awarded the try!

We were furious. We'd been in the lead until a few seconds ago, and lost because of a couple of refereeing calls. Steve McNamara vented his anger to the press afterwards, saying we were 'cheated'—in hindsight, if we'd have been as enthusiastic as the Leeds players were in the final few seconds, maybe we wouldn't have put ourselves into that position, but we were all annoyed about it. Our chairman at Bradford, Peter Hood, even asked for Leeds to hand over the two competition points! To make it worse, I had my mates at the RFL disciplinary on hand to rub salt into the wound for a challenge I'd made on Jamie Thackray, the Leeds forward.

Steve Mac had told us that Jamie was great at returning the ball and challenged us to put a big shot on him. During the match, I saw Jamie driving the ball in, so I flew out of the line to try to knock him down. Just as I got near him, he slipped, and I caught the top of his head. I got penalised—which was fair enough, because it was a high tackle. After the game, while everyone was cursing Ganson, Jamie came up to me to shake my hand and I said, 'Look, I'm sorry for catching you . . .'

'Don't worry about it', he said. 'I slipped.'

Any player will tell you that at the Millennium Stadium, when the roof is closed, the pitch becomes really slippery because of condensation. He said, 'If you want, I'll write a letter to explain.'

I thanked him for that—it spoke volumes about what a top bloke he is. Sure enough, on the following Monday, he sent a letter to Bradford and one to the RFL to explain what had happened. I thought that would be the end of it, but I still got cited! Even then, I thought they were just going through the motions, so the following day I went to Red Hall for the disciplinary hearing with Steve Mac. I'd been there plenty of times before and this was the most confident I'd ever been of getting off.

We watched the footage and it was clear Jamie slipped—his body dipped before I got to him. They read the letter from Jamie, too. I thought, 'I'm a free man'.

But when they returned their verdict, they fined me and gave me a three-match ban for a reckless high tackle!

Reckless high tackle? He bloody slipped!

I couldn't believe it. It was the stupidest decision. What more proof could they want? There was a letter from the guy I'd hit to explain that he'd slipped, and they still slapped me with a three-game ban! I was convinced they'd made the decision before they'd even seen me.

I walked out of Red Hall in tears. I said to Steve Mac, 'I don't want to play anymore. I've had enough'. I was completely demoralised. I copped the previous suspensions, but this time I felt like they had it in for me. I went home that night thinking I'm going to retire. It really knocked the stuffing out of me. I was done with rugby league—screw 'em.

Steve told me not to make any rash decisions while I was emotional, and he was right. I went to see Steve a day later and he was great with me. He told me he'd help me get through it. Bradford said they'd appeal the decision, which worried me a little bit because I'd appealed my ban for the hit on Longy 18 months earlier and been stung with a bigger punishment. Deep down, though, I knew I was innocent, so we appealed, but it fell on deaf ears. They wouldn't listen.

Rather than force me to retire, though, I made a conscious decision to use it to my advantage. I wasn't going to let them beat me. I trained the house down while I was banned, and when I returned I was in great shape as we beat Catalans and Huddersfield quite convincingly. We were travelling really well, which was a good omen because we were desperate to win our next match at home against Hull FC—Lesley

Vainikolo's last match before he switched to rugby union.

In the final team run, all the lads got together and when he got the ball on an unopposed run, we all gathered around him and jumped on him! He said, 'What are you doing?'

I replied, 'You'll have to get used to this in rugby union, Les'.

The fans turned out in force to say farewell to the big fella, which was no surprise because he'd become a real crowd-pleaser. Les was certainly one of the best wingers I played with. He wasn't nicknamed The Volcano for nothing!

He had speed, strength and power . . . the only thing he lacked was stamina, which was fine because he was out on the wing. Because he was so big, some people didn't realise just how quick he was, but he was lightning. He averaged nearly a try a game during his career with Bradford, and in his last match we were determined to get him over the try-line. In the end, though, he didn't score and I ended up getting four tries—I actually felt bad for stealing the limelight from him.

At least he kicked a goal at the end of the match, which brought a big cheer. I hope I never have to do that—my knee would go further than the ball!

Les arranged a leaving party, with the instructions that we had to turn up dressed as seventies gangsters. The lads who drove over from the North West met up at TGI's restaurant in Prestwich. We used to leave our cars in the car park and all travel over in one car. Matt Cook, typically, turned up late, and when he pulled into the car park, Simon Finnigan ran to his car, pulled his toy gun out of his jacket and yelled, 'You're late Cooky! You're late!' We all had a laugh, squeezed into Cooky's car and went to the party.

At the end of the night, when we dropped Simon off to pick up his car, there was a police transit van in the car park. Nothing too unusual about that. But when Simon walked to his car, armed police jumped out! Apparently, an old dear across the road had seen him pulling a gun on someone, got quite worried and called 999.

Luckily, the police saw the funny side of it and let him off. But about three weeks later, it was Simon's turn to drive, which I never looked forward to—not that he was a bad driver—but he had a Ford Fiesta and it was a real squeeze to get five big rugby blokes in it! We pulled out of Odsal to head back to the North West and hadn't gone a mile when we heard a police siren and saw flashing blue lights behind the car. The police officer asked Simon to step out and took him into the police car to interview him. We all wondered what was going on. A few minutes later he came back and told us that the police had made a note of his details because of his 'firearms' caution!

Bradford should have recruited a couple of those coppers for our Challenge Cup campaign. We played Saints in the semi-final at Huddersfield—and the club made a real balls up. At Wigan, for big games, our team coach was always given a police escort to stadiums. But for some reason, Bradford didn't arrange one for that match and it took us nearly an hour from leaving the M62 to get to the McAlpine Stadium. To make matters worse, as we were queuing in traffic, I looked out of the window to see flashing blue lights and the Saints team bus go past us! I couldn't believe it.

By the time we'd arrived at the ground, the Saints lads had changed and warmed-up. Little things like that can disrupt players—I'm not saying it was the reason we lost 35–14, but it didn't help.

Still, we recovered well. We'd already battered Leeds at Headingley 38–14 in mid-season—to say we were fired up for the game after what happened at Cardiff was an understatement—and during a strong end to the season, we drew 16–16 against them in September.

Leeds had played well all year, and just sneaked into second place ahead of us. But the fact we'd performed so well against them really gave us the confidence to feel we could make an impact in the play-offs. We had home advantage for a sudden-death game against my hometown club Wigan, who only got into the play-offs after a last-day win over St Helens.

David Solomona scored our first try after three or four minutes and we completely bossed the first-half. As the game approached the hour-mark we were 30–6 up and well in control. I knew that Wigan had arranged to have their Mad Monday party at my local pub, the Eckersley Arms, whenever their season finished. I'm not normally one for banter but, at one of the scrums, I said to Gaz Hock, 'It's a good job I ordered your buffet for tomorrow, Gaz.'

But Steve Mac made one of the most puzzling coaching decisions I've ever known, by substituting Solomona and me. Paul Deacon was injured for that match, so we were already short of play-makers—the last thing we needed was for him to take off Solomona and me. I can only think that, with such a healthy lead, Steve Mac assumed the game was in the bag.

I was sat on the bench and, when Mark Calderwood scored a try for Wigan, I looked across at Solomona and he looked at me, and we were both thinking the same thing—the game wasn't won. Some Aussies come to Super League for a big pay packet but Trent Barrett certainly wasn't one of them. He'd been outstanding all season and in that game, he kicked us to death. Late in the game—I think we were still leading by six points—Steve decided to put Solomona and me back on, but the snowball effect had taken place and it was impossible to stop their momentum. We had to force passes to try to kill them off, and in the end Wigan won the game 31–30, having trailed 30–6 midway through the second-half.

I was gutted. I saw afterwards that Steve defended his decision to take off Solomona, saying he needed the break. Break from what? Scoring tries!? He'd scored a hat-trick and was absolutely murdering Wigan before he went off. A rugby league match can change in an instant, especially when you're facing players like Barrett, Pat Richards and Sean O'Loughlin.

As I stood there, absolutely heartbroken, Gaz Hock came up to me and said, 'Tez, you can eat all that buffet yourself mate'. I felt like killing him, but I knew I deserved it! I was so pissed off. We'd played well all season, only just missed out on second spot and, in an instant, our season had gone down the pan.

Steve Mac surely must have thought deep down that he made a mistake. He was new to the job, fair enough, but everyone knows a game's not won until the end and it was another year gone and another chance blown.

For our Mad Monday we went to Blackpool for the day and then got the coach back to Leeds. Michael Platt told us he'd heard of a great club called Vibe. We only found out when we got there that it was a popular haunt with gays, so God knows who'd told him it was a good place for us to go. The gays in the club must have thought all their Christmases had come at once when a bunch of ripped rugby lads turned up!

I'd been happy with my form for Bradford in 2007. Even though I'd had two suspensions—one justified, one a complete joke—I'd scored 10 tries in 26 games, and I wasn't surprised to be named in the Great Britain squad for a home, three-match series against New Zealand.

Tony Smith had taken over from Brian Noble as GB coach. I'd had the impression that he wasn't a fan of mine, and though I put that down to paranoia I really wanted to make a good impression on him. He picked me for a warm-up match, the Northern Union v the All Golds, which was billed as a big celebration to mark 100 years since the first Kiwi tour. In truth, it was a complete non-event. We lost the game 25–18 and admittedly, I didn't play to my potential in that match.

Afterwards Tony pulled me to one side and said I looked sluggish, and that I needed to lose some weight before we played the Kiwis. Which would have been fine except for the fact the first Test was the following week! I don't know what he expected me to do—try Weightwatchers!

He picked me for the opening Test at Huddersfield, which was a fiery affair. Leading up to the game, there was a lot of paper talk about Fui Fui Moi Moi. He's not only got arguably the coolest name in rugby league, but he's an animal of a player. Sam Burgess was making his Great Britain debut in that match and I was next to him when Sam floored him with one of the best legal hits I've ever seen. It looked like Moi Moi had been in a car crash—his braided hair nearly came off his head!

We won that game, but in my view we cheated. How? Because Tony gave a Great Britain Test cap to the St Helens forward, Maurie Fa'asavala. How the hell could he play for England? The rules may say it's fine, but in my eyes it's cheating. I was embarrassed about it, and the lads I spoke to weren't happy about it. We had an Australian coach and he picked a Samoan—it was wrong.

This is no disrespect to Maurie, because he's a lovely bloke. It's the people who picked him I had a problem with. I should have called up the Samoan rugby league to see if they'd pick me. I can guess now what their answer would be. I can understand it when I see lads representing other countries if that's where their parents are from, or if they've lived in a different country for most of their life. But Maurie was Samoan and had even played for Samoa in the Rugby Union

World Cup. Now, four years later, he was learning the words to the British National Anthem—it's wrong. The fact he scored a try, and we only won by six-points, didn't sit comfortably with me.

Tony never picked me again. He went with Jon Clarke for the next two Tests. I didn't spit my dummy out—I congratulated Jon—but I was upset not to play, especially as we destroyed the Kiwis 44–0 in the second Test in Hull. I could accept Tony's decision not to play me, because every coach is entitled to their opinion about different players, but it really irritated me that he didn't give me a reason.

We won the series 3–0, our first series win for more than a decade, but I felt a bit of an outsider. Had I played in the last Test, instead of the first, maybe I'd have felt differently.

After the series, we had a function and Tony told my wife, Stacey, that he didn't pick me for the second and third Tests because he wanted to see how I reacted. I would have respected him if he'd told me that, but he didn't; instead, he waited until after the series had finished and told my wife, which I thought was out of line. I've not really spoken to Tony since, and I can't say I was shocked that he never picked me again.

He's a good tactical coach, without question, but I didn't like his personality. I found him hard to approach and difficult to talk to. Other players will have different opinions—it's only fair to say that some lads preferred Tony Smith to Nobby— but I wasn't one of them. I felt like I was back at school when Tony was in charge. In one of the first meetings I was involved in, he stood at the front and told all the players that we weren't allowed to fart in front of him! How weird is that? We were a team of rugby lads, not bloody Morris dancers. Had I known how he was going to be with me, I'd have gone out for a madras every night!

Paul Deacon

*IT'S FAIR to say Terry Newton made a lasting first impression
on me. I was 12 years old and playing for Hindley amateur
team, against our great rivals Orrell St James. Stakes were
high. It was easily the biggest game of the year. I set off on one
of my typical runs at the defensive line when I was collared,
lifted up and driven face first into the dirt by their growling,
chunky bulldog of a prop. After that, I always tried to avoid
running at Tez!*

*Hindley and Orrell St James were the two best teams at that
age group in the country. As well as Terry, they had Warren
Stevens, Chris Causey and Martin Carney, who all later signed
for Warrington, as well Salford's future skipper Malcolm Alker.
We had a brilliant side, with future pros Jon Clarke, Paul
Johnson and Tony Stewart in our ranks.*

*Terry will admit we were the rugby playing side, while
Orrell St James were the bruisers! Up until 12 or 13, our
Hindley team held the upper hand. But then puberty hit,
players went through growth spurts—not me, mind!—and
then Orrell were able to dominate us physically. Terry was an
absolute powerhouse and, if I'm honest, lads were scared of
playing against him. He was a hot-head, and he used his
aggression to his advantage. In one final, he kicked off a fight
at a scrum and incredibly, he stayed on the pitch while our
prop—David Webb—was sent off! Webby was so mad, he
broke a toe kicking the wall in the changing room. Fortunately,
the best players of both sides came together to form the Wigan
town team and we blitzed everybody—and I discovered for
the first time just how good it is playing alongside Terry. He
was as hard as nails and had so much determination, which I
already knew, but I discovered just how much skill he had as
well. He was a high quality player, and a great passer—the*

231

fact he captained England schoolboys, and walked off with the man of the match, underlines just how highly he was rated. There's no wonder Warrington and Leeds were fighting for his signature.

Over the years, Tez and I always had a chat when we bumped into each other, but we only became close friends when he joined Bradford in 2006. Right away, I noticed he'd matured a lot. He'd got married and had kids. Maybe the Sean Long incident had shaken him up and changed him, I don't know. What I do know is that there was a big change in his mentality, and it showed because he hardly got into any trouble on the field, or off it, while at Bradford. In fact, only once did I think he was going to get into a fight—and that was definitely not his fault. It was a Mad Monday, and Terry had already surprised me by staying up past 10pm—usually he's tucked up in bed by then. One of the lads had taken us all into a gay bar in Leeds. To this day, I don't know why. Anyway, it wasn't exactly my scene, or Terry's, so we left. We stood outside as we waited for a taxi, when a car drove past and pulled over. The driver wound down his window and eye-balled Tez. Then he shouted something and I thought it was going to kick off. 'This is the last thing I need,' I thought. 'A scrap outside a gay bar!'

Tez was chilled about it all but just to be on the safe side, I went over as a peace-keeper.

'What's up mate?' I said to the guy in the car.

He was staring at Tez intently. I could feel the tension. I had visions of him getting out the car, pushing me aside and charging at Tez.

'Do me a favour,' he said to me. 'Your mate, over there. Go and tell him I think he's fit.'

I couldn't believe it! I'd never heard a bloke call Terry fit before! I told Tez and he pretended to be embarrassed about it—but deep down I knew he was chuffed.

As we both lived in Wigan, we travelled over to Bradford together. He picked me up every morning, and I thank him for that. He moaned at me because I never drove, but he loved driving and I was happy for him to take the wheel.

It was probably safer that way, because when he picked me up at 6.30am, I was always half asleep. Not Tez. He's early to bed and early to rise—he's normally tucked up by 7pm, then he watches all the soaps—Emmerdale, Corrie, Eastenders—in bed before going to sleep. The upshot of that is he gets up at the crack of dawn. Once, he picked me up as usual at 6.30, I opened his boot to throw my boots in and it was full of Asda bags—he'd only done a big shop before picking me up!

I hardly ever drove, but I'll never forget one of the few times I did. We were on the M61 at Horwich, heading south towards the M60. I was in the outside lane, and we overtook a car in the middle lane which had two girls in it. They gave us cheeky smiles, so Tez said, 'Pull in Deacs, pull in'. I cut into the middle lane, in front of the two girls' car. The next thing I knew, they overtook us in the outside lane—and the girl in the passenger seat had her tits out!

I've never seen a man get so excited in my life!

'Deacs, Deacs, did you see that!' he yelled. He was practically jumping up and down in his seat.

'I saw it Tez, I saw it,' I said. 'What's going on?'

'I don't care,' he replied. 'Get your bloody foot down and get past them again.'

And so for a few miles until we turned off, it was like the Wacky Racers, with these two cars overtaking each other . . . and Terry chuckling all the way!

We'd spend three hours a day together most days, talking about anything and everything, and we saw some strange things on our trips across the M62. Once, there was one guy who was playing the saxophone as he was driving!

I also learned a lot about Tez. His daft sense of humour, his love for his family . . . not to mention his networking skills! I'm not kidding, it was like listening to Arthur Daley sometimes! If there was a deal to be done, Tez was the man. He never let me in on that side of his life, and in all honesty, I never wanted to be! But whatever I needed, Tez could get it for me, and nothing was ever too much for him. I can't tell you the number of times his phone rang with a mate or a family member on the other end asking for a favour—'No problem', he'd always reply. 'No problem.' That's the kind of mate he is.

He's also a great dad. You probably wouldn't expect him to be good with kids because of his tough persona, but he's brilliant with them. Some people don't know what to do or say with kids, but Tez has got a way with them. He's brilliant.

23

GOING WEST:
M62 TRAVELS

BY THE MIDDLE of 2008 I'd stopped enjoying my time at Bradford. Steve Mac had approached me while we were on our pre-season training camp at the start of the year and told me that Wigan had made an enquiry about me, but nothing materialised. I was gutted. I'd spoken to Brian Noble, who was still coaching Wigan, a few times and he knew I'd jump at the chance to go back to my hometown club. At the start of the year, Nobby phoned me and asked if I would be interested in coming back if they made an offer.

Negotiating rush hour traffic in the mornings when travelling to Bradford took more than two hours. The environment and the facilities weren't great either—it felt like a massive step back from Wigan. I told Nobby I would love to go back to Wigan. But I said I wanted to agree a deal first before I asked Bradford for a release—if a move fell through, Steve Mac would have been within his rights not to pick me. I've never been a top earner, but I also wanted to make sure Wigan offered me a decent contract. I told Nobby that if he got me a contract offer on the table, I'd go to Bradford the following day to tell them I wanted a release. A firm offer never materialised, though, and when Steve Mac told me that the Wigan chairman, Ian Lenagan, had asked his Bradford counterpart Peter Hood about me, I told him a white lie and said I was happy at Bradford.

I think Wigan wanted me to tell Bradford I wasn't happy so they'd release me—or at least be open to the idea of selling me on the cheap. But I wanted the security of knowing there was a definite deal. I had a young family to support, and I was gutted they failed to come to me first with a figure. Had they done that I'd have told Bradford that I wanted to leave.

I felt a bit sorry for Micky Higham, the Wigan hooker, because he was oblivious to it all and it wasn't his fault that Wigan were trying to replace him three weeks before the season started. He must have felt awful about it. Bradford put out a press statement, quoting me saying: 'I'm at Bradford now and want to win trophies. I think Bradford is the place to do that. I'm enjoying myself here, the squad is excellent and we're going places.'

That was pretty much what I'd told Steve, but I never believed it myself. I felt then we were on the slide. We lost four of our opening five games and were slaughtered 44–2 by our arch-rivals Leeds at Easter. My good mate, Kris Radlinski, says a losing run is like a comfy bed—easy to get into and hard to get out of, and he's spot on. It's a tough cycle to break, and after a defeat, players go home and mentally beat themselves up—it's hard to keep positive.

Steve Mac arranged a team-bonding night out to try to raise morale. Michael Platt, Paul Deacon and I—who travelled over—decided to go as Hawaiian boys and because my wife's a hairdresser, I suggested dying our hair blonde. In our grass skirts and tropical shirts, we really looked the part. But the dye was still on the following week when we played at Hull KR, and I looked a complete idiot. I started that game as a substitute, and when I got the call that I was going on, I did a typical warm-up jog up and down the touchline. The crowd in the main stand at Craven Park is really close to the pitch, and as I was jogging, someone yelled out, 'Newton, you're a big enough prick without your hair dyed blonde!' All the fans started laughing their heads off. I went as red as a beetroot, making me look even more ridiculous. The day after, I shaved my hair off.

Some of my best times at Bradford were the laughs we used to have on the journeys over from the North West. At first it was Paul Deacon, me and Paul Johnson. Then, when Johnno left to join Warrington, Michael Platt, Simon Finnigan and Matt Cook would cadge lifts with me and Deacs.

But it was always me and Deacs. We'd been mates for years and after those trips across the M62 we became good friends. We're different. He's more sensible and he looks younger, for a start. He came with me to buy some sunglasses from the Trafford Centre before I got married. I was in a shop, trying on different pairs. It was autumn so I looked daft no matter which ones I tried on! Deacs waited outside the shop while he checked his messages on his phone. When I found a pair I liked, I went to pay and the woman behind the counter asked why I was buying sunglasses in winter.

'I'm getting married in Jamaica,' I told her. She looked at Deacs over my shoulder and said, 'How nice. Are you taking your son with you?' I looked over my shoulder, and saw that she was looking at Deacs! I was in hysterics. Deacs came in, wondering why I'd gone to pay for some sunglasses and ended up nearly pissing myself. I know they call Deacs 'babyface', but that took the biscuit!

We made the play-offs in 2008 and again we got Wigan. Unlike the previous year, when they pulled a win out of a magician's arse at Odsal, they had home advantage. Trouble was, Dave Whelan—who virtually owns the ground, and also bankrolls Wigan Athletic—wouldn't let them play there so soon before a big Premier League match and so the game was switched to Widnes.

It caused an absolute shit-storm. Some of my Bradford team-mates thought it would work in our favour—in a sense, we were playing them at a neutral ground—but the fans were really pissed off with Whelan and rallied behind their team. I knew it would work in Wigan's favour, which it did. They used it to their advantage and blew us off the park that day. We had a decent team but it helped that Brian Noble had previously coached at Bradford and he knew our defects—he helped their cause.

Bradford had another mass clear-out at the end of the year. They didn't just change two or three players, like St Helens or Leeds tended to do. They ditched the stability in search of a quick fix and I found it disruptive. Even when they brought in better players, it took time for the new players to get into rhythm with the rest of the lads. There was one signing, though, who I was definitely happy about: Steve Menzies.

He seemed to have been around forever, Beaver. I played in the first Super League season in '96 and Beaver had been playing for Australia well before then. He's a legend of the game, and rightly so. In one of our early matches, against Catalans, we were trailing and Paul Deacon got the ball at first receiver and launched down the field, to the left corner. Menzies was on the right-hand side of the field, but he got there and scored a try! I couldn't believe it. That try showed me not just how well he read a game but how fit he was, to pull off a play like that in the final minute of the game. He may be old—when he came over, that's all everyone was talking about—but what does that matter when someone can still play well? Steve has obviously looked after himself off the field, and more than that, he was a real down-to-earth fella. He'd have a laugh, too. He did a piece in one of the Sydney papers about Sam Burgess. Someone read it out and Sam was made up when he said, 'He could become one of the best forwards in the game'. He was smiling from ear to ear.

'Good judge, is Beaver,' Sam said.

Then they carried on reading the article and Beaver put, 'He also has the biggest head in the world', which got us all in hysterics. Sam saw the funny side, too.

Sam was getting a lot of attention, and rightly so. When I heard rumours he might be going to Australia I thought, 'No way will Bradford let him leave'. At this point, Bradford had offered me a new one-year deal on reduced money and I'd turned it down—I wanted a two-year deal, plus I was ready for a fresh challenge. If I was going to sign a one-year deal, it was with Wigan and nobody else.

Bradford already knew I would be going as well as Glenn Morrison and a couple others—I couldn't believe it when they let Sam go too. I think the decision will backfire on them, big time. Sam went to meet Russell Crowe on the set of his Robin Hood film and he took a couple of lads with him and they all had their pictures taken with him. Rugby lads mingling with Hollywood stars, who'd have thought it? Mind you, I wasn't jealous—I let them all know that Jennifer Love-Hewitt had once taken a liking to me!

Things didn't work out for us on the pitch in 2009. Something that annoyed me was the way Bradford got rid of Tame Tupou, the former Brisbane winger who they'd signed to replace big Les Vainikolo.

He'd been injured for a while and, under the terms of his contract, they could offload him. It really left a bitter taste in my mouth. I thought, 'How would they treat me if I got injured?' We even had a meeting of the senior players and they all agreed that it was wrong, but what could we do? We wanted to stick with Tame but we were powerless. I think that's why our season fizzled out—the morale of the team was so low. Fans were disappointed and saying the players weren't good enough, but I disagree—I think the quality of the players was good enough and we all got along fine. The problem was when we got together, the first thing we'd ask was, 'What's the latest with Tame?'

I didn't finish the season. When we played Harlequins away, I kicked a ball from dummy-half. Chris Melling collected it and was running it back. Glenn was on one side, I was on the other—I tackled him and WHACK!

'Bloody hell', I thought. 'What was that?'

It felt like an elbow had gone through the side of my face. Melling's a good player and a clean one—he's not the type to clean an opponent out. The next thing I knew I was being picked up by the physio and helped off. Once in the dressing room, I asked what had happened. 'You banged heads with Glenn Morrison,' he said.

'Where's he then?'

'He's still out there—his head must be harder than yours.'

I looked in the mirror and there was a big dint in my cheek—it was like a car bumper had been knocked and pushed in! I'd suffered a depressed fracture of the cheekbone.

My season was over.

The op went well. I asked the surgeon if he could make some improvements to my looks while he was at it, but he didn't! The one blessing about having a facial injury was I could carry on training. Had I been coming back from a knee op, or a shoulder op, I think clubs may have been reluctant to sign me.

There were rumours Wigan were coming in for me, so I got in touch with Shaun Wane—who was their reserve coach at the time—and asked if he would put in a good word for me. Waney's a legendary fella who, like me, loves Wigan to death.

He was supportive and said he would have a word, but they already had two hookers on their books and nothing came of it. I was gutted—I'd never wanted to leave Wigan in the first place and, after four years away, I would have loved to have gone back. A few months later, I was at a Wigan Schoolboys Dinner and Ian Lenagan, the club's chairman, came to me and said if the time had been different he may have signed me.

Catalans made an enquiry and it actually appealed to me, but when Wakefield came in for me it was an easy choice. They'd gone great that year, I knew they were going to sign Glenn Morrison, Ben Jeffries and Johnno, plus I'd worked with John Kear before with the England academy and at Wigan, and liked him a lot.

There was no emotional farewell from Bradford, but I'd made some good mates there and the fans were always alright with me. There was a lot going right at the club, but there was a lot going wrong as well. The morale was low and the facilities we trained at were amateurish. The gym at my local club, Wigan St Judes, was better. Little things like that added up and frustrated me. On the plus side, they have some great staff in the offices and Steve Mac had some very good ideas, though he's young and he's still learning.

During the season, all the squad put £40 into a kitty, and each week we'd take turns in placing bets, with any money we won going back into a pot to pay for our Mad Monday celebrations. We had a decent run with the bets (none on rugby league). I didn't win us anything—I'm an awful gambler—but we managed to collect enough to pay for a trip to Magaluff for a few nights at the end of the season.

We were on the ale before we'd set off from Manchester Airport, and we were pretty tuned in by the time we hit the bars. We ended up in one place which had a hypnotist on. We all got the beers in to watch the show, thinking it would be a good laugh. The hypnotist asked for volunteers to come onto stage. A few tried to nudge me forward but I was having none of it. Wayne Godwin's not as shy as me—especially after a day on San Miguel—and he didn't need any persuading. In a shot, he was up on the stage next to half-a-dozen tourists, shirt off, showing off his lobster-red skin. The hypnotist did his usual trick to put them under his spell, and then made all the people on stage look like complete idiots.

We were in stitches watching Wagga. He's a funny guy anytime—seeing him when he was pissed up and hypnotised was hilarious.

'Now,' the hypnotist said, 'I want you to pretend you're in love with your chair.'

The others all got on their knees and started cuddling, caressing and kissing the backs of their chairs. Wagga didn't— he got behind it and started shagging it! The sight of Wagga making love to a chair will, sadly, stay with me until I die. For his finale, the hypnotist told everyone on stage to close their eyes, and then said that he was a chainsaw killer. They all opened their eyes, saw the hypnotist, screamed their heads off and cowered behind each other, shrieking like little girls.

All, that is, except Wagga, who saw the hypnotist, screamed, then got up and legged it!

We all laughed our heads off, it was one of the funniest things I've ever seen. The look on his face was one of genuine fear. One of the lads ran after him down the beach, but Wagga's no slouch, and he came back a few minutes later and said he couldn't find Wagga. We ordered another round of drinks and waited for him to turn up. After about half an hour, there was still no sign of him, and we began to worry. Somewhere out there was a hypnotised pissed up bloke convinced that a mad murderer with a chainsaw was chasing him—God knows what he was going to do. After two hours we were really panicking. The hypnotist was worried sick—he couldn't leave the bar, because he needed to get Wagga out of his spell. Eventually, we found Wagga and the hypnotist brought him back to the real world.

24

FINDING LEANNE

I'D JUST finished training at Bradford one day when I got a call from my dad.

'Terry, it's your sister,' he said. 'She's not well.'

That was nothing new. She hadn't been well for a while.

'It's serious,' my dad told me. 'She's in intensive care.'

My dad explained that he'd gone to see her as usual, and she was on the couch in agony. She had pains in her stomach, and she couldn't walk. My dad pleaded with her to go to the doctors but she wouldn't budge; in the end, he took her to Wigan Infirmary himself. There was something wrong with her heart, and they moved her to the intensive care unit.

I drove straight to the hospital. I hadn't seen Leanne in six months; hadn't spoken more than two words to her in years. I'd completely cut her off.

'What am I going to say to her?' I thought, as I walked to her ward.

I was a bag of nerves, but as soon as she saw me coming through the door, she started crying. I broke down in tears as well and walked over to her and gave her a big hug. I had my sister back.

In an instant, all the anger I'd felt disappeared. As I hugged her, my mind flashed back to the time I'd said I didn't have a sister—I hated myself for saying that. It's something I'll regret until my final day. We hugged for ages. It felt like I'd not seen my sister in years—in effect, I hadn't. Not really. My mum said to her, 'Look what you've done. You always used to make Terry cry'. Then we all laughed. That feeling, to have my sister back, was incredible. Amazing. It beat any Challenge Cup Final.

We sat around her bed, my mum, dad and I, laughing and enjoying being together as a family. Everything was forgotten and forgiven, we were all close. I told Leanne I loved her and she said she loved me, and then she said 'sorry' for what she'd done.

I said, 'Don't worry about it, just get better'.

And she did.

She stayed in hospital for a couple of months and her condition improved. She was clean of drugs, and they moved her from intensive care to a regular ward. I've got to give credit to the doctors and nurses—they were brilliant with her. I took Stacey and the kids up to visit her all the time, and Leanne got to know my girls. It was great. Stacey and I were there when a nurse came and said she was free to go home, so I drove her to my mum and dad's house. Everything was better again.

But a couple of days later, my mum called me and said, 'Leanne's not herself'.

I rushed around to their house and found Leanne on the couch. She could hardly move. She couldn't even get up the stairs and she was complaining of pains in her leg.

I even had to carry her upstairs so she could use the toilet. I told my mum to call her an ambulance, and they rushed her straight back to intensive care. I went to see her and told her, 'We'll get through this'. We were with her, 100 per cent. They wired Leanne up to all sorts of machines. I visited her every day that week, but she became weaker. She must have been tired of fighting all the time.

On the Friday, it was my birthday, and when I went to see

her she apologised that she hadn't got me a present. That's how close we'd become. We hadn't bought each other gifts for years—we'd not even spoken to each other—and suddenly she felt bad for not buying me a present. She was stuck in a bed in intensive care, I don't know where she expected to buy something from! I told her not to worry about it.

'Have a drink for me tonight,' she said. Stacey had planned a party for my birthday.

'I'm not going to that now,' I told her. 'I'll call it off.'

Leanne looked mortified. 'Go to it, please,' she said. 'Don't cancel it for me—I'll feel awful. Please go. For me.'

I wasn't exactly in the party mood, but I went to the party to please Leanne. I didn't want her feeling guilty on top of everything else she was going through. The following morning, I woke up and called my dad to see how she was, and he told me her condition had deteriorated. She'd slipped into unconsciousness in the night and they'd put her on a life support machine.

I rushed up to the hospital. At first I felt bad that I'd been at my birthday party while she was going into a coma, but then I remembered how insistent she'd been that I went to the party. I know this might sound silly, but it felt like she'd hung on for me. It was as if she didn't want to go on my birthday.

I met my mum and dad at the hospital, and we sat around her bed. I was waiting for a doctor or a nurse to tell us she'd be okay. But when a nurse finally came to us, that's not what she said. 'She's not got long left, I'm afraid.'

Seven words that hit me like a sledgehammer. It tore my guts out.

I broke down into tears, right there and then. I was holding Leanne's hand and my dad held her other hand, and my mum kissed her head and stroked her hair. And I was still holding her hand, hours later, when the machine that monitored her heart stopped pulsing and the line on the monitor went flat, when Leanne finally stopped fighting, and slipped away.

Pneumonia killed Leanne. Her body was so weak from all the drugs over the years, it just couldn't go on. It was the only time I'd experienced someone so close to me dying so young. My nan had passed away a few years earlier, but she was old—it was different. Leanne was still in her twenties. She had three kids and everything to live for. Her death hit me like I can't explain. If my mum, dad and Stacey hadn't been there for me, I don't know where I'd be now.

I went through the days after her death, and the funeral, in a daze. I was more concerned about my parents than myself, so I didn't really grieve straight away. Over time, I got worse, not better.

Steve McNamara, the Bradford coach, was brilliant and said I could have as much time off as I wanted. But sitting at home thinking about Leanne made my depression worse, so I returned to training soon after—I wanted something to focus my energies on. Whenever I had a minute to myself, my mind would automatically start thinking about Leanne. And it wasn't just happy memories of her—I couldn't help being angry. I found it one of the hardest things ever. At some time every day, I looked back and thought, 'Could I have done something different? Would she still be here now if I had?'

I still do it now, and I can't help myself. I knew the people she was knocking around with were real scum. Should I have gone and sorted them out? Would it have made a difference if I'd tried to scare them off? I don't know. Probably not. She did it to herself.

I'm so glad we made up when she was first admitted into hospital. I only had my sister back for a few weeks but that time was great. At least we'd said that we loved each other before she died. I dread to think how I'd have coped if she'd died from an overdose during the years we weren't speaking— I honestly don't think I could have forgiven myself.

That's why I'm always shocked when I hear about people who haven't spoken to family members for years because of silly fall outs. I wish I could get them and bang their bloody heads together, and make them realise how lucky they are to have a brother or a mum or a son who is still alive. They bicker over little things and it's not worth it, because anything could happen.

My performances for Bradford in 2009 weren't up to scratch, I wasn't enjoying training and I think a lot of it was to do with Leanne's death. I decided, when I signed for Wakefield, that I would start afresh and get my career back on track.

My old mate, Paul Johnson, also signed for Wakefield and one day, for no obvious reason, I wasn't myself. I didn't say anything but Johnno knew what was wrong with me. He'd gone through a similar thing when his brother Craig died a few years earlier. We had a good, honest chat in the sauna. I asked him how he handled it and he said there was no secret formula, but speaking to him—to someone who's been through a similar thing—really helped. He's a champion fella, Johnno.

I've also got to mention Paul Deacon and Brian Carney, too. Brian's not just a walking one-liner, he's a top bloke and— like Deacs—a great listener. It can't have been easy on them, but they were great.

I'm not embarrassed to admit I went to see my doctor about my depression. He's been good, as have my family. My mum and dad have been terrific but how they're coping, I don't know.

They raise Leanne's son, Callum, and I think that gives

them a lot of the fire to carry on. He's a great little lad and he's like another son for them. They love him to bits. Leanne also had twins, Molly and Matthew, a few months before she died. They've been adopted by a lovely couple, Kirsty and Simon. They're still in touch with us, and as a family we couldn't be happier. They're brilliant parents and they bring the little ones round to my mum and dad's place, which is great. They're an absolutely brilliant family.

Stacey Newton

IT DEFINITELY wasn't love at first sight. My first impression of Terry was probably the same as thousands of opposition fans over the years—I never really liked him!

It wasn't personal, it's just that I never wanted to go out with a rugby player. I used to think they were show-offs and big-heads, and when Terry started visiting my step-dad's pub, where I worked, I had no reason to think he would be any different.

Over time, his visits to the pub became more frequent. He'd come in with his dad and order orange juice or Coke. It was obvious that he was shy because he never spoke to me; he used to write me little notes on beer mats instead! He eventually plucked up the courage to ask me out, and we've been together ever since.

Terry, like me, gets quite nervous. He's guarded, and that's why I was so shocked when he said he wanted to release his autobiography. I suppose he wanted a chance to put his side of his life across. I know people have different opinions of him, and while it never really bothered him that people judged him without knowing him, it really bothered me.

I used to work in a hairdressers in Orrell, which is a village in Wigan but close to the border with St Helens, and so quite a few Saints fans came to the salon. I never advertised the fact that Terry was my husband, but there were a few occasions when Saints fans spoke to other girls about rugby and inevitably, Terry would come into the conversations. The customers would say things about him being nasty or being a thug—not knowing his wife was a few yards away—and it really annoyed me because I knew he wasn't like that

I felt like saying to them, 'You don't know what he's like as a person', because if they did know him they'd see he's nothing like the player he was.

He's a big softy, really. And I'm not saying that because he's my husband—anyone who knows him would say the same.

We've been together more than a decade and he still manages to surprise me. Like the time I woke one Christmas morning to find a brand new Renault Clio—complete with red bow on top—parked on the driveway for me.

Or the time we dressed as old people one Boxing Day night (it's always fancy dress in Wigan). He managed to find a zimmerframe from somewhere, and he hit on the idea of switching costumes—he went as an old lady, I went as an old man. Terry, worryingly, managed to pull it off quite well, so much so that when we walked past an old people's care home, Terry decided to shuffle his zimmer into the middle of the road and lie down, motionless, on the floor. Seconds later, a car coming the other way screeched to a halt. I thought the driver was going to get out and give Terry a piece of his mind for his prank, but instead, he and his passenger rushed over to him and said, 'Are you alright dear?' Terry, being the sod that he can be, went along with it and the next thing I knew, he was inside the residential home having a cup of tea!

Terry's a really good husband, and a great dad.

He chips in with the cleaning and does a lot of cooking, and tries his best at DIY. He's got better over the years, even if—whenever he put shelves or pictures up at home—I have to phone his dad afterwards and ask him to fit them properly. He point-blank refuses to use rawplugs!

Terry's a brilliant dad. Our girls mean everything to him.

I'm sure all dads love their own kids, but Terry really does go out of his way and dedicates so much of his time to them. He's always taking them swimming, or reading them stories. He even takes them to the cinema, which is hard for him because he hates, absolutely hates, the cinema! Having to listen to people munching their popcorn in his ear annoys him more than anything else. He always wanted two girls, and he's brilliant with them. Anyone who thinks of him as some kind of 'bad boy' should see him as a dad; they'd change their mind, because he's normal most of the time.

He has his quirks, like everyone. He goes to bed at 7pm every weekday night, SkyPluses the soaps and gets up at 5.30am to watch them before work. Terry is a soap addict. And he doesn't keep a car for more than six months. He's always on the Autotrader website, looking for a different motor. It's his obsession. But with everything else, he's pretty normal!

I'm obviously disappointed at the way his playing career has ended. It was awful when he told me what he'd done. I was gobsmacked, because he's always criticised athletes who've cheated. I'm not going to justify what he did at all but I will say that Leanne's death hit him hard. He hadn't been himself for the last two years of his playing career.

The suspension has obviously been a testing time but, if anything, Terry seems happier now he's not playing. He's really enthusiastic about making a real go of the pub he's bought with my step-dad, the Ben Jonson. He knows he's got a lot to learn but he also has a natural business sense. I can't count the times I've walked in at home to be greeted by crates of things—rugby boots, socks, you name it—that he'd got because someone was selling them cheap. But he always got rid of them! Brian Carney calls him Del Boy, and he's right.

These last few years, because he's been playing for Yorkshire clubs, we haven't spent as much time together. He's been constantly tired from all the travelling and I know it upset him that he couldn't see the kids as much as he'd liked.

Loads of girls think it's a WAGs lifestyle being married to a rugby league player, but it's definitely not like that. There's only one time of year you can go on holiday, a three-week *window in October or November. Every time I received an invite for a friend's birthday, wedding, or Christening, I could guarantee that eight times out of 10 I'd be there alone, apologising to people because Terry had a game, or a training session, or a rehab session. It annoyed him as much as it did me.*

We could never just go away for the weekend with the kids, or jet off somewhere on Valentine's day as a couple. And don't get me started about the food! Terry always ate healthy food—he's actually a good cook—and so whenever I wanted a takeaway and maybe a glass of wine, Terry used to sit next to me eating grilled chicken, salad and sipping a protein shake while I tucked into my Chinese or Indian.

He always used to say that if he ate takeaways, he'd put a stone on. Well, now we can find out!

25

AN UNDETECTABLE SOLUTION?

'TERRY, HAVE you seen the *TV Times*?'

It was May 2007, and I was on my way down to the second Magic event in Cardiff with my Bradford team-mates when my old man phoned. Yep, I thought, my dad had finally lost the plot.

'Funnily enough dad, I've not read it this week,' I said to him. 'I was just about to rush out and buy it.'

'Stop being a sarcastic git,' he said. 'There's a thing in there about you.'

That got my attention. No matter what any player tells you, it's still nice to get a bit of recognition in the press, especially when it's a national publication and not just the local rag or the *League Express*.

'I'll read it to you,' he said. 'Newton has recently returned from a two-year ban for failing a drugs test.'

Fuck me, I didn't expect that!

'Why the hell have they put that?' I asked, but before my dad replied, the answer came to me. Bradford had signed Ryan Hudson, a hooker, just before he was banned for failing a drugs test. The *TV Times* must have confused the pair of us.

We had a team meeting in Cardiff, and I mentioned it to Steve McNamara. He told me he knew about the story the previous day, but he didn't want to let it be a distraction from the game. It wouldn't have been—I'd played some of my best rugby at Wigan with the threat of court action hanging over my head—but I saw where he was coming from. Bradford contacted the *TV Times* a few days later and they apologised. They also paid me £15,000 in compensation which paid for a new car for the missus, thank you very much.

At the time, it really pissed me off. Being called a drugs cheat was the lowest of the low. When I was called 'dirty', or 'fat', or a 'thug'—or even a 'dirty fat thug'—I wasn't bothered. Saints fans called me 'wanker' all the time and it was water off a duck's back. But being wrongly labelled a drugs cheat in that magazine really stung. I was so pissed off and embarrassed. Yet by the end of that year, I'd changed my mind about performance enhancing drugs completely.

I'd never really known about drugs during all of my time with Leeds and Wigan. I was piss-tested a squillion times, and every time I was clean. I never took anything and, truth be told, I never knew anyone who took the performance enhancing drugs like steroids.

We all heard rumours about so-and-so being on cocaine, just like now, but that's all they were—rumours. I certainly never came across it.

Around 2007, though, players started to hear more and more about human Growth Hormone (hGH). Rugby league is a close-knit sport—every player has either a mate or a former team-mate at another club, and we all talk. And like a game of Chinese Whispers, it doesn't take long for rumours to be spread through the game. I can't remember exactly how I found out about it—it wasn't like someone walked in one day and said, 'Listen lads, have you heard about hGH?'. That's not how it worked. Like a lot of things, I picked up little bits of information over time. All we knew—or thought—was that it was undetectable, because it's a substance that's produced naturally by the body.

It really annoyed me that others might be using it. I know there have been times in games that I've crossed the line and broken the rules. And when I've seen a referee turn his back, I've thrown a couple of digs at opponents. But I'd never cheated by taking a banned substance and I'd never seen the need to. I was happy with how I was performing.

At the end of 2007, after my second season with Bradford, Great Britain played a Test series against the Kiwis. During that series, I changed my mind about hGH.

There was a player involved in that tournament who I'd heard was taking hGH, and he played alright throughout the series. But what struck me was, in truth, I knew he was a nothing player. Average at best, in my opinion. I can't say who it is—he'd sue my ass for having no proof and, if you've not heard, I'm not on a player's salary anymore! But quite a few knew about it. Actually, that's a lie: no-one *knew*—but a few suspected, including me. And he got away with it.

I was angry at first, but over time it helped change my opinion of it all. I didn't make a complete U-turn, but I went from being 'Mr anti-cheating, completely dead against it' to thinking, 'Well, if it helps, and you can get away with it . . .'

While I didn't take any banned substances for 18 months, that instance planted the seed in my mind.

I was dropped from the GB side for the last two Tests in 2007 and I never got back in the international team. I struggled for form in 2008. I wasn't enjoying my rugby, and I was down in general. I was constantly hearing more about hGH. And it wasn't just some of the older guys who were supposedly on it. By my final year at Bradford, in 2009, I'd heard players talking about young lads at other clubs doing it—academy lads I'd never even heard of. I finished games and—particularly if I'd struggled—I used to think 'Is he taking it? Is he taking it?' The players may not have been, but I was so paranoid that I thought, 'If they're playing better than me on this stuff, how the hell am I supposed to get back in front of them?'

I was struggling to motivate myself. I'm not using this as an excuse, but after Leanne died I just wasn't the same person. It really hit me hard. My doctor diagnosed depression, and put me on a course of anti-depressants. Again, I want to stress, I'm not using that as an excuse, but as a way to highlight my mind-set at the time. Basically, my head was up my arse.

When I broke my cheekbone playing for Bradford in July 2009, the club agreed to pay me up and release me. Bradford had offered me a one-year deal for the following season, which I'd rejected. I wanted to look after my family's future. I wanted a two-year contract, minimum. And, to be honest, I wanted to get away from Bradford. The 80 minutes on the pitch were good, the laugh with the lads was good too, but I wasn't happy. It was nothing personal against the staff or coaches who were there, it was just the way I felt. A combination of poor form, poor results—plus my depression—just got me down. When Wakefield came in for me, I saw it as a chance to start afresh. It would be a clean slate—a chance to get back to being the player I once was.

When Bradford paid me up, I thought, 'Now's my chance'. I decided to use hGH to help me recover from the injury, and help me get fit, too. I wanted to be in the shape of my life for the time I started training with Wakefield in November.

From being released by Bradford, I had three months to get myself sorted.

I asked a couple of lads who I knew were taking hGH, and they swore that—not only did it help their recovery—but that it was undetectable. No-one would ever know. I still knew it would be wrong, of course I did. But I suppose it's the equivalent of if you were walking down a street and you found a wad of cash on the side of the road—you know it's wrong to take it, but if no-one was looking and you'd never get caught, would you take it? I know I would.

I thought more and more about hGH. I searched the web to see if any athlete had ever been caught, and no-one had. The internet gospel that is Wikipedia informed me that it is used clinically for children with growth disorders but, crucially for me, it couldn't be detected by urine tests. I convinced myself that I'd be fine. Rugby league is a small sport, compared to baseball, American Football and sports like that. I thought, 'If none of those athletes have ever been caught, what are the odds that I'll be caught?'

They're all tested, just like we are. Even if there were only 1,000 athletes in the world, across all sports, on hGH—and let's be honest, I bet it was far more than that—then the chances of being the first to be caught were miniscule.

'Fuck it,' I thought. 'I'm doing it.'

I didn't tell anyone. Not Stacey, not my mum and dad. In doing my 'online research'—well, I Googled hGH—I discovered you could buy it over the internet, no problem. There are firms in China and places like that who ship it in. I know, to speak to, a couple of gym-monkeys and I knew they'd be able to get it. But the last thing I wanted was word getting out that I'd bought some, so I asked another player at another club who was taking it. I phoned him one day, and asked for it. I must have sounded casual, but inside I was bricking myself.

'That stuff you take . . . could you get me some?' I said.

'No problem.'

hGH, I read on Wikipedia, helps speed up a body's rate of

recovery, which was just what I needed. My face was fucked, after I'd smashed my cheekbone, plus after 14 years of top-flight rugby I had more niggling injuries than I could count. More knocks than a bloody fairground dodgem car.

It had all taken its toll. It had got to a point where, if I played on a Sunday, I'd struggle to walk on the Monday. By the Tuesday, I could just about jog. In pain. Wednesday would be a day off, and by Thursday I'd be just about back to normal. Ready to go again.

The older I got, the harder it became. When I was a kid, I could play every day. It seemed I'd have a game for my school, my club and the town team, every week, and I'd be fine. Then when I started playing pro, all the way through my Leeds and Wigan days, it never bothered me. I bounced back easily from games . . . the morning after I'd be sore, but ready to go again. When we played over Easter, when there were two games— one on Good Friday, one on Easter Monday—I used to hear some of the older lads moan about the quick turnaround and I'd think, 'Whinging gits'.

But when I got to about 29 or 30, gradually it became harder. I'd be stiffer for longer. I've torn both biceps and some days, I'd struggle to lift the covers off me in the morning! Anyone who saw me the morning after a game wouldn't have thought, 'He's an athlete', they'd have thought, 'He looks like an old man'.

My hope was that the hGH would help clear up some of those niggles before I started with Wakefield. And so, a couple of days later, I met the player at a motorway service station on the M62, and he gave me my hGH. It cost £150 for a month's supply. Dearer than protein shakes!

It looked the real deal. All professional. The hGH was clear, and came in tiny little syringes—just like insulin shots that diabetics take—each in sterile wrap.

They were packed neatly in a padded box which contained 100 IUs—international units—worth. 'Take five IUs a day for five days, then have two days off,' the player said. Bloody hell, I thought. Five injections! Then I noticed there were only 20 syringes—even a mathematical idiot like me worked out that each syringe must contain five IUs. 'The best place is your stomach,' he said. 'Or, if you want, you can inject it into your groin, right . . .'

'Stomach's fine,' I said, not waiting for him to demonstrate how to move your balls to the side and put a needle where a needle should never go.

It wasn't like some dodgy, back-alley drug deal. It was as if I was buying a stereo off a mate. Really casual.

I was fine with it, he was too, but I knew Stacey wouldn't be if she found out. At home that afternoon, I went inside, my new friends in my hand, and locked the door. Why, I don't know—Stacey was out at work, she's a hairdresser—and the kids were at school. But I still knew in my mind that I was doing something wrong. That I was crossing the line. I made myself a brew, and flicked on *Sky Sports News*. It was just background noise—all I was thinking was, 'Should I do it? Am I really going to do this?'

I'd like to say that I wrestled with the decision, but I didn't. My mind was made up. But first, I needed a place to hide it— I couldn't leave it on the kitchen side for when Stacey came back. I could just imagine her walking in on me now—it'd be just my luck she finished early that day.

'What's that Terry?'

'The kettle? Oh, you mean that box . . . that dear, that's just my human Growth Hormones.'

It felt weird. Stacey and I are both as daft as brushes, but more than anything, we're best mates and we're dead open and honest. If one of us has got a problem, we say it. We're not like those couples who are nicey-nice to each other, and then they go and bitch about their partner to their mates. She's the one person in the world I can tell anything to, and yet for the first time, I had something I had to hide from her. I can only imagine I was feeling what it must be like when a person is having an affair, trying to cover their tracks and hide stuff.

The hGH came with storage advice on its label—'keep refrigerated'. I opened the fridge, looked in and thought, 'Not a chance'. Where will she never find it? Where's quite cold? The garage! She'd never stumble across it in there, and surely that must be cool enough to keep it okay.

I grabbed the box from the kitchen side, and walked through the door into my garage. I pulled my toolbox from the shelf—I'd like to say I'm handy at DIY, but I'm bloody useless!—and slotted it behind. It fit, perfectly.

Sorted. I took it out again and took one of the little syringes from the box. I handled it carefully—they're so small, they look fragile. Rugby league players are injected with pain-killers all the time. Needles are part of the job. I'd had hundreds of pain-killing injections, but that was the first time I'd actually held a syringe. I'd certainly never injected myself before! I lifted up my t-shirt, biting the bottom of it to make sure it didn't fall down. I was calm and composed. No sweats. No regrets. I carefully removed the sterile wrap surrounding the syringe, took the cover off the end of the needle, and without thinking about it, I slowly pushed the needle into my abdomen, about an inch or two above my belly button. I wasted no time. Smoothly, but quite quickly, I pushed on the end of the syringe . . . and kissed my career, my reputation and a six-figure two-year salary, goodbye.

26

COCK-WATCHERS AND COMING CLEAN

'EH UP—the cock-watchers are here,' I said, as the drugs-testers walked in.

Cock-watchers was my name for them because, obviously, when a player does a urine test they actually have to watch you pissing. Apparently, a few years ago, an American firm had started selling fake dicks—complete with 'clean' urine inside—that athletes could use to trick the testers!

I always had a laugh and a joke with the drugs-testers, even the one I nearly killed in the middle of the night outside my house years back. They're good lads, doing their jobs. And they took it on the chin that I called them 'cock-watchers'!

When they walked into a non-descript gym in Featherstone one November lunchtime, where some of the Wakefield lads had been doing wrestling training, I never thought anything of it. Even when our assistant coach, Paul Broadbent, said they wanted me.

I'd started taking hGH three months earlier to speed up the healing of my face injury, plus my other various knocks.

While I wasn't nervous the first time I took it, I was apprehensive—and even a bit sceptical—about it. I was going into the unknown. A part of me expected something radical to happen, but it was the opposite—nothing happened. Even the injection itself wasn't a big deal; the needle was so small, I hardly felt any pain. And when I squeezed the hGH into me, there was nothing. No buzz, no sensation, no light-headedness.

One thing I'd done, in researching it on the web, was check for any side-effects. I knew hGH was nothing like steroids but I wanted to make sure it didn't have any of the same perils. The last thing I wanted was my dick shrivelling up! I'd heard of Roid Rage, in which people taking steroids had gone into bad mood swings, and I didn't want to risk that. But the pieces I read on the medical websites said there was none of that, which reassured me. I'll be honest, my biggest concern about taking the hGH wasn't the effects—good or bad—or even whether the RFL managed to find out about it. I was shitting it in case Stacey found out! It's a weird feeling having to go to 'clear history' and remove from Google, 'Does taking hGH have any side effects?' If Stacey saw that, she'd have strung me up by my balls.

The morning after I first took it, I woke up at my usually ridiculous early hour. As normal, it took me a few seconds to find my bearings . . . then it came to me, what I'd done. There was no guilt. I'd blanked the severity of what I'd done—and what I was doing—from my mind. I had blinkers on. I'd convinced myself it was the best thing to do, for me, and that no-one would ever know. 'Right,' I thought, 'Let's see if this has worked.' Normally, I get a real ache in the joint between my biceps and my shoulders when I lift the covers back. Not a shooting pain—but enough to remind me of the two bicep operations I've had. I took a deep breath, pushed the covers back . . . and felt the exact same ache I'd had for the last two years. I thought it would feel different, but it didn't. Stacey was still asleep, next to me. I looked at my stomach, just to check there wasn't a rash or anything else that could give me away. When I squinted, I could just about see a small, round bruise where I'd injected myself. That was it. I felt exactly the same. Even when I went for a piss, I don't know what I expected, but I studied the colour of it to check it wasn't green or red or anything. But it was just the usual morning, piss colour.

That morning—the day after I'd taken it—I'd arranged to do a circuit session with a personal trainer. I was serious about getting myself fit. I thought, 'I'm going to fly it', but I didn't. It wasn't that I struggled; but I didn't kill it, either. It was just as normal, like before. And it was like that every day.

It stopped being a big thing, and just became part of my daily ritual. Have I showered? Have I brushed my teeth? Have I injected myself with hGH?

I carried on sneaking into my garage in the late afternoon, five days on, two days off, to inject myself. Still no effect. When I only had three or four doses left, I got a text from the player I'd bought it from asking me if I wanted any more.

I checked Stacey was out, locked the front door, and phoned him up.

'It's not working,' I said. I was a bit pissed off—I'd spent £150, and I might as well have been injecting water into my stomach for all the good it was doing me. I was going to tell him I didn't want any more, but he said, 'It's like everything— they don't work overnight'. He said it took four to six weeks to have an effect, so a day later, I met him and bought another month's supply, and carried on taking it.

He was right.

It didn't happen overnight. It wasn't like a switch—it was a gradual change. The best way I can explain it is, if you have a headache and you take an aspirin—it doesn't stop altogether, but a few minutes later you might be watching TV, and the adverts come on, and you realise your headache's gone. Well, it was similar to that. One day, I was wondering why I'd just spent £300 on something that was having as much effect as drinking lemonade. And the next day—well, next month—I was in my kitchen, waiting for the kettle to boil when a thought hit me: 'Did I just walk down the stairs forwards?'

My knees had been aching for the last few years. I'm fine on the flat, and even going uphill—but ask me to walk downstairs and it's like I'm walking on broken glass. That's why I walk down at an angle; it eases the pain. I walked back to the stairs, jogged up to the top, and then walked down again. No problem.

What the fuck!

It had worked. I spun my arms round, windmill style, expecting a grimacing pain to shoot from the biceps across my chest . . . but nothing. They felt fine. Normal. I don't want to be an advert for hGH, I want to be a deterrent from it. I'm living bloody proof you shouldn't take it! But I can't lie; it did make me feel refreshed.

It didn't help me run further or faster or lift more weights, it's not like that. But it speeded up the recovery, which meant that—where as usually I'd be stiff in the morning—I could train again the following day. I felt like I was 26 again. I only intended to take it for three months, before I started at Wakey. But it was helping me out and I was going so well in training that I thought, 'Sod it, I'll carry on'. So I did—five days on, two days off. I kept buying it from the same player, and kept it stashed behind my toolbox in my garage, a guarded secret from everyone who would bollock me if they knew.

As far as I was concerned, only four or five people would ever know: me, the guy I bought it from, and two or three other players who were on it.

It didn't cross my mind that I'd get done for it. Not even when I walked into the toilet with a couple of cock-watchers that November day. I was about to whip my todger out for the standard urine test when one of them told me I was having a blood test. Rugby league had brought blood-testing in the year before. I'd never had a blood test, but even when the tester stuck the needle into my arm and took my blood, I thought I was safe. The only thing that crossed my mind for a split-second—and this will sound so daft, now—was whether I'd taken any medicines, but I hadn't. That sounds stupid, I know, given that I was taking hGH, but the list of banned substances doesn't just contain drugs like steroids and cocaine—simple cold remedies that you can get from any shop can land you in the shit. I knew I hadn't taken any medicines—I never had, without checking with my doctor first—but in that split-second, I did a quick recap in my mind. I knew I was fine.

I'd last taken a dose of hGH the previous day, when I'd got in from training at 4pm. About 18 or 19 hours ago. Even the most sceptical of warnings about hGH had been that it was out of your system in 20 minutes. I was off the hook. As far as I was concerned, it was undetectable. It didn't even cross my mind that I might get done—the only thing I was thinking was, 'Hurry up, fella, I'm bloody starving and it's nearly dinner time'.

He didn't take long. He took the needle out, put a piece of cotton wool on my arm and stuck it down with tape.

'All the best for next season, Tez,' he said.

'Cheers, cock-watcher.'

And we both laughed.

They never got in touch with me, and I never expected them to. All the way through December. All the way through January. I played against my old club, Leeds, twice—in a friendly and in a Super League match—and all the while, I carried on taking hGH. Everything seemed to be going fine. I'd settled in well at Wakey. I was driving over from Wigan with my old mate Paul Johnson—another one who was shocked when he found out what I'd done—and I fitted in well. John Kear had assembled a decent squad; there were no big-name stars, but there was plenty of talent, and I genuinely fancied our chances of doing well.

That all changed, for me at least, with a letter to my home that fateful Wednesday, February morning.

After I'd broken the news to my dad, I phoned my agent, Andy Bailey, and I went to see my solicitor at Hatton's, a firm outside of Wigan, that lunchtime. He called someone at Wakefield, and they summoned the board of directors together that afternoon. I drove over to Wakey with Andy. They knew what was coming—or at least, they must have had a bloody good idea.

I walked into their boardroom and the directors were sitting there, as well as the coaches, John Kear and Paul Broadbent. I only had to tell them I'd failed a test—I didn't have to say anything else, or admit or deny anything—but I wanted to come clean. I wasn't going to bullshit anyone. I told them straight, and I held my hand up and said, 'Look, I've done it'. John and Paul knew I'd fucked up, they were in shock, but I think a small part of them respected me more for being honest about it.

Afterwards, John asked me if anyone at Wakefield had anything to do with it, and I told him, honestly, 'No'. It had completely been my choice.

As I drove back from Wakefield that afternoon, I didn't say a word. I was still numb. I knew I was staring at a two-year ban. I couldn't believe it was all over for me. I'd always thought I'd go out with a final game in front of my home fans—whoever I was playing for—and get a good send-off. I turned my phone on silent, turned the radio up and thought,

'How long have I got before everyone knows what I've done?'

About 10 minutes. That's all it took before my suspension was leading the radio sports bulletin. Wakefield had put a statement out, saying I'd been suspended for breaching anti-doping rules.

By the time I got home, I had about 30 missed calls on my phone. Many were numbers I didn't recognise—reporters, I presumed. I didn't call anyone back. I didn't want to speak to anyone.

When I got home, Stacey had calmed down a little bit, which is to say I didn't fear she was going to hit me! But I could tell from looking at her how disappointed she was in me. I cuddled my little girls so tight—it's amazing how just hugging your kids can make you feel better when you're down.

When the girls were in bed, I sat down with Stacey over a brew. She was still in shock. She couldn't believe I'd done it, because she knew what my thoughts on drugs cheats had been.

She kept asking, 'Why've you done it?'

I went to bed early that night but I hardly slept, and not just because Brian Carney burst into my bedroom to give me hell!

I avoided the newspapers the following morning, but I guessed about what they'd put. I started taking some calls, from mates and other players. Some advised me to deny it. They said I should have the B-sample tested and contest it, because no-one had ever been caught doing hGH before. I didn't want to do that. I thought I'd get more credit to just hold my hand up rather than lie and drag it out. Plus, all that anyone knew—from the press statement—was that I'd been found guilty of breaching anti-doping laws. It didn't say what it was I'd taken, and that did my head in, because—so soon after Leanne's death due to heroin—I thought, 'The last thing my mum and dad need are people in the street saying, "Their Terry's been on it, too"'. That wasn't the case.

Brian was brilliant. He came around to my house, and during our conversations, I told him that I wanted to get it over and done with, and come clean. I was honest. I realised I'd screwed up, what I'd done was bad enough without me lying about it. I'm always telling my kids 'You get in worse trouble for telling lies'—I wasn't going to be a hypocrite. A couple of papers offered me cash if I broke the story to them first, but it didn't take me long to decide against it. Brian helped me word a statement in which I owned up to taking hGH. We sent it to my solicitor, and he sent it out to the press.

There are three questions I got asked a lot, and I can't answer two of them.

Firstly, why did it take so long to get the results? I've no idea. I took the test in November, I got suspended in February. Believe it or not, I'm not all that up on science, and I'm not quite sure how they tested my blood and why it took so long. I even did a pre-match press conference at Wakefield, a few days before I was banned, to promote our upcoming game against Leeds. Do some people really think I'd have the balls to do that, knowing I was due to get banned? No chance.

Secondly, who dobbed me in?

I don't know. When it was released that I'd been caught, the anti-doping authorities made a point of saying I'd been targeted because of some 'intelligence' they'd gathered. In other words, someone had reported me. I don't know who it was, I don't even have any suspicions, because I thought the only ones who already knew I was taking it were also taking it. And, like me, they'd have thought it couldn't be detected. To be honest, I'm not all that bothered who it was—I'm the one who fucked up—but I just wish they'd been a man about it, and instead of dobbing me in like a grass, had approached me about it, or even got one of my mates to do it. If they'd have gone to Kris Rads, Brian or Moz, and told them on the QT, I know for a fact those guys would have given me absolute hell and made me see sense, and this whole thing could have been avoided. I can't look to blame whoever dobbed me in because it was all my fault. And, to look at the bigger picture, I suppose by dobbing me in instead of handling it directly, they did the game a huge favour.

I'll try to answer the third question: Why did I risk it?

I played the best rugby of my career when I was clean, at Wigan. I'd been picked for Great Britain, and for the Super League Dreamteam. A couple of team-mates had even talked me up as a contender for the Man of Steel. When I spoke to Stacey—as well as mates like Terry O'Connor and Brian—they couldn't understand it. They said, 'You weren't a below-average player, why d'you do it?'

Well, it goes without saying that I never thought there was a risk. I never thought I'd get caught, and that wasn't just cockiness—I honestly believed there was no way a test would have detected it. I'm not justifying it in any way, because what I did was wrong. But for anyone wondering why a bloke who'd been drugs tested a ton of times and seen 'cock-watchers' week in, week out—and even seen mates and team-mates suspended—would be so stupid, well . . . I thought hGH was different. On the episode of *Boots 'n' All*, the night I was banned, the Widnes coach Paul Cullen said there was a myth in rugby league that hGH couldn't be detected. But the thing is, it wasn't a myth—I got caught.

I've got a friend who was on it, and he had been blood tested a year earlier and his test came back negative. So it wasn't as if there was just a rumour going around that this super-dooper hGH couldn't be detected—I actually knew someone on it, who was taking it daily, and who had returned a negative test. I presume that, between him escaping and me getting caught, a new testing method had been found. I don't know.

Those who are close to me couldn't believe why I'd done it and, now I look back, I can't either. Some people say I'm only sorry because I've been caught but that's not true. It jolted me. It took me getting caught to make me see sense, and to make me realise I was representing other people, and not just myself.

But at the time, I wasn't seeing things sensibly. My head was up my arse. I was depressed, and rugby was making me worse, not better. I think, looking back, it was a bit of a chicken and egg situation—I wasn't playing my best because I wasn't happy, and I couldn't become happy unless I was playing my best. On top of that, age had caught up with me and I knew I wasn't the same player I used to be. My fitness and strength were okay but I didn't have that same zip or drive I used to have. That fuelled my depression.

I can't tell you how hard it was seeing players who had never been as good as me, start to creep ahead. And when I found out—or, more precisely, heard rumours—that some of the younger lads were on hGH too, I thought, 'I'm fighting a losing battle here'.

I only started taking hGH shortly after I'd signed for Wakefield, so it wasn't as if I was playing for a new contract; I could have strolled through my final two years at Wakefield and, playing good or bad, I'd still have got paid. But no-one wants to fade away. I didn't want to spend two years being an average player, I wanted to be as good as I used to be. I thought, 'If I'm playing well, it'll make me happier'.

I googled my name for the first time the other day.

Someone had told me I'd made news around the world with my suspension, and they weren't wrong. Because I was the first athlete ever to be caught doing hGH, the papers everywhere had pounced on it. I read a story in the *New York Times* that baseball was now introducing hGH testing, because of my case.

I'd spent 15 years wondering what a rugby league player had to do to get some global recognition, and now I'd found out! Even Lance Armstrong, the legendary cyclist, referred to my case on his Twitter page. I can't say I was proud about that. But I can't say I was too shocked, either, because—from what I read—hGH is a huge concern for sports in other countries, particularly America.

The chief executive of the US Anti-Doping Agency was quoted in one of the papers as saying 'Newton's case is proof the test works'.

I know what you're probably asking: how widespread is it in rugby league? I'm not sure. I'd be guessing. Rugby league is such a small circle that players have a decent idea about what's going on at all the clubs, and I'd heard about a number of players who were on it. Old, young, English, foreign . . . more and more were turning to it, believing they wouldn't get caught. Of course, it's all word of mouth—the one thing players definitely don't want other players to know about is if they're cheating—which is why I'm reluctant to put a number on how many were doing it when I was. It could have been 30, 50 or 100. I don't know, but nothing would surprise me.

All athletes get injured and they want to recover quickly. Their livelihoods and careers depend upon being out there on the field or the track and performing. hGH helps this and everyone believes, or believed, that there was no way of getting caught.

I'm not saying this to try to water down what I did.

Absolutely not. What I took was a banned substance, and the more testing rugby league does, the better. They can't test every player every week—they've not got enough coin to employ that many cock-watchers—but I've always been against banned substances and, as hollow as this sounds, I still am.

I was weak, and I cheated. But that doesn't mean I think what I did was right. I didn't need anyone telling me I'd been a dickhead. As it happened, I had mates queuing up to tell me that very same thing. They say you find out who your real mates are when you need them most, and that's been the case with me. Brian's not been off the phone since. Sean Gleeson, briefly a team-mate at Wakefield, has also been supportive. Adrian Morley came to see me, and he couldn't believe it. He's so dead against all of that—he was gutted that I'd become one of them.

Terry O'Connor and Kris Radlinski were the same. They were absolutely devastated. They're such professionals and they're dead against it. And—here's the scary part—I am too. But I say that with a clear, sensible mind. When I started taking it, I wasn't thinking sensibly. I was depressed, desperate and looking for a quick fix. It's no excuse. I can't believe I allowed myself to be seduced by something that promised me so much, when in the end it's taken so much.

What hurts, is that the people who played with and against me think I'm a cheat now. Which I am. I'm a cheat. And that's something I've got to live with. Just saying those words to myself now—'I'm a cheat'—hurts me more than any abuse the Saints fans used to dish out. Guys like Brian, Moz, Tez and Rads, I know they had so much respect for me, and it frightens me that—even in a few years from now, when we're all old men and reminiscing about good times—they won't have anywhere near as much respect for me as I have for them.

If there's one positive to come out of my case, I'm glad it

was me who was caught and not a player who's at the start of his career. I'd heard of young players taking the drug who have little money, who have done nothing in the game. They're not bad people for taking it. They're just feeling the pressures of being a sportsman, and they thought, like practically everyone else, no-one would ever know.

I hope they look at me and see that there is a way of testing for it. Two years out of the game is a long time. They should think of that. Next time they lift up their t-shirt and stick a syringe in their stomach, they should think about how much it would cost them—not just their reputations, but financially, too.

Rugby league was always pretty good at drug education but if anything puts others off taking hGH, it's me. They don't want to piss it all away, like I did. I know for a fact that, if someone else had just been banned doing hGH, there's no way I'd have taken it again. It's not addictive. It doesn't give you a kick. If I could rewind a few months to when I put Sky Sports on and if I'd seen a story about an athlete—in any sport—that had been caught, I wouldn't have hesitated to throw my hGH away. I'm serious. I'd have taken it from my garage, put it in my car, driven to a skip and binned it (although the tight bastard inside of me may have wanted to flog it instead!) I sincerely hope young players out there, in rugby league and other sports, think, 'I don't want to go the same way as Terry Newton'.

I know a handful of players who were taking it at the same time as me; to a man, they all told me they've stopped. Whether they have or not, I don't know. I'd like to think they'd not be so stupid as to carry on, playing the odds, but what else are they going to say to me?

Well, if they have carried on, they're even bigger fools than I ever was.

I'm sure there were plenty of players who could get their hands on hGH. The player I bought mine from was shocked when I was caught. He probably felt a tinge of guilt, too, but it was all my fault. No-one else's.

Whether he's still taking it himself, or selling it to others, I don't know. I suppose if no-one is buying, it would solve it, eh?

The clubs do their bit in educating players, but young players are under so much pressure to make it that they fall into that trap. I'd love to get involved and speak to young players—and old players for that matter—about it. I don't just mean about drugs, but the court stuff too. It's in my nature not to walk away from a fight, but how much has that cost me over the years? The stress, the money, the stares on the street . . . it's not been worth it. I know clubs may be reluctant to bring me in, because if anyone got wind of it they might think, 'There must be a problem at that club, if Terry's there', but I'd like to think some will, one day, look beyond that. Not every player will be like Sean O'Loughlin or Kris Radlinski or Paul Deacon, who had nice upbringings and were always sensible lads. There are also plenty of players who are on the same wavelength as me, and I'd love to speak to them. I know I wouldn't, as a young man, have listened to some suit from the RFL advising me not to fight. But maybe I'd have listened to a former Test international who'd been in the same place.

Rugby league is a rough game and of course it attracts people from rough backgrounds, but the game shouldn't be ashamed of that—it should be proud of it. Rugby league gave me a path out of trouble, and there are people in the game who grew up on rough estates like me, who probably need a bit of advice to put them back on the straight and narrow. If someone had taken Gaz Hock under his wing, would he have carried on? Who knows.

Gaz was stupid like me, though he took cocaine and not a

performance-enhancing substance, but we both got two-year bans. Some say what he did was worse, but it wasn't—in my view, he didn't deserve a two-year ban. He needed help, not a suspension. He had a problem. I didn't—I stone cold cheated to help my career. What I did was five times worse than whatever Gaz did.

Since Leanne's death in November 2008, I've thought a lot about drugs. After losing a sister to heroin, I suppose most people would expect me to be really anti-drugs, but I don't think like that. There's a part of me that understands why people go to raves, listen to shite music, take pills and dance all night. And part of me can see why others listen to miserable rock music and sit around smoking pot.

It's not for me, and if I ever found someone pushing it on my little girls, I'd break every bone in their body. But I'm not going to preach, because I can see why they do it. I'm not wired like that; others obviously are.

My only problem with social drugs is that they can lead to the strong drugs. Heroin and crack—they're the killers. There's no social side to drugs like that. Once heroin has a grip on someone, it destroys their life. Sadly, it's a subject that no-one likes to acknowledge, which is why no-one has a proper discussion about it. MPs would be committing political suicide if they suggested giving addicts free drugs, but that's what I think they should do, in organised centres where the users could go, get their fix, but on the condition that they'd stay over, be looked after and weaned off their addiction. That way, there'd be no addicts breaking into old people's homes to feed their habits. That's my view, anyway. I'm not expecting any changes any time soon, because people see heroin as something that happens to other people, and not to the people they love. They're wrong. Do those people think my sister started off on heroin?

She started off doing petty things, and if someone had asked her when she was younger whether she wanted to destroy her life with heroin she wouldn't have said 'yes'.

That's not how it works. They start off getting involved in petty crime and it escalates from there, as they chase the next buzz, and the next one. And it doesn't matter how much love they have at home—my mum and dad are proof of that. They did everything they could for Leanne, and more.

I class the term 'drugs' as something that does you harm. That's why I never saw hGH as a drug, because it was something that I saw was helping me. The same way aspirin has helped me. The same way the anti-depressants I was prescribed after Leanne died helped me. Again—please don't take that as an excuse in any way—it's completely right that hGH is a banned substance. I just never saw it in the same light that I see other drugs. I saw it as something that was helping me, not harming me.

Quite a few athletes have returned from doping suspensions and, after a while, no-one mentions the drugs any more. People forget about it. That's annoying for me, because I'll not have that chance to come back, and no-one wants to be remembered as a cheat. But that's my fault and no-one else's. In truth, if I wanted, I could probably make a comeback and play again. I'll have just turned 33 when my ban expires and, with no miles on the clock for two years, I'm pretty sure I could get a gig somewhere. The way I'm feeling, I'll not return to playing.

But maybe, when my ban is finished, I'll feel differently. The RFL sent me a letter a few weeks after I was suspended, saying that if I wanted to return when I'd served my ban, I had to fill out a form agreeing to have random drugs tests. At first,

I was going to throw the letter in the bin. I thought, 'I'm done'. But I spoke to Stacey and I've sent it back—and I've agreed to fill out the forms, detailing where I will be for an hour of every day, every month. Just in case I change my mind. I'm not sure I will . . . we'll have to wait and see.

I didn't enjoy my rugby the same after I left Wigan and, when my time at Bradford had come to an end, I'd fallen out of love with the game. I wasn't at Wakefield long enough to know whether it would have been rekindled, but the game wasn't the same to me. Don't get me wrong, I still like to watch rugby league and I loved playing it—the 80 minutes on the pitch was great. It was everything else that went around it that I'd stopped enjoying. I'd been doing weights and sprints as a full-time job for 15 years and it had become boring. In the days after I got banned, people thought I would spiral into a depression, but I went the other way. I was smiling. Some said they'd never seen me happier. It felt like a burden had been lifted from my shoulders.

By chance, a couple of months before I was banned, I bought a pub with my father-in-law. He's been in the pub game for years and it was always an ambition of mine to get into pubs when I'd hung up my boots, I don't know why. Probably the prospect of all the free ale!

The pub's a couple of miles outside of Wigan town centre, and it's called the Ben Jonson (no 'h'). It was called that long before we bought it. Apparently it's named after a famous poet, and not the Canadian athlete drugs cheat—but I must admit the name is quite ironic! I planned to be a silent partner while I carried on playing but, after my ban, I put all my energies into making the pub a success. So far it's gone well. The building alone is worth what we paid for the pub, so I'm feeling confident about it. I've got a couple of other investment properties, but the pub was the biggest new venture for me. I'm a big believer that things happen for a reason, and the pub has given me something else to throw myself into. I've already done the odd stint behind the bar, though it took some getting used to—the first pint I pulled had a bigger head than Terry O'Connor's!

It's certainly been a steep learning curve for me. The first time I locked up, Keith left a note telling me not to forget to take the trays out of the tills, and to lock the money upstairs in the safe. But when I went to take the till drawers out, they wouldn't budge. I yanked on them, hit them, cursed them, and still they wouldn't shift. In the end, I unbolted both tills and lumbered them upstairs—I'm surprised I didn't put my back out, they were so heavy. I explained to Keith the morning after and he said, 'Tez, you don't take the whole drawer out the till, look . . .' and, of course, he opened it up and lifted the inside, 'cutlery-tray style' moulds out of the drawers! That aside, I'd like to think I'm an improving bar-man. I'm always willing to learn, at least, and it's given me something to concentrate on.

One lesson I learned, pretty early on, was to separate work from pleasure. I'm well known around town, and when I was behind the bar, customers kept offering to buy me a pint. I've never been one to turn a drink down. But the problem was that, I'd have a pint here, a pint there, and by the end of the night I was pissed! A couple of times, I went to work in the car and came home in a taxi. When I told Stacey I'd had too much to drive home, she said, 'Terry you're working, you can't get pissed'. She was right, too. Everyone's heard the stories about the ex-sportsmen who buy a pub and end up drinking all of the profits, and I don't want to become one of those. I want to make a real success out of the pub, so I've decided not to drink in my pub.

The more I look back, the more I get upset about what I did.

No matter how many times I think about it, it's not going to change anything. I've decided it's best to look forward, and be positive. It's tested my relationship with my mum, dad and Stacey, but we've come through it stronger.

Those three people have always been there for me, and it's because of them that I've had the career and life I've had. I know my career ended badly but I don't feel hard done-by— if anything, I feel lucky. Rugby's given me a great life, and it makes me so glad that I chose that path. I'd already broken into factories and nicked bikes before I started focussing on my rugby. I'm not saying I would have gone down the crime and hard drugs path if I didn't have rugby, but I can't say I wouldn't either. Without naming names, a couple of the lads I used to mate around with are still taking drugs. They've been inside. They've served some hard time. I think I had something inside me that makes me think I could have gone down a bad path, had it not been for rugby. There's nothing hard about going to jail. Where I was from, when I grew up, the hard bit was keeping out of jail!

I also had Stacey from being 20, and she's been great. With my mum and dad's support, and Stacey alongside me, I chose the right path.

I know I've not been an angel. I know I've had my scrapes and my brushes with the law, and I know I've done some stupid things. But I also know only too well that things could so easily have panned out a hell of a lot worse if I'd chosen a different path. If I'd chosen the path that my sister took.

A few weeks after Leanne died, I had a sleeve tattoo designed, with her name on a crucifix. I'm not Mr Religious, I don't go to church, but I do believe in God. The tattoo has also got the names of Stacey and our two little girls, and their birth dates, on it, and it's also got in writing, 'I don't care how poor a man is, if he has his family, he is rich'. It's something I came up with after Leanne died, and it's true. That's how I feel—rich.

That's why, while I'm ashamed that I cheated, I'm not going to spend the rest of my life hiding. I've not kept my head down. Taking a banned substance is a mistake I've made. But show me a man who's not fucked up once in his life and I'll show you a liar.

It's something I've got to live with, and my kids have to live with. My girls are a bit too young to understand what's gone on, thankfully. Maybe one day, when they're older, they'll read this book and see the mistakes I made, and they can learn from them. If it stops my two little girls going down the same path as Leanne, I'll be happy. As a player, I used to say a team is never as good as their best win or as bad as their worst defeat. In a way, it's like that as a man. I've got plenty of previous for being daft, and the way my career ended was the daftest thing I've ever done. But without getting all Jesus on you, if someone wants to judge me from my biggest mistakes, then screw 'em. If my girls ever read my story, they may even be proud of the way I handled the situation, I don't know. Hopefully they'll see the rugby side of my career, which they have known little about, and be proud of what their old man achieved.

EPILOGUE

Compiling this book gave me a chance to reflect on my career, long before I was banned. If someone had said to me as a kid, 'You'll win a Challenge Cup, you'll play at Wembley, you'll play for Wigan with Andy Farrell and Jason Robinson, you'll captain Wigan and you'll beat the Aussies in their own backyard' . . . well, I'd have taken that.

I achieved more than I ever thought I would. Sure, it would have been nice to win one of my four Grand Finals. I wish I'd stuck my heels in at Wigan and never left. And of course I wish I'd never taken hGH. But I still feel lucky for what I achieved. If I could have changed one thing from my career, it wouldn't be a game I played in but a game I was forced to miss.

The week after I got suspended, Wakefield's next game was against St Helens at Knowsley Road—I'm sure there were some Saints players who were glad I was gone! Lord knows I've hit enough of them over the years. I have to say, I've been fined a small fortune for smashing players high over the years, but when the fine was for hitting Saints players I never minded paying! I'd have given my right arm to play just one more time, for Wakefield, in that game against Saints. I'd have loved one more crack against the team I grew up to hate. One more run out in front of the Saints fans, who would have booed and hissed me. I'd have savoured every minute of it. They'd have given it to me good style—and that's what I'm going to miss. The duels with Keiron Cunningham. The fans on one side yelling encouragement, the fans on the other side yelling abuse—I know I was a bit of a pantomime villain but I bloody loved it. I used to love signing autographs, and chatting to the kids. If someone ever says I never had any time for a young kid, I'd wire 'em up to a Jeremy Kyle lie-detector test and watch them sweat, because no matter how long I played the game, I never tired of chatting to kids after matches. And when I saw a shy one who was too nervous to talk to me, I always used to think back to when I was in the same boots, outside Central Park, watching Shaun Edwards and Dean Bell walk past.

I'll miss all that. I'll miss the feeling of nailing someone with a great hit, or fooling someone with a dummy and cutting through the defence and sending a player over for a try.

My career didn't end the way I wanted it to, but when I think of everything I've done I feel blessed. And, thinking about it now, it shouldn't really be a shock that my career ended with controversy because it's been like that from the start. It seems like every season, something happened that would only happen to me. When I signed, I had two clubs fighting over me and got frozen out of the game for a year. Then when things were going well at Leeds I broke my leg, got sent out to Bramley and came back to play for Great Britain that same year. When I joined Wigan it had to go to a tribunal and when I left, it was via a ridiculous merry-go-round transfer involving Micky Higham. With all that, when I started taking hGH, I ought to have known I'd become the first person in the whole damn world to get busted for it!

But out of the many texts I received in the days after I got banned, the one that struck a chord was one from my former Wigan team-mate, Matty Johns: 'We all make mistakes . . . the bigger men get over them.'

And I have done.